LOST KINGDOMS

LOST KINGDOMS

Celtic Scotland and the Middle Ages

John L. Roberts

EDINBURGH UNIVERSITY PRESS

© John L. Roberts, 1997

Edinburgh University Press
22 George Square, Edinburgh

Typeset in Bulmer
by Pioneer Associates, Perthshire, and
printed and bound in Great Britain

A CIP record for this book is available from the
British Library

ISBN 0 7486 0910 5

CONTENTS

ACKNOWLEDGEMENTS

For the sake of consistency, all clan names such as MacDonald have been spelt with a capital letter as shown, while the earlier form of kindred names such as Ewan macDougall have been used. Names of the form Ewan macDougall mean literally Ewan, son of Dougall.

I am grateful to Professor G. W. S. Barrow, who kindly and very generously agreed to read an earlier draft of the typescript, despite the pressure of his own work, meticulously correcting my errors and giving me the benefit of his unrivalled knowledge of medieval Scotland. Needless to say, I remain responsible for whatever errors of style, substance and interpretation may still be found in the text. David Caldwell kindly discussed the latest findings of the Finlaggan excavations with me. Charles MacLean of MacLean Dubois (Writers and Agents) gave me much useful advice, for which I am very grateful. A. A. M. Duncan, J. M. and R. W. Munro, W. F. H. Nicolaisen and C. W. J. Withers kindly allowed me to use the copyright in their figures and genealogical tables, and A. A. M. Duncan made useful corrections to my own illustrations. The book could not have been written without the unfailing encouragement of my wife Jessie, who painstakingly drafted all the figures and diagrams, while her forthright criticisms greatly improved the text.

Figures 1.2, 1.3, 1.4, 1.5 and 1.6 are redrawn from *An Historical Atlas of Scotland, c. 400–1600* (edited by P. MacNeill and R. Nicholson, 1975) with permission of the Trustees of the Conference of Scottish Medievalists. Figures 1.7, 3.1, 3.2, 3.4 and 4.1 are redrawn from *Scotland* (*Volume 1: The Making of a Kingdom* and *Volume 2: The Later Middle Ages*) with permission of Mercat Press.

PREFACE

The underlying theme of *Lost Kingdoms* concerns the struggles of the
Canmore kings, and later the Bruce and Stewart dynasties, to impose their
authority over what may be called Celtic Scotland. It starts with a brief but
wide-ranging introduction to the history of Celtic Scotland from Roman
times onwards, dealing in turn with the legacy of the Picts and the Scots, as
well as the impact of the Angles and the Vikings, and ending in the eleventh
century with the reign of Macbeth, 'Son of Light', the greatest of all the
Celtic kings of Scotland. Still a Celtic kingdom with a predominantly
Gaelic-speaking population when Macbeth was killed by his dynastic rival
Malcolm Canmore in 1057, Scotland then underwent profound changes
over the next 240 years under the feudalising rule of the Canmore kings,
before the struggles for independence against England came to define
Scotland's own national identity in the fourteenth century. Subsequent
chapters record the impact of these changes upon Celtic Scotland, as its
autonomy became ever more constrained, ending with the downfall of the
Lordship of the Isles under Clan Donald in the late fifteenth century.

The death-knell of Scotland as a Celtic kingdom was first sounded by
Malcolm Canmore when he married Margaret, sister of Edward Ætheling,
as his second Queen. Although England had still to be conquered by
William, Duke of Normandy, when Malcolm Canmore seized the throne in
1057 the feudal ideals of the Normans had already crossed the Channel.
Soon they came to affect Scotland, especially under the influence of Queen
Margaret, who set about reforming the Celtic Church. But it was her sons
Edgar, Alexander I and especially David I, as well as her great-grandsons
Malcolm IV and William the Lion, who first established the feudal system in
Scotland during the twelfth century, triggering what has been called the
Norman Conquest of Scotland. Its introduction was accompanied by a great
influx of Anglo-Norman and Flemish settlers into the country, who founded
many of the most aristocratic families in the realm, including the Bruces and
the Stewarts.

English was already the language of the Lothians south of the Forth, and it gradually penetrated farther north throughout the eastern lowlands of Scotland, where it was used as a lingua franca by these French-speaking magnates when speaking with their feudal tenants and by the inhabitants of the newly established burghs. Under these pressures, Gaelic started its long decline in lowland Scotland, before its final retreat into the Highlands and Western Isles. Equally the impact of the new regime upon the ancient earldoms of Celtic Scotland meant that they first came to be held by feudal tenure, and then often passed by marriage into the hands of the Anglo-Norman aristocracy. Only a few Celtic earldoms survived in their ancient line long after the Wars of Scottish Independence, since the Scottish peerage came to be dominated by the Stewarts during the second half of the four-teenth century, before it was completely recast in the fifteenth century.

Not surprisingly there was a violent reaction to the new regime, marked by a long history of rebellions in Moray and farther north, as various Celtic claimants attempted to seize the throne from the Canmore kings. Only with the reign of Alexander II did these rebellions finally come to an end, as the Canmore kings slowly imposed their own authority as far north as Caithness. As they did so, they planted the country around the fringes of the Highlands with their own Anglo-Norman and Flemish followers, granting them land in return for military service. Several such families eventually took on all the trappings of a Highland clan, including the Grants, the Chisholms and the Murrays, as well as the Frasers, the Gordons, the Menzies, the Stewarts and the Sinclairs, who later settled in the Highlands. Only rarely was a native Celtic family such as the Rosses rewarded with much territory and power for its service to the Canmore kings.

It was Alexander II who first turned his attention to Argyll and the Western Isles, early in the thirteenth century. Ever since the expedition of Magnus 'Barelegs' in 1098, the kings of Norway had claimed sovereignty over the Western Isles of Scotland. But dynastic quarrels in Norway and the apparent weakness of the Canmore kings had allowed Somerled in the twelfth century to carve out a Celtic kingdom for himself in Argyll and the Southern Hebrides. His descendants, progenitors of Clan Dougall and Clan Donald, held their island territories from Norway as the 'Kings of the Hebrides'. They only came under the sovereignty of Scotland after the victory of Alexander III over King Hakon of Norway at the battle of Largs in 1263.

Despite the occasional conflict, especially during the reign of William the Lion, the Canmore kings enjoyed close ties with England, often marrying the daughters of its Anglo-Norman aristocracy, or even the sisters or daughters of the English kings, and giving Anglo-Norman names to their offspring. Their sons and daughters often made equally good marriages south of the Border, or even across the English Channel in France. Only when the direct line of the Canmore dynasty ended in 1290 with the death of Margaret, the 'Maid of Norway', was Scotland threatened with the outright hostility of Edward I of England, 'Hammer of the Scots'. But it was the national identity of Scotland that was ultimately forged during the ensuing struggles for Scottish independence, culminating in the campaigns of King Robert the Bruce. Thereafter, apart from the diplomatic marriages made by David II and James IV with English princesses, the kings of Scotland often looked abroad for their brides, and especially to France (and Denmark), while their younger sons and daughters usually married into the aristocratic families of the Scottish realm.

King Robert the Bruce attempted to restore the ancient earldoms of Scotland, while rewarding his own loyal supporters with territories in the north confiscated from his Comyn enemies. However dynastic accidents and political misfortunes during the fourteenth century thwarted his intentions. Disorder became endemic in the north, culminating in the lawless career of Alexander Stewart, 'Wolf of Badenoch', younger son of Robert II. It was the Gordons, 'Cocks o' the North', who were eventually given responsibility as the King's lieutenants for restoring order, first as the Lords of Badenoch and then as the Earls of Huntly. They even gained the earldom of Sutherland under dubious circumstances in the early sixteenth century, and their power in the far north went unchallenged except by the Sinclairs, Earls of Caithness.

Farther west, the Campbells and the MacDonalds were almost the only families in what remained of Celtic Scotland who profited from their support of King Robert the Bruce in the struggle for national independence. John MacDonald of Islay not only inherited the territories in Argyll and the Inner Hebrides granted to his father, but his marriage with Amie macRuari brought him the proud title of 'Lord of the Isles' with all its territories. Then he allied himself by a second marriage with the Stewarts, gaining Knapdale and Kintyre when his father-in-law became Robert II. After his death in 1387, his three successors at the head of Clan Donald pursued such an avowedly separatist course as the Lords of the Isles (and Earls of Ross after 1437), often acting in alliance with England, that they eventually suffered forfeiture. First they lost the earldom of Ross in 1476, and then the Lordship of the Isles in 1493. Their downfall left the Campbells, created Earls of Argyll in 1457 after their long rise to power and influence, to contest the proud claim of Clan Donald to the Headship of the Gael. By then, however, Celtic Scotland had turned full circle, shrinking on itself until it only held sway over the Highlands and Western Isles, comprising little more than its ancient heartlands of Dalriada, first settled by Gaelic-speaking Scots from Ireland nearly a thousand years earlier.

Chapter One

ANCIENT CELTIC KINGDOMS

The Romans first penetrated as far north as the central lowlands of Scotland under the command of Julius Agricola, after conquering the south of Britain in the first century AD. There they found, in the words of Tacitus, his son-in-law and biographer, that

> the estuaries of the Forth and Clyde, carried far inland by the tides of opposite seas, are separated by but a narrow strip of land, which at this time was strengthened by garrisons, and the whole tract of nearer ground was held, the enemy being removed as it were into another island.

The Romans later built the Antonine Wall across this narrow waist of Scotland. But it was the Firth of Forth, and the wide flood-plain of the River Forth with its boggy and poorly drained ground, especially of Flanders Moss, which was the true frontier to Roman Britain. Stretching inland to within a few miles of Loch Lomond, it remained a formidable barrier to communication and a natural frontier, until drainage works reclaimed the land in the seventeenth and eighteenth centuries. Until then, it could only be crossed easily at Stirling Bridge, where the broad valley of the River Forth narrowed abruptly as the river forced its way between two volcanic outcrops. Stirling Castle was built on the volcanic rocks to the south and long remained of strategic importance. Indeed William Wallace and his compatriot Andrew de Moray won a famous victory against the English in 1297 guarding this very crossing to the north. Afterwards the Firth of Forth was called the Scottish Sea, and the whole country beyond its shores was known throughout the Middle Ages as Scotia, or Scotland north of the Forth.

Roman Campaigns in the North

Agricola himself campaigned north of the Forth, winning a great victory in AD 84 over the Caledonian tribes under their leader Calgacus at Mons Graupius, fought somewhere in north-eastern Scotland. The remains of

1

marching-camps even now mark his advance north by way of Perth and the fertile lowlands of Strathmore and the Mearns, and then into Buchan and farther west towards Moray. Later invasions by the Romans followed virtually the same route north, as did Edward I of England, invading Scotland north of the Forth more than 1,200 years later, and the Hanoverian army of the Duke of Cumberland, prior to his victory at the battle of Culloden in 1746. Agricola took great care to protect his advance north by building a defensive line of forts, brilliantly sited at the mouths of Highland glens, guarding his left flank between Callander and the River Tay. They lie along a segment of what is now known as the Highland Line, separating the Highlands and Western Isles of Scotland with its once Gaelic-speaking population from the fertile lowlands of Scotland to the east and south-east, where even the common people spoke Scots as a vernacular language akin to English by the end of the fourteenth century.

After Agricola was recalled to Rome in AD 87, the Roman legions withdrew under attack from the northern tribes, eventually to Hadrian's Wall, built after AD 118 as a defensive line across northern England. Further attempts were made to subdue the Celtic tribes of lowland Scotland over the next two centuries. The Antonine Wall was built after AD 142, but it was soon abandoned in favour of Hadrian's Wall after the Brigantes farther south had revolted against Roman rule. Perhaps briefly re-occupied towards the very end of the second century, when further rebellions occurred in the north, the Romans finally withdrew from the Antonine Wall after the four-year campaign of Emperor Severus to conquer Scotland north of the Forth ended with his death in AD 211.

Peace then returned to the Roman frontier for the next eighty years, until attacks were renewed by the Picti and other northern tribes in the years after AD 297. Repulsed at first, but without any lasting effect, they became ever more devastating during the fourth century until the native Picts and the Scots from Ireland overran Hadrian's Wall in AD 367. Despite their counter-attacks, the Romans eventually abandoned Hadrian's Wall around AD 400, and soon afterwards they left the native British to fend for themselves. By then the Angles and the Saxons from northern Germany were already attacking the south of Britain.

Origins of the Celts

The Celtic tribes who defeated the Romans in their vain attempt to conquer Scotland were the descendants of an Iron Age people who had started to disperse from their European heartland several centuries earlier, around 700 BC. Little more than two centuries later they had reached Scotland, where the first examples of their distinctive metalwork and pottery date

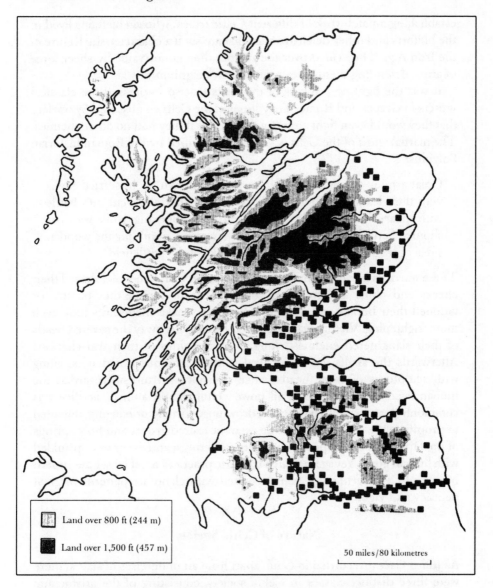

FIGURE 1.1 *Topographic map of Scotland showing the sites of Roman forts and marching camps (after Jones and Mattingley,* An Atlas of Roman Britain, 1990)

from around 450 BC. They brought with them their Celtic languages and a warlike aristocracy who ruled as military chieftains or tribal warlords over a hierarchical society. Most likely roving bands of Celtic warriors were the first to arrive, forcing the earlier Bronze Age inhabitants of Scotland into submission. They seemingly colonised the country in a piecemeal fashion, establishing a patchwork of different Celtic tribes, whose chieftains lived in the hillforts and other defensive sites that are such a characteristic feature of the Iron Age. They ruled over the surrounding countryside by sheer force of arms, defending themselves against their neighbours.

It was the fighting prowess of the Celts that so impressed the classical writers of Greece and Rome. They thought the Celts so obsessed by warfare that they would even fight amongst themselves if they had no other enemies. The martial spirit of the Celts was vividly described by the Roman historian Polybius:

> Great armies of frightful-looking warriors, drawn up in serried ranks with their leaders mounted in horse-drawn chariots, went into battle with spears flying, swords clashing, and horns blowing, while warriors shouted fierce battle-cries and women screamed, pounding the wooden sides of wagons drawn up along the flanks of the battlefield.

These warriors bleached their hair and spiked it with limescale, shaved their cheeks and chins and cultivated their moustaches, while they painted or tattooed their bodies with fantastic designs to make themselves look even more frightening. Victory was celebrated by carrying away the severed heads of their slaughtered enemies, slung along the sides of their war-chariots. Afterwards the skulls were displayed in their religious sanctuaries, along with sculptures of stone heads, since the cult of druidism regarded the human head as the source of all power. Human and animal sacrifice was commonly practised by acts of ritual drowning, burning or hanging, intended to propitiate the spirit world, while even the sacred groves and holy springs of the Druids were 'heaped with hideous offerings, and every tree sprinkled with human gore'. Yet against such barbaric practices must be set the superb beauty of Celtic artifacts, often decorated with elaborate patterns of great delicacy and vigour.

Nature of Celtic Society

As Julius Caesar recorded in Gaul, apart from an underclass of slaves, there were three distinct classes in Celtic society, consisting of the aristocratic *equites*, the priestly *druides* and the more lowly *plebs*. Such a hierarchy remained typical of later Celtic societies, as found in Dark Age Ireland. Indeed our detailed knowledge of Celtic society mostly comes from the Irish law-tracts, which appear to date from the eighth and ninth centuries, when the oral traditions of earlier centuries were first written down. They describe how Ireland in pre-Christian times was divided into perhaps a hundred petty kingdoms, varying greatly in size and importance. Each kingdom was known as a *tuath* and was ruled over by a *ri tuaithe*, or 'tribal king'. There were distinct degrees of kingship, so that the *ri tuaithe* as the 'under-king' of a petty kingdom might well owe allegiance to a *ri ruirech*, or 'high-king', who ruled over a much larger province, and paid tribute to him as his overlord. Later an *ard-righ*, or 'high-king', emerged to rule over the whole country.

No doubt Celtic kings in pre-Christian times had a ritual function to perform as well as their other powers and duties. They ruled over a warrior aristocracy who were landowners and the patrons of religion and the arts. Of equal status were the pre-Christian druids or priests, along with bards and poets, jurists, physicians, historians, artists and skilled craftsmen, known as the *aes dana*. Below this was a class of freemen and commoners, mostly small farmers, lesser craftsmen and other artisans, who formed the basis of society as the vassals of the landed aristocracy. Such a caste-ridden society was doubtless supported by an underclass of slave labour, who tilled the ground among their other menial tasks.

Emergence of the Picts

By Roman times the Celtic tribes of northern Scotland had achieved some degree of political cohesion, since they were apparently able under Calgacus to form a confederacy in opposition to Agricola. Afterwards the Romans entered into treaties with the more southerly tribes, such as the Votadini of the Lothians, buying off their hostility with gifts. But the military threat posed by the Romans may well have forced the Celtic tribes north of the Forth into alliance with one another, so explaining the emergence of the people known to history as the Picts, or the 'Painted Ones', to give them the nickname first coined by the Romans in AD 297. By the time the Romans had left Britain, or soon afterwards, the Picts had established two distinct kingdoms, separated from one another by the mountains of the Mounth, as the barrier of the Grampian Mountains was later known, running east from Ben Nevis towards the coast at Stonehaven. The southern Picts were the more powerful, perhaps exercising a degree of political sovereignty over the northern Picts. The next few centuries saw the ebb-and-flow of armed struggle, as the Picts came into conflict not only with the Gaelic-speaking Scots invading their territory from Dalriada in the west, but also with the Britons of Strathclyde and the Angles of Northumbria, who penetrated well north of the Firth of Forth before they were defeated at the battle of Nechtansmere in 685.

Our knowledge of the Picts is fragmentary in the extreme. They left no written records apart from a king-list in Latin, known rather grandly as the Pictish Chronicle, of which only very late copies survive, dating from the tenth century at the earliest. What inscriptions appear on their sculptured stones are mostly in Latin, apart from a few others written in Ogham, which was a primitive form of incised script introduced into Pictland at a very late date from Ireland. Transcribed into Latin the language appears quite unintelligible, apart from some personal names and what might be Gaelic words. Thus what we know of the Picts comes from beyond the boundaries of Pictland and especially from the laconic entries written in the monastic annals of the time, augmented by other chronicles which were mostly written down in later centuries. Only Bede's *Ecclesiastical History of the English People* dates from the early years of the eighth century. Indeed we do not even know what the Picts called themselves. Quite possibly they were not even a single people with well-defined origins and cultural background. Surprising as it may seem, place-names provide us with our best evidence that they were a people who spoke a Celtic language.

The Celtic Languages and Pictish Place-Names

Only a few place-names in Scotland are the ancient survivals of a pre-Celtic language, mostly occurring as the names of rivers and other natural features. Otherwise the earliest place-names have their roots in the Indo-European language known as Celtic. It split into two branches, perhaps after the Celts had settled in Ireland, where the Goedelic or Q-Celtic language now known as Gaelic diverged from the main stem of Celtic languages. Elsewhere the Brythonic or P-Celtic language gradually evolved into the distinctive dialects later preserved as the Welsh, Cornish and Breton languages. Gaelic as a Q-Celtic language treats the guttural *q* or *k* of Indo-European languages as sounding like the *c* in *ceithir*, meaning 'four', whereas Welsh as a P-Celtic language treats it as sounding like the *p* in its synonym *pedwar*. The equivalent in Latin is *quattuor*, preserving the original *q*-sound.

It is a striking fact that place-names with P-Celtic roots are found not just in Wales, but much farther north in Scotland, as emphasised most recently by W. D. F. Nicolaisen (1976). Perhaps the most obvious and widespread example is the prefix *aber*, meaning the mouth of a river, which occurs in such well-known Scottish place-names as Aberlady, Abernethy, Aberfoyle, Arbroath, Aberdeen and Aberdour, corresponding to Aberystwyth and Abergavenny in Wales. It is the same word as *inbhear* in Gaelic, later corrupted to *inver*, as seen in Inverness, Inverewe and Inveraray, for example. Of special interest is Inverbervie, known as *Haberberui* in 1290, showing that the P-Celtic root was later replaced by its Gaelic equivalent.

There are several other P-Celtic roots preserved in Scottish place-names, even if they often occur in a corrupt form, such as: *tre(f)*, a 'village' or 'homestead', which occurs as a prefix in Tranent or Traprain, or as a suffix in Fintry or Menstrie; *penn*, 'head' or 'end', as in Penicuik and Pencaitland;

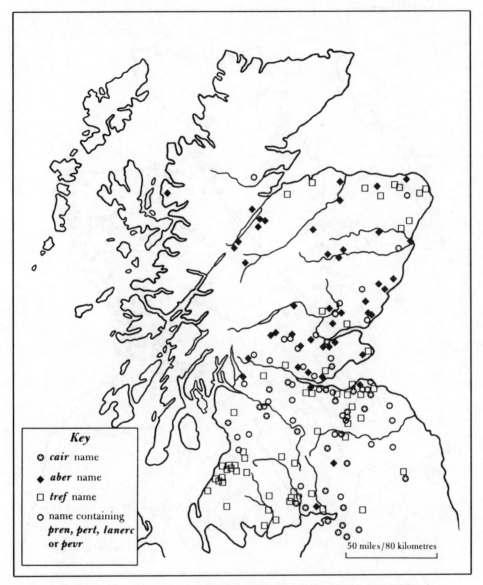

FIGURE 1.2 *Distribution of P-Celtic (Cumbric) place-names in Scotland*
(after Nicolaisen)

cair, a 'fortified homestead, as in Cramond and Carfrae; *carden*, a 'thicket',
which occurs as a suffix in Kincardine or Pluscarden, but as a prefix in
Cardenden; *pevr*, 'radiant' or 'beautiful', as in Strathpeffer; *lanerc*, a 'glade'
or 'clearing', as in Lanark; *pren*, a 'tree', as in Pirn; and *pert*, a 'wood' or
'copse', as in Perth.

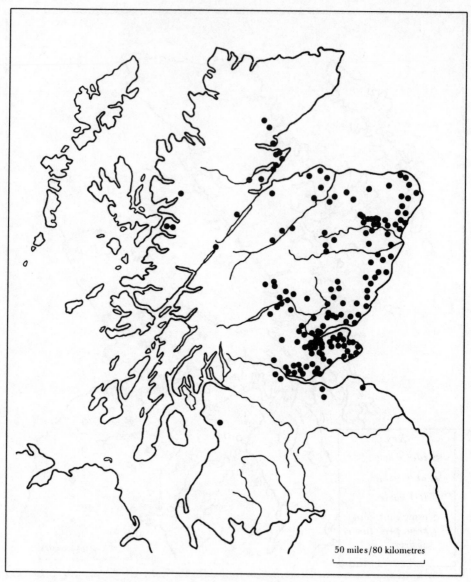

FIGURE 1.3 *Distribution of* Pit-*names in Scotland (after Nicolaisen)*

Such place-names could only have been coined if a P-Celtic language akin
to modern Welsh was spoken throughout the lowlands of eastern Scotland,
stretching from the Scottish Borders to the Moray Firth and beyond, wherever these place-names are found. As Gaelic-speaking Scots from Dalriada
colonised much of Scotland north of the Forth, starting in the eighth century,
if not earlier, such a language can only have been spoken by the Picts.

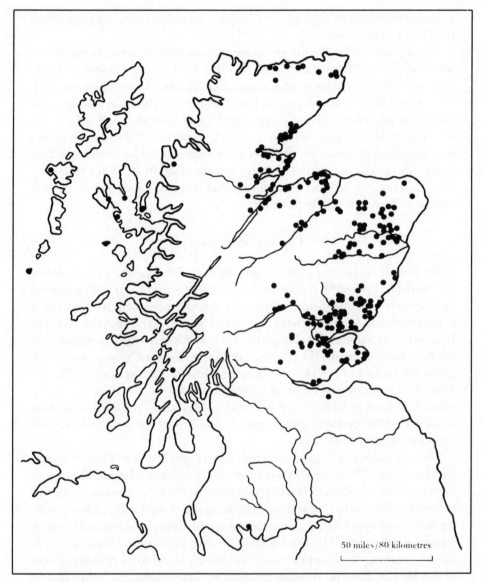

FIGURE 1.4 *Distribution of Pictish symbol-stones and sculptured cross-slabs in Scotland (after MacNeill and Nicholson (eds),* An Historical Atlas of Scotland, *1975)*

Farther south, much the same P-Celtic language was spoken as the dialect known as Cumbric by the Britons of Strathclyde, albeit with regional variations. Such place-names could only be preserved if they were adopted by the Gaelic-speaking incomers, who took to using them even as the older language died out, so arguing for a lengthy period of bilingualism between the Picts and the Scots.

Equally distinctive are the settlement-names starting with the prefix *pit*, which is derived from the P-Celtic word *Pett*, meaning a 'piece of land'. Almost without exception such a prefix is followed by a Gaelic element. This gives rise to place-names such as Pitcaple and Pitcastle, among many others, in which the second element is derived from such Q-Celtic words as *capul*, 'a horse', and *caisteal*, 'a castle', respectively. Such place-names presumably originated after the Picts were dispossessed by Gaelic-speaking Scots, who perhaps retained a Pictish system of landholding for their own use. They only occur where standing-stones and later cross-slabs with their enigmatic Pictish symbols are found.

Coming of the Scots

Apart from their ancient place-names, the Picts left only their monumental sculptures as a powerful testament to their existence when they disappeared mysteriously from the historical record in the mid-ninth century. According to later traditions, the Picts were conquered by the Gaelic-speaking Scots of Dalriada in 843 under their king Kenneth mac Alpin, popularly regarded as the first King of Scots. The Scots were themselves a Celtic people, who spoke the variant of the Q-Celtic language known later as Gaelic. Like the Picts, they were given their name by the Romans, who described the Celtic tribes of Ireland as *Scotti*. They migrated to Argyll from the north of Ireland around AD 500, perhaps following an earlier settlement from Ireland over the previous two centuries.

The new colony in Argyll was founded by Fergus Mor mac Ercc, or Fergus the Great, son of Ercc, and his two brothers, Oengus and Loarn. They came from the Irish kingdom of Dal Riata, situated in the far north-east of Antrim around the fortress of Dunseverick. Crossing the North Channel, but retaining their links with Ireland, they established the Celtic kingdom of Dalriada, ruling over the Inner Hebrides and the ancient province of Argyll, or *Airir Goidel*, meaning 'Coast of the Gael', stretching south from Ardnamurchan to the Mull of Kintyre. It lay to the west of *Drumalban*, the mountainous backbone, or 'Ridge of Scotland', now identified as the watershed running south from Cape Wrath close to the western seaboard of the Scottish Highlands.

Early Gaelic Place-Names

W. F. H. Nicolaisen (1976) has shown how the early settlement of Gaelic-speaking Scots from Ireland can be traced wherever the Gaelic word *sliabh*

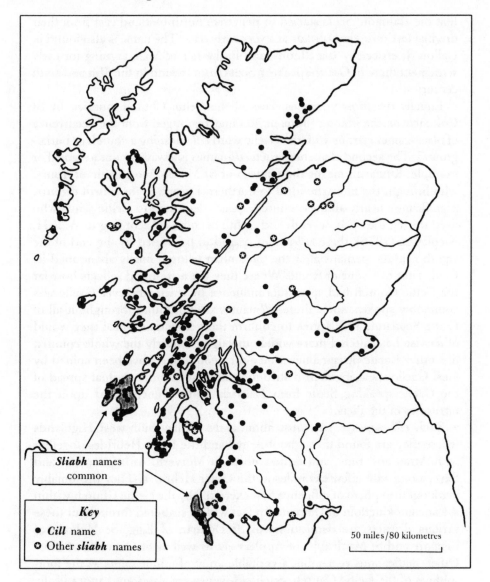

FIGURE 1.5 *Distribution of Gaelic place-names containing* Cille *as a prefix (after Nicolaisen)*

and its corruptions are used for a hill or mountain. Found as Slieve in present-day Ireland, *sliabh* is found most commonly in Islay and Jura, as might be expected, and elsewhere in Colonsay, Lismore, Kintyre, Knapdale, Arran and even Canna. It also occurs very sparsely in Badenoch and Atholl, drained by the upper reaches of the River Spey and the River Tay, suggesting that the Dalriadic Scots started to penetrate north-east and east from their original territories in Dalriada at a very early date. The name is also found in Galloway, especially the Rhinns, and in the Isle of Man, arguing for early settlement there of Gaelic-speaking Scots from Ireland in the fifth and sixth centuries.

Equally the proselytising success of the Celtic Church founded by St Columba on the island of Iona in 563 may be judged from the occurrence of place-names starting with the Gaelic word *cill*, meaning a church or burial-ground. The second element in such *cill*-names is always a saint's name. For example, Kilmartin means the Church of St Martin, most likely of Tours, who brought the monastic ideal to northern Europe in the fourth century. Significantly nearly all these churches were dedicated to Celtic saints who lived during the sixth, seventh and eighth centuries. According to W. F. H. Nicolaisen (1976), these *cill*-names ceased to be coined by the end of the eighth century, perhaps after the Columban Church finally abandoned its Celtic rites in favour of Rome. Where they are now found reflects how far the Celtic Church had spread its influence by then, wherever Gaelic was commonly spoken, since these *cill*-names are not found throughout all of Celtic Scotland. This serves to confirm their early date, since they would otherwise be scattered more widely throughout nearly the whole country, like other Gaelic place-names. Since they could only have been coined by local Gaelic-speakers, their distribution must reflect the gradual spread of the Gaelic-speaking Scots from Dalriada as they encroached upon the territories of the Picts.

Such *cill*-names occur most abundantly in the south-west Highlands where they are found throughout Argyll and the Inner Hebrides, together with Arran and Bute, and farther north in Morvern, Ardnamurchan and Skye, along with a few examples in the Outer Hebrides. They presumably mark out the sphere of influence first exercised by the Celtic Church within the ancient kingdom of Dalriada. In fact widely scattered throughout these various districts are dedications to St Donnan of Eigg, St Moluaig of Lismore and St Maolrubha of Applecross, as well as St Columba of Iona. Other dedications remember a veritable army of minor saints as the foot-soldiers of the Celtic Church. Such *cill*-names are also found sporadically along the Great Glen to the north-east, and beyond into Easter Ross and the south-east of Sutherland. Evidently the Great Glen acted as the route whereby Dalriadic influences penetrated into the northern kingdom of the Picts, just as St Columba journeyed to the Pictish kingdom of Brude. They are also found farther south, not only in Galloway, where they are especially abundant, but also in a broad swathe from Strathclyde and farther east into Menteith, Strathearn and Fife, as well as farther north in Atholl and Breadalbane.

Gaelic Settlement-Names

The Scots of Dalriada eventually came to rule over the southern Picts by the time of Kenneth mac Alpin in the mid-ninth century, if not earlier. Exactly how this happened remains a matter for scholarly debate, but the place-name evidence suggests that the Scots had already gained much ground to the east, perhaps from quite an early date if not permanently, penetrating along the Perthshire glens into Pictland. Indeed the Pictish province of Atholl was originally known as Athfotla, or *New Ireland*, and since it is first mentioned in 739, it must have been settled from Dalriada by this time. Later the ascendancy of the Scots over the Picts is mirrored by the widespread use of Gaelic as the language spoken throughout nearly all of mainland Scotland and by the coining of Gaelic settlement-names.

Settlement-names starting with the Gaelic word *baile*, typically found as the prefix *bal-*, are especially revealing. Whether *baile* means 'homestead', 'farm', 'hamlet', 'village' or 'town', it always refers to a place of permanent habitation. Ballachulish is a typical example, meaning the 'homestead of the narrows'. Such place-names are now only found where a well-settled population spoke Gaelic in the past, often farming the better ground along the river valleys. Such evidence is augmented by the occurrence of place-names containing the Gaelic word *achadh*, meaning a 'field'. Typically occurring as a prefix, it has often been corrupted into a variety of different forms, especially in lowland Scotland, giving rise to such place-names as Auchendinny, Auchintool, Achmelvich and Achnaclioch. Even if these *achadh*-names are now given to farms, hamlets, villages or towns as settlement-names, they were originally coined as field-names such as Auchmore, meaning the 'big field' from the Gaelic *Achadh mor*. Typically they are found as settlement-names wherever marginal land, originally only cultivated as out-fields, has been colonised by Gaelic-speaking farmers at some time in the past. As might be expected, they occur rather more widely than the *baile*-names, especially in the Scottish Highlands.

Taken together, as W. F. H. Nicolaisen (1976) has shown, such Gaelic place-names occur throughout nearly all of Scotland, apart from Orkney and Shetland and the lowlands of north-eastern Caithness, where settlement-names are nearly all Norse. Evidently Gaelic-speakers had only just reached the far north-east of the Scottish mainland before Caithness was settled by the Vikings in the ninth century. Likewise only a few *baile*-names are found in the Outer Hebrides, while *achadh*-names are almost entirely replaced by Norse settlement-names. Most likely the Vikings had overrun the Outer Hebrides before they were colonised to any extent by Gaelic-speaking Scots. Such place-names and their later corruptions are also absent from south-eastern Scotland, beyond the watershed lying south-east of the Clyde

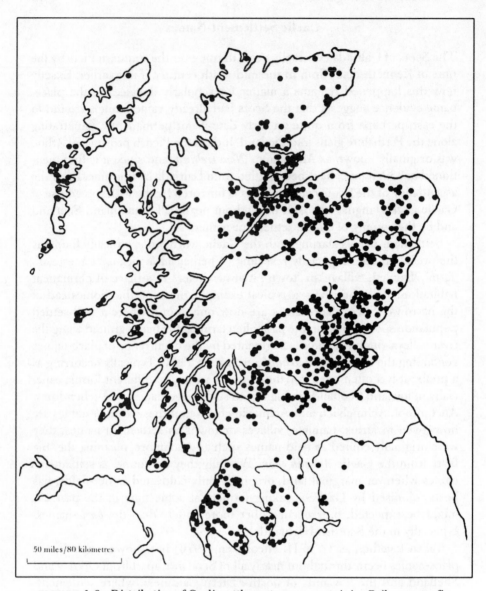

FIGURE 1.6 *Distribution of Gaelic settlement-names containing* Baile *as a prefix*
(after Nicolaisen)

and the Nith, where Anglian place-names take their place, except for a
scattering of *baile*-names in the Lothians and around the upper reaches of
the Tweed and its headwaters.

North of the Forth *baile*-names are found most frequently around the
coastal lowlands of eastern Scotland, corresponding to the very best of

agricultural land in what was the very heart of Pictland. They occur most densely in the lowland districts of Menteith, Fife, Kinross and Angus, while extending farther inland towards Breadalbane and Atholl. They are nearly as dense in north-east Scotland, especially along the valleys of the Dee, the Don and the Spey, along with the district of Buchan. Farther west *baile*-names are abundant in the lowland districts at the head of the Moray Firth, and farther north-east along its western shores towards Sutherland and Caithness. Elsewhere such names are widely scattered through much of Argyll and the Inner Hebrides, including the Isle of Skye. Their presence is clear evidence of a prolonged and sustained period of permanent settlement by Gaelic-speakers throughout this entire region, perhaps starting as early as the ninth century, even if these *baile*-names were still being coined in the seventeenth and eighteenth centuries.

Union of the Picts and the Scots

Popular tradition often traces the origin of Scotland as a separate nation to the conquest of the Picts by Kenneth mac Alpin around 843. Such a view largely rests upon the Scottish chronicles written in the Middle Ages, perhaps following much earlier sources. They depict a very abrupt transfer of power when they simply record with laconic brevity the 'destruction of the Picts' by Kenneth mac Alpin, who was 'the first king from among the Gaels to gain the kingdom of Scone', after which 'the Scots passed into the lands of the Picts'. Equally late is the story of how Kenneth mac Alpin destroyed his Pictish rivals by treachery, after he had invited them to a feast at Scone. During the banquet the Scots somehow managed to withdraw the wooden pegs holding up their seats, which had been loosened beforehand, so allowing them to collapse. The Scots then slaughtered all their Pictish guests in the ensuing confusion, leaving Kenneth mac Alpin to rule without any rivals as King of the Picts.

Following the studies of M. O. Anderson (1973), it is now thought more likely that, when Kenneth mac Alpin gained the Pictish throne of Fortriu, as the province of Strathearn and Menteith was then known, Pictland had already been ruled by Scottish kings from Dalriada for more than fifty years, after Causantin mac Fergus had established a new dynasty ruling over both kingdoms. Indeed, Kenneth mac Alpin only became King of the Picts, after Constantin's nephew Eogainn mac Oengus was killed in battle with the Vikings in 839, leaving no close descendant to succeed him. His succession may even have occurred in a peaceful manner, since there are no other battles mentioned in the contemporary records of the time. Once Kenneth mac Alpin had gained the throne of Fortriu, he reigned over the newly united country from Scone near Perth, rather than the old Pictish capital of

Forteviot. Tradition has it that he brought relics of St Columba from Iona to Dunkeld, where Constantin mac Fergus had already established a church by 820, perhaps reviving an earlier foundation, and which soon afterwards became a bishopric.

Known in Gaelic as *Alba*, the kingdom of Kenneth mac Alpin stretched south to the Firth of Forth, beyond which were the Angles of Northumbria, while the Britons of Strathclyde held the country farther south-west, centred on the fortress of Dumbarton near the mouth of the River Clyde. How far his kingdom stretched to the north of the Mounth remains uncertain, since the Vikings had already settled Shetland, Orkney and Caithness by this time, raiding the whole of the eastern coast as far south as Whitby. Moreover although very little is known about the history of Moray during the next two centuries, it was most likely held by descendants of the *Cenel nLoairn* from Dalriada, who had travelled along the Great Glen to settle around the Moray Firth, probably by the end of the eighth century, as suggested by the place-name evidence.

When the Scottish kingdom of Dalriada was first established by Fergus Mor mac Ercc around AD 500, his brother Loarn had settled in the district of Argyll still known as Lorne, where his princely descendants became known as the *Cenel nLoairn*. Their strongholds were the ancient fortresses of Dunollie and Dunadd. This dynastic family had the *Cenel nGabrain* as its greatest rivals. They were the descendants of Fergus's grandson Gabran, who had apparently settled in Kintyre with his strongholds at Dunaverty and Tarbert. However it was Gabran's son Aedan, consecrated by St Columba in 574, who founded the powerful dynasty that was to rule as the *Cenel nGabrain* over Dalriada for much of its history. Only during the late seventh century did the *Cenel nLoairn* challenge their supremacy under their king Ferchar Fota and his grandson Muiredach. Even so the *Cenel nLoairn* then disappear from the historical record for the next three centuries, after their defeat in 736 by the Picts under their great king Oengus mac Fergus.

Oengus mac Fergus had already defeated a rival Pictish dynasty to become high-king of the southern Picts, and after his victory over the *Cenel nLoairn* of Dalriada he attacked the Britons of Strathclyde. However, any Pictish ascendancy over the Scots of Dalriada did not last for very long. After Oengus mac Fergus died in 761, Aed *Find* mac Eochaid of the *Cenel nGabrain* was sufficiently powerful to invade the Pictish province of Fortriu in 768, when he defeated Oengus's son Talorgen. Such attacks by the Scots continued over the next few years, eventually culminating in the victory of Causantin mac Fergus over the southern Picts in 789. It was after this victory that the *Cenel nGabrain* of Dalriada came to rule over the southern Picts. Their rule was continued by the MacAlpin dynasty after 843, since Kenneth mac Alpin belonged to this kindred as the great-grandson of Aed *Find* mac Eochaid. Meanwhile it seems the *Cenel nLoairn* had established themselves in Moray. Indeed the men of Moray later traced their ancestry back to Ferchar *Fota* of the *Cenel nLoairn*, who had reigned over Dalriada at the very end of the seventh century, as did several other Highland clans in the Middle Ages.

Viking Raids and Settlement

What power Kenneth mac Alpin and his successors exerted over their ancestral kingdom of Dalriadia must have been limited in the west by the Vikings, who had founded the Norse kingdom of Dublin in 853, after dominating the seaways of the Western Isles with their longships for the previous half-century. They had begun raiding in 793, when the monastery of Lindisfarne off the coast of Northumbria was first attacked and destroyed. As the Anglian churchman Alcuin later wrote of Lindisfarne's destruction: 'Never before has such a terror appeared in Britain as we have now suffered from a pagan race. Nor was it thought possible that such an inroad from the sea could be made'. The entry in the Annals of Ulster for 794 records the 'devastation of all the islands of Britain by the gentiles', as the pagan Vikings were known, suggesting that such attacks were not just isolated incidents. The monastery of Iona was raided in 795, along with the island of Skye and the monasteries off the coast of Ireland, while there were Viking raids in 798 throughout the Hebrides and Ulster. The Vikings returned to pillage Iona in 802, and again in 806, when sixty-eight members of the religious community were massacred, and yet again in 825, when its abbot Blathmac was put to death after refusing to reveal the hiding-place of St Columba's shrine. The terror that such raids evoked is clearly expressed in the prayer 'From the fury of the Norsemen, O Lord, deliver us!', used in Church services during these years. As an Irish chronicler wrote: 'Neither honour nor mercy for right of sanctuary, nor protection for Church, nor veneration for God, nor for man was felt by this furious, ferocious, pagan, ruthless people'.

Even if the Vikings first appeared as piratical raiders intent on ravaging and pillaging the land, and carrying away the spoils of battle as booty, they soon started to settle down permanently in Shetland, Orkney and Caithness. Indeed the Norse earldom of Orkney was first established by Sigurd the Mighty during the later years of the ninth century, and its southern borders soon stretched as far south as the Kyle of Sutherland. The Norse name of Sutherland may well date from this time, since it was then known as *Sudrland*, or 'South-Land', as it would appear to the inhabitants of Caithness and Orkney to the north. However after the death of Sigurd the Mighty in 892, the Norse earldom of Orkney was much weakened by bloody feuds and internecine struggles between rival families and it did not revive until the time of Sigurd the Stout, nearly a century later.

Sigurd the Stout is best remembered in the Norse sagas as a powerful warrior and a great Viking, who went each summer to plunder the Hebrides, Scotland and Ireland. He drove the Scots from Caithness, establishing once again the borders of his earldom along the Kyle of Sutherland, and perhaps pushing even farther south to rule over Ross and Moray, while he brought the Western Isles under the influence of his Norse earldom of Orkney, perhaps for the first time in their history, although they had long been settled by the Vikings, to judge by the place-name evidence. Eventually he raised a great fleet of longships to challenge Brian Boru, High-King of Ireland, but his attempt to conquer Ireland ended with his defeat and death at the battle of Clontarf in 1014. Even so he was succeeded by his son Thorfinn the Mighty, known to his contemporaries as a great warlord, who eventually overcame all his rivals to reach an even greater pinnacle of power than his father.

After the death of Thorfinn the Mighty in 1065, the independence of the Norse earldom of Orkney was increasingly challenged by the growing power of Norway, and eventually Magnus 'Barelegs' mounted his great expedition to the Western Isles of Scotland in 1098. It succeeded in its purpose of bringing all the Western Isles and the Isle of Man under the suzerainty of Norway, which lasted for the next 165 years until the Norse defeat at the battle of Largs in 1263. Indeed Magnus 'Barelegs' was apparently able to force a formal treaty upon Edgar, King of Scots, recognising that all the islands off the west coast of Scotland between which a galley could be sailed with its rudder shipped belonged to Norway. The sagas even recount how he was drawn at the helm of his longship across the isthmus at Tarbert so that he could lay claim to the peninsula of Kintyre. However this ploy appar- ently failed since the diocese of Sodor, which later came under Trondheim, did not include Kintyre. Otherwise it included nearly all the islands lying off the western seaboard of the Scottish mainland, apart from Lismore, as well as the islands of Arran, Bute and the Cumbraes in the Firth of Clyde. Somerled and his descendants were later to abide by this treaty after they had come to power as the Kings of the Isles in the twelfth century, recognising that they owed allegiance to Norway for their island possessions, while they held their mainland territories in Argyll from the Scottish crown.

The virtual lack of any Norse settlement-names along the western seaboard of the ancient province of Argyll certainly suggests that the Gaelic-speaking Scots still retained control of their ancestral territories in Dalriada after 843. Only later did Fordun suggest that the Scots of Dalriada were driven east to conquer Pictland by the Viking attacks. Long after Kenneth mac Alpin came to rule over the Picts, there are scattered references in the Irish Annals to the western origins of several macAlpin kings who ruled after Kenneth mac Alpin, while Iona was even patronised by the eleventh century by such kings of the Scots as Malcolm Canmore and his queen Margaret. Indeed if it was the burial-place of the macAlpin kings, which now seems less certain than once thought, it could hardly have lain beyond the authority of these kings. Equally there are records of Viking raids on Iona and Dalriada throughout these centuries, and perhaps only towards the very end of the tenth century did Sigurd the Stout, and his son Thorfinn the Mighty, bring the Western Isles under the suzerainty of their Norse earldom of Orkney.

Moray: Province or Kingdom?

What control the MacAlpin kings of Alba exercised over Scotland north of the Mounth is a tantalising mystery. Apart from the Irish annalists, who still retained an interest in Moray and its neighbouring provinces, we have hardly any information about its history during the two centuries after Kenneth mac Alpin became king of the southern Picts. As the descendants of the *Cenel nLoairn* in Dalriada, the men of Moray may well have maintained their traditional hostility to the MacAlpin dynasty and its *Cenel nGabrain* ancestry, thus perpetuating the ancient divisions between the two Pictish kingdoms, separated from one another by the Mounth. No doubt the MacAlpin kings preferred to describe the rulers of Moray as underlings, holding the northern provinces of Pictland under the authority of the Scottish Crown. Yet it is not clear that the rulers of Moray saw themselves in such a light. But while the Irish Annals call them 'kings', they could have been under-kings who owed allegiance to the MacAlpin dynasty as their overlords.

Even so, the historical record suggests that Moray managed to exist as a powerful kingdom in its own right until the reign of Macbeth came to a bloody end in the mid-eleventh century. Neither the Norse earls of Orkney, nor the MacAlpin kings of Alba, were able to hold its territory for very long. Sigurd the Mighty, first Earl of Orkney, and his ally Thorstein the Red defeated Maelbrigte, who was probably King of Moray, in 892 when the Vikings first established their southern frontier at the Kyle of Sutherland, if indeed not farther south. But while Norse place-names are found throughout Easter Ross, if only rarely, they hardly ever occur south of the Cromarty Firth, suggesting that the Vikings were unable to settle Moray itself permanently in any numbers. Soon afterwards in 900 the MacAlpin King Donald I was killed at Forres, presumably on an expedition north into Moray, perhaps to collect taxes. When Athelstan, King of Wessex, invaded Scotland in 934 Constantine II retreated only as far north as Dunnottar, perhaps sug-

gesting the Mounth was then the northern frontier of his kingdom, while
Malcolm I is recorded as invading Moray in 943 when he killed Cellach,
who may well have been its king at the time.

Thereafter it is not clear what power the MacAlpin kings wielded north
of the Mounth for the next hundred years. Malcolm I himself perished in
954, possibly in Moray, even if there is an earlier tradition that he was killed
in the Mearns, while it seems that his son Dubh (962-6) was slain in Forres
by the men of Moray in 966. Further attempts by the MacAlpin kings to subjugate Moray evidently occurred during the reigns of Kenneth II (971-95),
or his son Malcolm II (1005-34), who indeed was known in the Irish annals
as 'King of the Mounth'. The last of the MacAlpin kings, they may well have
taken advantage of the internal rivalries that marked the early eleventh century in the north, since the men of Moray were soon afterwards described in
the Irish Annals as the subjects of Duncan I (1034-40). Indeed Malcolm II
was evidently powerful enough to marry his sister to Findleach, ruler of
Moray, and the father of Macbeth.

The internecine struggles in Moray culminated in the death of Findleach,
murdered in 1020 by his two nephews, Malcolm and Gillecomgain, the sons
of Maelbrigte. Thereafter Malcolm ruled over Moray until he died in 1029,
when his brother Gillecomgain succeeded him before he was killed in 1032,
burnt alive with fifty of his own followers. Macbeth most likely committed
this atrocity in revenge for the murder of his own father Findleach. As well
as his son Lulach, who reigned briefly over Scotland after the death of
Macbeth in 1057, Gillecomgain left a widow called Gruoch, granddaughter
of the MacAlpin King Kenneth III. Macbeth married her soon afterwards,
even if he had killed her husband Gillecomgain, who was also his own first
cousin, hoping to strengthen his own position as ruler of Moray.

If the MacAlpin kings held the ascendancy over Moray during these
years, it was certainly reversed in 1040, when Duncan I was killed by Macbeth
in a skirmish near Elgin. Macbeth then made himself king of all Alba,
becoming the only ruler of Moray to reign as king over the MacAlpin territories in the south. By doing so he perhaps acknowledged that Moray was
itself a part of Scotland, not a separate kingdom. Even after his death in 1057,
the Canmore dynasty made little attempt to crush Moray for nearly a century,
until the time of David I. Meanwhile several kings of Moray apparently
reigned peacefully over their territories, even if Lulach, Macbeth's step-son
and his immediate successor to the kingdom of Alba, was pursued north
by Malcolm Canmore and killed near Essie in Strathbogie in 1058. Even so
according to the Irish Annals, Maelnechtai, Lulach's son and successor,
died peacefully in 1085 after a long reign as the King of Moray, after which
little is heard of Moray until the early decades of the twelfth century.

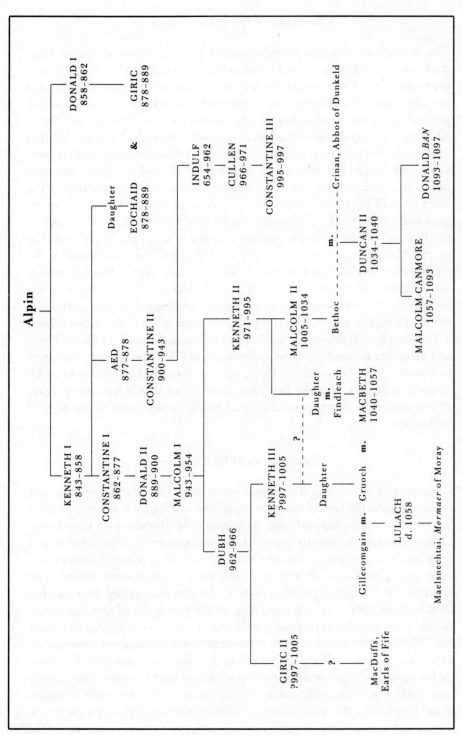

FIGURE 1.7 *The macAlpin Kings and the succession in the eleventh century*

Evidence of the Viking Sagas

The strength of Moray as an independent province if not a separate kingdom when the MacAlpin kings ruled in the south can also be glimpsed from
the pages of the Viking sagas. Even after the time of Thorstein the Red and
his ally, Sigurd the Mighty, the Norse earls of Orkney were often sorely
pressed by their neighbours to the south on the Scottish mainland.
Although the opponents of the Norse were often described as Scots, there is
little doubt that they were the men of Moray. The battles between them were
commonly fought in Caithness, not farther south, and the Norse warlords
were often defeated or forced to retreat to Orkney, especially during the
latter years of the tenth century. It was only when Sigurd the Stout and his
even more powerful son, Thorfinn the Mighty, ruled as Earls of Orkney in
the first half of the eleventh century that the Vikings made any headway
against Moray. Sigurd was even described after his death in Ireland at the
battle of Clontarf in 1014 as ruling over Ross and Moray. Once Thorfinn
the Mighty had finally gained control of Orkney in the years after his
father's death, his position was eventually challenged by the mysterious
figure of Karl Hundison, who was probably none other than Macbeth. Even
if Thorfinn the Mighty defeated Karl Hundison at the battle of Tarbat Ness,
and thereafter ravaged Scotland as far south as Fife, he eventually withdrew
to Orkney. After his death in 1065, the earldom of Orkney was riven by
dynastic struggles between two rival families, so that it was never again
strong enough to threaten the rulers of Moray to the south of the Kyle of
Sutherland.

Celtic Laws of Succession

Contrary to longstanding tradition, it is not clear if the MacAlpin kings ever
followed the Celtic laws of inheritance, at least in a formal manner. The Irish
law-tracts of the eighth and ninth centuries only describe how kingship in
earlier centuries apparently passed between brothers or first cousins and
then back to a nephew or a more distant cousin, all descended from a common great-grandfather. It gave an equal right of inheritance to the male
members of a kindred group known as the *derbfine*, rather than passing
directly from father to son according to the principles of primogeniture.
All the sons, grandsons or great-grandsons of a king were eligible to inherit
his office, down to the fourth generation, so that brothers, cousins or
nephews were just as likely to succeed to the kingship as his sons. However
by favouring collateral branches of a royal house such a system often gener-
ated conflict between rival claimants to the throne. Such disruptive struggles
could be offset by the ancient Celtic custom of tanistry, whereby a successor

to the reigning king was selected by him during his own lifetime, as agreed by the *derbfine*. Yet this gave the king-to-be yet another incentive to murder his predecessor, so that he was able to gain the throne all the sooner. Indeed, as Professor Barrow (1975) writes: 'the blunt truth is that each new king came to power, and was expected to come to power, by rebelling against his predecessor and either killing him, or having him put to death.' Royal sons-in-waiting commonly suffered a similar fate to their fathers, since they too were often killed off by rival claimants.

Quite likely Kenneth mac Alpin succeeded to the Pictish throne in 843 by virtue of such Celtic laws of inheritance. He was himself the great-grandson of Aed *Find* mac Eochaid, who had ruled over Dalriada before his own death in 778, when the kingship passed first to his brother Fergus mac Eochaid, and then to his nephew Causantin mac Fergus, who conquered the southern Picts in 789. There is thus no need to invoke a Pictish mother, as commonly done, to explain why he had a hereditary claim to rule over the Kingdom of the Picts, if indeed the Picts ever practised matrilinear succession, which now seems much less certain.

Kenneth mac Alpin was himself succeeded by his brother Donald I, who was followed in turn by his own son Constantine I, nephew of Donald I. The succession then passed very briefly to Constantine's brother Aodh, nephew of Donald I, who was overthrown by Eochaid of Strathclyde, who ruled jointly with Giric, son of Donald I. It then reverted back to Constantine's son Donald II, followed in turn by his cousin Constantine II, son of Aodh. Thereafter the succession started to alternate between ever more distant cousins over more than four generations, so that there were two distinct branches of the MacAlpin dynasty, each descended from Constantine I and Aodh as the sons of Kenneth mac Alpin. Some stability was possibly encouraged by allowing the heir-apparent to the throne to rule over the province of Strathclyde, after it had been conquered, perhaps from quite an early date. Notwithstanding the history of the MacAlpin kings was very bloody, if not unusually so for the times, since they nearly all gained the throne by the simple expedient of murdering their predecessors. Apart from Constantine II (900-43), Kenneth II (971-95) and Malcolm II (1005-34), no king after Kenneth mac Alpin reigned for more than a dozen years and several were overthrown within a year or two of their accession.

Malcolm II was the last of the MacAlpin kings. He had no sons, but he did have a grandson Duncan through the marriage of his daughter Bethoc to Crinan, the lay-abbot of Dunkeld. Breaking with Celtic tradition, Malcolm II arranged that Duncan should succeed him as king through the female line. Pursuing this ambition, Malcolm II had the grandson of Kenneth III murdered in an attempt to exterminate any rivals to his own grandson. Even so, following the death of Malcolm II in 1034, his grandson

Duncan I reigned for only six years before he was killed in battle by Macbeth, who was then ruling over Moray.

Macbeth, King of Alba

Contrary to Shakespeare's legend, Macbeth had just as strong a claim as Duncan I to the throne, and proved himself among the greatest of all the Celtic kings of Scotland. Not only was he the grandson of Kenneth II and the nephew of Malcolm II, whose sister his father Findleach had married, but his wife Gruoch was also the daughter or granddaughter of Kenneth III, whom Malcolm II had assassinated in 1005 to win the throne. Thus just as Duncan I's mother Bethoc was the daughter of Malcolm II, so was Macbeth's mother the daughter of Kenneth II, so that they were both shared exactly the same relationship to their grandfathers, Malcolm II and Kenneth II, respectively. No doubt Macbeth thought that he should inherit the throne through his mother, just as Duncan I had done, while his marriage with Gruoch as Kenneth III's granddaughter strengthened his claim. He probably regarded Duncan I as a usurper, depriving him of his right to rule over all of Scotland.

Why Shakespeare presented such a travesty of the truth can easily be explained. Although the playwright based his *Tragedy of Macbeth* upon Holinshed's *Chronicles of Scotland*, Holinshed himself derived his material from such medieval chroniclers and historians as Fordun and Wyntoun. They drew on even earlier sources, now lost, which were written down after Malcolm Canmore had founded an outstanding dynasty of strong kings, who ruled with great authority over much of Scotland for more than two hundred years after the death of Macbeth in 1057. Nevertheless the men of Moray still remained strong enough to challenge the power of the Canmore dynasty for much of its long life. Indeed the threat only ended when an infant heiress to the house of Moray had her brains dashed out against the Mercat Cross of Forfar in 1230.

Faced with such prolonged resistance, as the men of Moray and their descendants revolted time and again against central authority, the Canmore kings evidently engaged in a deliberate campaign to discredit the name of Macbeth. This they achieved by using the court bards, or poets, who employed the black arts of propaganda to destroy Macbeth's memory with such scurrilous and venomous attacks upon his character as later appeared in Holinshed's chronicle. Although the records of his reign are fragmentary in the extreme, they certainly suggest that Macbeth was a good and wise ruler. Even his name has the meaning 'Son of Life'. He is best remembered as the last of the Celtic kings of Scotland, apart from Donald Ban, since after the death of his ill-fated stepson Lulach he was succeeded by Malcolm Canmore, who introduced the alien language and customs of Anglo-Saxon

England to the Scottish court under the influence of his second wife, Queen Margaret. Unlike Duncan I, whose abortive siege of Durham in 1040 may well have contributed to his downfall and death later in the same year, Macbeth was apparently strong enough to resist an invasion of his kingdom by Earl Siward of Northumbria in 1045, when a battle was fought between the Scots in which Duncan I's father Crinan was killed, along with 'nine score fighting men'. Despite this revolt, Macbeth evidently felt secure enough to go on pilgrimage to Rome in 1050, like many other rulers of the time, where he 'scattered money like seed to the poor'. Indeed Macbeth's reign was marked by times of plenty, as described in the prophecy of St Berchan:

> The ruddy-faced king . . .will possess Scotland.
> The strong one was fair, yellow-haired and tall.
> Brimful of food was Scotland, east and west,
> During the reign of the ruddy, brave king.

Four years later, however, Macbeth faced another invasion of his kingdom by Earl Siward of Northumbria, now acting with the authority of Edward the Confessor. The attempt this time was to place Duncan I's son Malcolm Canmore on the throne. Unlike his younger brother Donald *Ban*, who had sought refuge from Macbeth in the Celtic west, or possibly in Ireland, Malcolm Canmore had fled south to the court of the English king when Macbeth had gained the Scottish throne. The two sides encountered one another in 1054 at the hard-fought battle of Dunsinane Hill in the Sidlaws, some miles east of Scone, and within sight of Birnam Wood. Macbeth was decisively defeated by Malcolm and his ally Siward, Earl of Northumbria, despite the support of a band of Norman knights who had taken service with him. After his defeat, Macbeth evidently withdrew north, abandoning his southern kingdom to Malcolm Canmore. He evidently still ruled over Moray, since it was not until 1057 that he was killed at Lumphanan in Mar. Even then, Macbeth's stepson Lulach, grandson or great-grandson of Kenneth III, was accepted by some Scots as King of Scotland. But he too was killed by Malcolm Canmore at Strathbogie after a reign of only a few months in 1058. By his death, Malcolm Canmore gained the throne as Malcolm III, finally establishing the royal house of Atholl, which reigned as the Canmore dynasty for nearly 150 years over the country which afterwards became known as Scotland.

Chapter Two

MALCOLM CANMORE AND
THE NORMAN CONQUEST

When Alexander III, then only a boy of nine years of age, was enthroned in 1249 as the last of the Canmore kings, his inauguration took place near Perth at the foot of the Moot Hill of Scone. Since David I had 'abhorred the obsequia' at his enthronement in 1124, the ceremony may once have been more pagan than Christian, perhaps even involving the sacrifice of a mare and the eating of its flesh, as described from Ireland in the twelfth century. Even if St Columba had insisted that such pagan rites be abandoned in consecrating Aedan mac Gabran as King of Dalriada in 574, it seems that the Christian ceremony still retained vestiges of ancient Celtic rituals for many centuries afterwards. Indeed it was only in 1329 that the Pope in Rome recognised the right of the kings of Scotland to be anointed with holy oil at their coronation.

Thus no crown was place upon Alexander's head in 1249, and he was made king by the magnates with the active participation of the clergy in what was essentially a secular ceremony. Once the newly enthroned king was seated upon the sacred Stone of Destiny, a Celtic genealogist or *seannachie*, holding the high office of the King's poet, or *Ollamh rig Alban*, then stepped forward to hail him in Gaelic, proclaiming him King of Scots with the words *Beannachd Dhe, Ri Alban*; 'The Blessing of God, O King of Scotland'. He then praised his illustrious ancestors by reading out his royal pedigree back in time to Kenneth mac Alpin, and then down the ages to Fergus the Great, son of Ercc, and even further back into the legendary mists of Celtic mythology, as proof of his right to rule.

Yet the reality was very different. Malcolm Canmore (1058–93), and more especially three of his sons by his second wife Margaret, who each reigned in turn as Edgar I (1097–1107), Alexander I (1107–24) and David I (1124–53), his great-grandsons Malcolm IV (1153–65) and William the Lion (1165–1214), Alexander II (1214–59) and Alexander III (1249–86) over the next two generations were all deeply imbued with the feudalising

26

influences of the Anglo-Normans, which almost without exception they had learnt at the English court. Marriage ties bound them to the royal family of William the Conqueror and his successors, or to the great Anglo-Norman families of England, while several held land in England as the Earls of Huntingdon from the English crown. Nearly all had been knighted by a king of England before they even gained the Scottish throne. Although they paid homage to their Celtic forebears, they had effectively turned their backs upon their Gaelic inheritance. Indeed as one English writer commented in 1212, perhaps unfairly, Malcolm IV and his brother William the Lion 'profess themselves to be rather Frenchmen in race, manners, language and outlook; and after reducing the Scots to utter servitude they admit only Frenchmen to their friendship and service'.

Malcolm Canmore and Queen Margaret

Malcolm Canmore gained the Scottish throne in 1058 after a four-year struggle against Macbeth and his stepson Lulach. The young king had been brought up at the Anglo-Saxon court of Edward the Confessor from an early age after his father Duncan I had been killed by Macbeth in 1040. The Anglo-Saxon king had himself mostly lived in France until 1042, when he became king of England, and his mother was herself a Norman. Admiring all things French, and with an abiding love for the Catholic Church in France, it was Edward the Confessor who first introduced French ideas and institutions into England, following the example of his strong-minded mother, well before the Norman Conquest of 1066. By then Normans and other Frenchmen had entered into England, often achieving high office in their new country. This influx became a flood when William, Duke of Normandy, conquered England in 1066, bringing with him a great entourage of Norman noblemen and their followers. Many of their descendants, especially their younger sons, along with the descendants of even later arrivals from Normandy and elsewhere, settled in Scotland during the years after 1124, when David I first came to rule over Scotland. We shall call them the Anglo-Normans, even if they included Bretons and Flemings as well as Normans.

We do not know if Malcolm Canmore was much influenced by the Anglo-Norman surroundings of his youth, but the late fourteenth century chronicler Fordun commented that the Scottish king could speak French and English as fluently as Gaelic. Such influences were reinforced when he married Margaret as his second wife, probably in 1069, after his first wife Ingibjorg had died. Queen Margaret was the great-niece of Edward the Confessor, and a sister to Edgar the Aetheling, by then the last surviving contender for the English throne from the ancient Anglo-Saxon house of Wessex. She was raised to an intense life of religious devotion while still a child at the royal court in Hungary, where her father had taken refuge. Later she came to share the French sympathies of her great-uncle when she returned to the Anglo-Norman court of Edward the Confessor in 1057.

After the Norman Conquest of 1066 her brother Edgar the Aetheling submitted to William the Conqueror, only to flee north to Scotland with his two sisters and their mother in 1068. Her marriage to Malcolm Canmore a year or two later was a historic act, not least because of the reforming zeal and conspicuous piety of three of her sons, Edgar, Alexander and David, born of this marriage, and sometimes known disparagingly as the Margaretsons, who each ruled Scotland in turn during the first half of the twelfth century. It marked the start of profound changes in the fabric of Scottish society, which occurred as the old Celtic institutions were slowly abandoned in favour of the feudalising influences of the Anglo-Normans.

It was Queen Margaret who first sounded the death knell of the Celtic Church in Scotland, attempting to rescue it from what she saw as its doctrinal ignorance and spiritual decline by bringing its archaic customs and traditions into line with the Church of Rome. The matters under dispute were significant but hardly central to Christian doctrine. Perhaps of most concern to the ecclesiastical authorities in Rome were irregularities in the consecration of bishops. The Celtic Church in Scotland had an episcopal structure, but its bishops took it upon themselves to consecrate their new members by virtue of their own office, without invoking the higher authority of a metropolitan archbishop at York. Turgot records that Margaret pressed the Celtic Church to reform these various malpractices at a council attended by Malcolm Canmore, who acted as her interpreter as she spoke no Gaelic. Yet contrary to tradition, Margaret did not neglect the Celtic Church. She not only encouraged the veneration of native saints but she is said by Orderic Vitalis, perhaps correctly, to have restored the monastery of Iona, which had fallen into disrepair, and where she may have commissioned the building of St Oran's Chapel. She also gave liberally with her husband to the *celi De* communities of celibate clergy, often simply known as Culdees or the 'servants of God', which had spread throughout Scotland as a religious order observing greater strictness in the Celtic Church.

What Queen Margaret achieved in practice was perhaps less important than the influence she was able to wield, especially over her husband Malcolm Canmore. This is clearly seen in the Anglo-Saxon names from the royal house of Wessex given to her six sons: Edward, the eldest, who was killed in 1093, was named after her father; Edgar I, who ruled as king (1097–1106) after the broken reign of his uncle Donald *Ban*, was named after her brother; Edmund, who allied himself with Donald *Ban*, and ended his days in religious seclusion, was named after her grandfather; Ethelred, who became the Abbot of Dunkeld, and perhaps the Earl of Fife, was named after her great-grandfather; Alexander I, who reigned as king (1106–24) after Edgar I, was perhaps named after Pope Alexander II or even Alexander the Great; and David I, the youngest, who reigned as king (1124–53) after Alexander I, was most likely named after the Biblical psalmist of the Old Testament. None was given the name of a MacAlpin king, but they all shared the religious devotion and intense piety of their Anglo-Saxon mother. She was eventually canonised as St Margaret in a ceremony held after the inauguration of Alexander III in 1249.

Donald *Ban*, Last of the Celtic Kings

The death of Malcolm Canmore in 1093 triggered a Celtic reaction to the Normanising ways that had started to affect Scotland during his reign. It was led by his brother Donald *Ban*, meaning the 'Fair', the son of Duncan I (1034–40). He claimed the throne by virtue of the ancient Celtic traditions of inheritance, which preferred brothers to sons under its laws of lateral succession. After many years spent in exile, following the murder of his father Duncan I by Macbeth in 1040, he raised a powerful fleet of galleys in the Western Isles, and took possession of the Scottish throne, apparently with the full agreement of the Celtic aristocracy. He expelled the 'English' followers of Malcolm Canmore from the country, and it is likely that their number included all the surviving sons of Queen Margaret, except perhaps for Edmund. Indeed it is likely that Edmund ruled over Lothian and Strathclyde on behalf of his uncle, the Scottish King, while Donald *Ban* himself held Scotia, north of the Forth, just as the macAlpin kings had divided their power. Such a division of power occurred in subsequent reigns when the eldest surviving brother of the reigning king came to hold Lothian and Strathclyde. It suggests that Scotia, lying north of the Forth, still remained at the very heart of Scotland.

While Donald *Ban* ruled in Scotland, several of Margaret's sons took refuge at the Anglo-Norman court of William Rufus, who now ruled over England after the death of William the Conqueror in 1087. Also living at the English court was their half-brother Duncan, eldest son of Malcolm Canmore by his first wife Ingibjorg. He had earlier been held hostage for the good behaviour of his father Malcolm Canmore, who had submitted to William the Conqueror at Abernethy in 1072. Trained as a knight, Duncan swore fealty to William Rufus, who in return gave him a sufficient force of Anglo-Norman knights to invade Scotland in 1094, when he defeated Donald *Ban*. Although enthroned as Duncan II, the Scots aristocracy only accepted him as king after he had agreed not to keep any English or Normans in the country and not to allow them to perform any military service for him. Deprived of such support, Duncan II was defeated within a few months by the native Scots who rebelled against his rule. Soon afterwards Duncan II was slain at Mondynes near Stonehaven by Maelpetair, the *mormaer* or Celtic earl then ruling over the Mearns, and Donald *Ban* was restored as king of the Scots.

After the death of Duncan II, William Rufus turned to Edgar, the eldest son still surviving of Malcolm Canmore and his second wife Margaret. Faced with the hostility of Donald *Ban*, he invested Edgar with the kingdom of Scotland in a ceremony held probably in 1095, in which Edgar became a vassal of the Norman kings of England. A full-scale invasion of the country was mounted in 1097, when Edgar and his Anglo-Norman knights defeated Donald *Ban* in a pitched battle. Edgar was supported by some Scots at least, since Constantine of the royal family of MacDuff, and afterwards Earl of Fife, was among his party. After his capture Donald *Ban* was mutilated by blinding, but he still had enough standing to be buried on Iona after his death as the last of the Celtic kings of Scotland to be accorded such an honour. Even though Celtic claimants to the Scottish throne were to revolt time and again over the next 130 years, they never succeeded in ousting the later kings of the Canmore dynasty.

Edgar's reign was uneventful, except that he was forced to recognise the Norse claim to the Western Isles, as well as Orkney and Shetland, following the great expedition of Magnus 'Barelegs' in 1098. The holy island of Iona and its ancient burial ground, where all but two of the MacAlpin kings are reputed to be buried, was abandoned. Edgar died childless in 1107 and the succession then passed to his younger brother Alexander I, who ruled over Scotland until his own death in 1124. He acted more independently of England, building royal castles to secure his realm instead of relying upon mercenary forces of Anglo-Norman knights from the south. His reign is best remembered as a time of religious foundation, when an Augustinian priory was founded at Scone, after his mother had earlier established a Benedictine monastery at Dunfermline. But it was also during his reign in 1114 that his younger brother David entered into a momentous marriage that profoundly influenced the subsequent history of Scotland.

David I and his Anglo-Norman Followers

David was already the brother-in-law of Henry I of England, who had succeeded William Rufus in 1100, when the English king married David's sister Matilda. Indeed David I had spent much of his youth in England, perhaps from the age of eight, receiving a royal upbringing at the court of William Rufus, while Donald *Ban* reigned over Scotland. His sister's marriage meant that he was now a favoured member of the royal household, witnessing the charters of Henry I as 'David, the Queen's brother' and acting as a justice. Knighted by Henry I it is likely that he saw military service with the English King in Normandy. Then as a mark of special favour from the English King, to whom he swore an oath of fealty and homage as the epitome of Norman knighthood, he was given in marriage to Matilda, daughter and heiress of Waltheof, Earl of Huntingdon and Northampton, herself a grandniece of William the Conqueror.

Even before he became king in 1124, David I already possessed lands in the south of Scotland, stretching from Strathclyde to Northumberland, bequeathed to him by his brother Edgar. He first started to settle Anglo-Norman families on these territories, later making them grants of land by royal charter in return for military service as his vassals. This influx of French-speaking foreigners marked the start of what has been called the Norman Conquest of Scotland. It proceeded gradually from within, slowly destroying the fabric of the ancient Celtic society and replacing it with the structures of a feudal kingdom. The ensuing changes not only profoundly altered how the country was governed and the nature of its institutions, but they also introduced an entirely new stratum of aristocratic Anglo-Norman families into the uppermost levels of Scottish society. These French-speaking incomers and their descendants often founded aristocratic families that rose to great power and influence within medieval Scotland. Indeed the Bruces and then the Stewarts were eventually to rule over the country, while the Balliols and the Comyns were to play an equally important role in its history.

Nature of the Feudal System

The great strength of the feudal system was that the grants were heritable, passing down the generations from father to his eldest son by the agreement of the king, as were the obligations for services to be rendered in return. It cemented the bonds that existed between the king and his barons, for it provided the king with a military force of knights and their followers, while the barons profited from their estates and the patronage of the king. Any estate granted to a baron could be further divided among his own retinue of knights, who then became his vassals or tenants, taking on similar obligations of military service to their lord as he himself owed as their superior to the king. The honourable ties of knighthood and chivalry which bound the lord to his vassals, and vice versa, greatly reinforced the feudal system. Equally it gave great powers to the king, since estates could also be forfeited by their holders for treachery or high treason. If an estate passed to an unmarried heiress, the king had the right to arrange her marriage as he thought fit, since her husband would then hold her lands as his own vassal.

Burghs and Sheriffdoms

As well as settling his own followers upon the land, David I was apparently the first king of Scotland to create royal burghs and sheriffdoms as a deliberate policy aimed at extending his own authority more widely throughout his kingdom. Burghs were privileged communities holding a monopoly of industry and trade under a royal charter, set up to provide the royal exchequer with a much needed source of income from excise duties and other taxes. Often a burgh was the *caput* or headquarters of a sheriff, appointed by the king to exercise royal authority in civil and military matters over the surrounding countryside, since the burghs were subject to their own laws. Sheriffs were not just legal officers, who held a court in the king's name, dealing with civil cases and criminal charges, but even more importantly they administered the king's estates, collecting the king's revenues in money and kind. Typically the office was held by men of great substance drawn from the highest ranks of the Anglo-Norman nobility, even if a few of the earliest sheriffs in the north had Gaelic names.

The burghs established by David I show the gradual imposition of his authority northwards around the eastern fringes of the Highlands, which quickened during the reigns of his immediate successors, Malcolm IV and William the Lion. Berwick and Roxburgh were described as burghs before David I even gained the throne in 1124, while Edinburgh, Stirling, Dunfermline, Perth and Scone were elevated to this position by 1130. They were followed soon afterwards by Montrose, Aberdeen, Elgin and Forres in the north, along with several others in the south of Scotland, such as the ecclesiastical burgh of St Andrews. However it was only after the death of David I in 1153 that a substantial number of burghs were established around the coastal fringes of Buchan and Moray, as well as farther south in Angus. Banff, Cullen, Auldearn, Nairn and Inverness all became burghs during the later reigns of Malcolm IV (1153–65) and William the Lion (1165–1214), together with Inverurie and Kintore, inland from Aberdeen. Burghs were also established in Angus around this time at Brechin, Forfar, Arbroath and Dundee. Rosemarkie, Dingwall and Cromarty also became burghs in the years up to 1314, as royal authority gradually spread over Ross as well as Moray. There were none in the Western Highlands until very much later, when Tarbert became a royal burgh during the reign of Robert I in the early years of the fourteenth century.

The sheriffdoms first established by David I over wide areas of the country were also intended to strengthen his royal authority over what was still a very diverse and turbulent realm. Not all can be easily dated, but his reign probably saw sheriffs established at Berwick, Roxburgh, Edinburgh, Stirling, Clackmannan and Scone (which later became united with Perth), as well as farther north at Forfar, Kincardine, Aberdeen, Banff and Inverness. All these sheriffdoms may date from 1136 or slightly later. The north-eastern sheriffdoms roughly correspond with the old Celtic earldoms or provinces of Angus, Mar, Buchan and Moray, but it is not clear if the Celtic earls themselves ever acted as sheriffs. Indeed it seems likely that sheriffs took over much of the power once exercised by these earls. It was only much later during the thirteenth century that other sheriffdoms came into existence at Dingwall and Cromarty, while the sheriffdom of Moray was split into smaller units based upon the royal castles at Elgin, Forres and Invernairn as well as Inverness. After an Act of Parliament in 1305 had stipulated that sheriffs should hold their office for life it tended to become hereditary in certain families.

Sheriffs may well have taken over the powers once exercised by thanes in medieval Scotland. It seems likely that thanes were first introduced as royal officials by Malcolm II (1005–34) as part of the Anglo-Saxon system of local government, which broke the country down into self-contained shires. They had charge of royal estates, known later as thanages, especially north of the Forth, administering its affairs, leading its inhabitants in war, supervising justice and paying tribute and taxes to the king. Originally held by men with Gaelic names, such as Macmallothen of Dairsie, Macbeath of Falkland, Gilys of Idvies, Dugall of 'Molen', Ewen of 'Rathenach' and Lorne of Uras, thanages eventually became part of the feudal system. Many were granted out to the Church, while others came into the possession of Anglo-Norman settlers or the Celtic nobility. Several in the north became the *caputs* of sheriffs. Even if thanages survived into the fourteenth century they were then held in a variety of different ways, while they had declined greatly in importance.

Office of the Justiciar

Sheriffdoms and free baronies were placed under the jurisdiction of a king's officer who later became known as the Justiciar, who had the important task of representing the king in the country at large. Such royal officers of the Crown went on twice-yearly circuits of the country, trying the serious crimes of arson, robbery, murder and rape which lay beyond the jurisdiction of the sheriffs. They were responsible for the perambulation and measurement of land and for other administrative duties central to a feudal state. They also supervised the work of the sheriffs, hearing appeals against their judgements. There were two Justiciars at first, one for Scotland north of the Forth and one for the Lothians to the south, but later a separate justiciar was appointed for Galloway.

While David I was laying the foundations of royal authority in matters secular, he was even more forward in reviving the religious life of the country. Often given credit for creating an entirely new system of episcopal dioceses throughout the country, David I merely restored many existing dioceses to greater activity, simply by appointing bishops in regular succession to one another, often encouraged by generous endowments. Only the dioceses of Moray, Ross and Caithness were definitely created by Alexander I and David I, while Argyll was later separated from the diocese of Dunkeld. Such foundations had a strategic function, intended to strengthen civil government by bringing the authority of the Church to bear upon the far-flung frontiers of the kingdom, especially in the north. Thus the Bishop was often moved before the Knight on the chessboard of Highland politics, or so it has been remarked. Yet it may be doubted how effective was this policy, since several bishops appointed to these remote dioceses were only titular figures, often absent for long periods at the royal court, and exercising little authority over their dioceses.

The Anglo-Norman Families of Scotland

David I and his successors Malcolm IV and William the Lion could not have undertaken the feudal settlement of Scotland in the twelfth century without a ready source of high-born followers, eager and willing to seek fame and fortune in a new country. They came from his vast estates in Huntingdon and Northamptonshire in the English Midlands, gained by his marriage with Matilda. Attracted north by his great strength of character coupled with his evident abilities, they indeed came from all over England, since we find families settling in Scotland from Yorkshire and Somerset, Shropshire and East Anglia, while others came directly from Normandy or elsewhere in France. Often they were the younger sons of the great Anglo-Norman barons, together with their dependents, who could not expect to inherit the patrimony of their fathers. They may well have come north to Scotland with selfish interests, seeking rank, privilege and fortune in what they regarded as a land of opportunity. Yet it seems likely that they also felt themselves bound to David I by the idealistic ties of knightly chivalry and brotherly fellowship, engendered by his own strong personality.

When David I first became king of Scotland in 1124 he granted Annandale in the south of Scotland to the Anglo-Norman family of Robert de Brus, whose descendants were later to feature so prominently as the **Bruces** in Scottish history. They take their name from their ancestral lands of Brix in Normandy which his father Adam de Brus left for England with William the Conqueror in the Norman Conquest of 1066. The lands he afterwards gained in the north of England passed on his death to Robert de Brus as his elder son. He was granted even more lands in Yorkshire as well as Annandale. When Robert de Brus died in 1141 his eldest son Adam de Brus inherited his English estates, while his second son and namesake Robert de Brus had already received the lordship of Annandale as his patrimony. Other Anglo-Norman families were later to hold the lordships of Eskdale, Ewesdale and Liddesdale as his neighbours. Annandale then passed around 1194 to his son William de Brus and afterwards in 1215 to his grandson Robert de Brus. He married Isabel, second daughter of David, Earl of Huntingdon, and the younger brother of Malcolm IV and William the Lion. It was through this marriage that his son Robert de Brus, known as the 'Competitor' and grandfather of the future king, was able to assert a claim to the throne of Scotland after the death in 1290 of Margaret, Maid of Norway.

Another baron greatly favoured by David I was Walter fitz Alan, ancestor of the Stewart family which came to rule over Scotland after 1371. Traditionally the **Stewarts** traced their origins to Banquo, Thane of Lochaber, and beyond him to the ancient kings of Scotland and especially to Kenneth mac Alpin. But the truth is more prosaic since they are Breton in origin, descended from the hereditary Senescals or Stewards of the Household to the Counts of Dol in eleventh century Brittany. It is just possible they have a remote claim to Celtic ancestry living as they did just beyond the borders of Normandy in Brittany, which was colonised much earlier by the Celts of Cornwall. Nonetheless their early history was much like many other Anglo-Norman families who first settled in England after the Norman Conquest of 1066.

Granted land in Shropshire by William the Conqueror it was a younger scion of the family who came north to serve David I after 1124, when Walter fitz Alan was granted the vast estates of Renfrew, Mearns and Strathgryfe in what is now Renfrewshire. He was also made High Steward to the Royal Household and his descendants later took their name from this office, which Malcolm IV made hereditary to his family in 1157. It was probably also Malcolm IV who granted Walter fitz Alan the lands of North Kyle farther south in Ayrshire, where he became the neighbour of another Anglo-Norman family who held the lordship of Cunningham. Walter fitz Alan may even have received the island of Bute after the death of Somerled in 1164. Such feudal grants of territory along the eastern shores of the Firth of Clyde were evidently intended to guard the hinterland of Scotland from seaward attack, not only by the Norse kings of Man, or by the Lords of Galloway but also by Somerled's descendants from Argyll and the Western Isles. After the death of Walter fitz Alan in 1157, his descendants held the office of High Steward of Scotland for another six generations until Robert the seventh High Steward ascended the throne of Scotland in 1371 as King Robert II, the only-surviving grandson of King Robert the Bruce by the marriage of the

King's daughter Marjorie with his father Walter, sixth High Steward of Scotland.

Many other Anglo-Norman families of lesser degree settled in Scotland during the reign of David I and indeed for long afterwards, along with Bretons and Flemings and even native Anglo-Saxons. They mostly came in the train of the great magnates making up the personal entourage of the king such as the Bruces and the Stewarts. Often they became the feudal tenants of these magnates, holding their lands as free and honorable vassals of their lord in return for military service. Although some families died out, so that their names now mean nothing to us, while others remained in relative obscurity over the ensuing centuries, many such families rose to prominence during the later years of the Canmore dynasty, often seeking fame and fortune in the service of the Crown. Indeed nearly all the royal officers of state, as well as many of the bishops appointed by the Canmore kings, were drawn from these families. Occasionally after entering Scotland these Anglo-Norman families continued their northerly progress, settling in the Highlands or around its fringes over the next two centuries. Several such families with their feudal origins came to regard themselves as true clans in the Highland sense, eventually taking on all the trappings of what was originally a Celtic institution.

Angles and Scots

It was the influx of these Anglo-Norman and Flemish settlers in the twelfth and thirteenth centuries that acted as a catalyst, triggering the long decline in the Gaelic language which has continued virtually to the present day. When they first arrived these French-speaking magnates shared only Latin as a written language in common with the Gaelic-speaking Scots, while it is likely that many of their followers spoke an early form of middle English. Already by the twelfth century Gaelic as the language of Celtic Scotland had been halted in its south-easterly advance when the Gaelic-speaking Scots encountered the Angles of Northumbria, or at least their descendants, who had settled the border counties of south-eastern Scotland, especially around the Merse.

By the end of the seventh century, after an earlier advance farther north into Pictland which ended with their defeat at the battle of Nectansmere in 685, the Angles of Northumbria had established their northern frontier along the line of the Pentland Hills, or perhaps farther north along the southern shores of the Firth of Forth. Farther west although they annexed the British kingdom of Rheged around the Solway in the seventh century, as well as the district of Kyle around 750, they otherwise made no headway against the British kingdom of Strathclyde. Then over the next century the

Anglian kingdom of Northumbria was very much weakened by dynastic struggles between its ruling families before the Danes attacked York in 866. They established their own rule over what was once the Northumbrian kingdom of Deira in the south, driving the Angles northwards beyond the River Tyne into their Northumbrian stronghold of Bernicia. However the Danish kingdom of York was itself soon threatened by the Anglo-Saxon kings of Wessex who succeeded Alfred the Great in 899. Indeed by the time of Alfred's grandson Athelstan Wessex was so powerful that Athelstan was able to invade Scotland in 934, reaching as far north as Dunnottar, while his fleet ravaged the Viking settlements in the Orkneys.

Even as the Anglian kingdom of Northumbria declined in power during the ninth century it was threatened from the north by the Scots. Once he had established his own authority over Pictland after 843, Kenneth mac Alpin invaded the country held by the Angles to the south of the Forth no less than six times. However it was not until the reign of his great-grandson Indulf (954–62) that Edinburgh was finally abandoned to the Scots, even if it did not become the permanent capital of Scotland until the reign of James III five centuries later. It was during the tenth century that the macAlpine kings were forced to enter into an alliance with the English kings of Wessex, as they overwhelmed the Danish kingdom of York, whereby the Scottish kings were to hold first Cumbria and then the Lothians, protecting the northern flanks of England against Viking attacks. The exact nature of this alliance was to plague Scotland for centuries, since it was held by the English kings at least that they were the overlords of the Scots. Eventually, however, the weakness of England under Aethelred the Unready was exploited by Malcolm II of Scotland, who won a famous victory over the English at the battle of Carham in 1018. The kingdom of Strathclyde was annexed around this time, stretching south into Cumbria, when Malcolm II set his grandson Duncan to rule over its people after the death of its last king. Thus Malcolm II had effectively established the border of Scotland from the Tweed to the Solway, even if the province of Cumbria itself was later lost to the English.

The Scottish acquisition of Lothian first brought an Anglian-speaking population within the borders of the still Celtic kingdom of Scotland long before the time of David I. However given the scarcity of *baile*-names and the absence of *achadh*-names in the south-east, there is no evidence that this early Anglian-speaking population of farmers and small landowners was ever dispossessed throughout East Lothian and the basin of the River Tweed, where it had already settled over the previous centuries. Indeed it was perhaps reinforced in the years after the Norman Conquest of 1066 when the whole country between York and Durham was devastated by William the Conqueror and its Anglian-speaking inhabitants expelled to take refuge in the south of Scotland, or so we are told by Symeon of Durham. Even so the presence of a Gaelic-speaking aristocracy throughout this Anglian-speaking region is suggested by the scattered occurrence of Gaelic place-names given to topographic features in the Lothians and the Border Counties. Moreover the occasional presence of such settlement-names as Makerstoun, Maxton, Comiston and Gilmerton, in which the Anglian ending -*tun* is linked with a Gaelic personal name, often now corrupted, even records the names given by the Anglian speakers to the estates owned by such Gaelic-speaking incomers. Indeed by the mid-twelfth century it appears that an English-speaking population was already established in the upper reaches of the Clyde valley, where the settlements established as Flemish fiefdoms during the reign of Malcolm IV have such names as Thankerton, Lamington, Roberton, Symington and Wiston, recording the names of their proprietors.

Introduction of Norman French

It was Malcolm Canmore when he gained the Scottish throne in 1058 who added Norman French to this linguistic *mélange*. He had learnt French as well as English at the court of Edward the Confessor where he had taken refuge after his father's murder by Macbeth in 1040, while still remaining a native Gaelic speaker. The introduction of Norman French as the aristocratic language of the realm was greatly accentuated when David I came to rule in 1124. Not only had he spent his youth at the Anglo-Norman court of Rufus of England, along with his elder brothers Edgar and Alexander, who each reigned in turn before him, but he started to settle feudal fiefdoms upon his Anglo-Norman barons. Nearly all these great magnates spoke Norman French as their first language, even if they had acquired some English as well, and it remained their chosen language for the next two centuries and even longer. Indeed there was a resurgence in the use of French during the Wars of Scottish Independence, when many of the great magnates had dealings in French with the English court, where it was the official language in which nearly all its business was conducted. Indeed even such an archetypal Celtic baron as Ewen MacDougall of Lorn, descendant of Somerled, wrote to Edward II in French. It was not until the very end of the fourteenth century that French ceased to be used by such magnates in Scotland. The reason then for its demise was explained most strikingly by George Dunbar, Earl of March, in a letter to Henry IV of England, when he excused his writing in the Scots vernacular as being 'more clear to my understanding than Latin or French', even if he still signed himself as 'Le Count de la Marche d'Escoce'.

Emergence of the Scots Vernacular

However it seems likely that the followers of these great Anglo-Norman barons were mostly native English speakers who bolstered the English-speaking population south of the Forth and brought its influence to bear elsewhere as the feudal system spread throughout much of lowland Scotland. The founding of burghs and other towns as well as monasteries and other religious houses, which were often settled by Flemings and Normans, Angles and Scandinavians, reinforced the use of English. Indeed it was recorded that the burghs and other fortified places of the Scottish realm were inhabited by English speakers in 1174 and by Flemings who had perhaps been expelled from England by Henry II in 1155, so that their inhabitants were never predominantly Gaelic-speaking. It was the linguistic fusion occurring within these communities that allowed the Scots tongue to emerge with great vigour as a vernacular dialect of northern English in later centuries, much influenced by the Scandinavian speech of the former Viking settlements in the north of England. The very early charters from the twelfth century were sometimes witnessed by men with Norse names, along with others with Anglo-Saxon and Celtic names, while witnesses with Norman names only became common from the time of David I onwards. Such charters were often addressed to 'French and English, Scots and Flemings', as the inhabitants of medieval Scotland were then called, where the Scots were the Gaelic-speaking population.

Northerly Penetration of English-Speakers

Once the feudal system became established as the common form of land-holding it seems from the evidence of place-names that English, or *Inglis* as it was then known, was used by the French-speaking magnates to communicate with their bailiffs, stewards and other servants, as well as their tenants, even where the common people still spoke Gaelic. Thus north of the Forth, W. F. H. Nicolaisen (1976) has shown that non-Celtic place-names first appeared during the early thirteenth century when Reidfurde was first recorded in Angus, along with Strype, Staneycroft, Muirford, Corncairn and Stobstane in Strathisla. Around the same time the names of Byermoss, Gledcairn and Crawcairn were given to boundary-marks in Aberdeenshire. Such names could only have been coined by English speakers, even if they evidently took over such Gaelic words as *cairn* in doing so. Yet these English names did not necessarily replace the older Gaelic names since many places in the Grampian foothills apparently had two names, one Gaelic and the other its English equivalent, such as Myllaschangly and Scottismill, Athyncroith and Gallow Burn, Tybyrnoquhyg and Blind Well,

Monboy and Yallow Pule, or Carnofotyr and Punderis Carne, which were all recorded from the Angus parish of Kingoldrum in the mid-fifteenth century.

There can be little doubt that speakers of Gaelic and English were then still living together side-by-side. Even if the very existence of native Gaelic-speaking families can only be glimpsed occasionally from the scattered pages of the historical record, it is likely that many people were bilingual. It may well be that native Gaelic-speakers gradually took to speaking English as the influence of the feudal system made itself felt in lowland Scotland, just as John Major recognised in 1521 when he commented that many Lowlanders had spoken Gaelic only a short time previously. It is even recorded that one family in Dunfermline abandoned Gaelic names for Norman ones in the thirteenth century, changing their names first from Gilgrewer to Gilchristin, who however had the Gaelic nickname of *Mantauch* the 'Stammerer', and then to Richard and finally to Maurice, all over four generations. Equally the Celtic earls of Scotland often adopted such Norman names for their children during these years. Nevertheless it was not just status that encouraged Gaelic-speakers to acquire English, but sheer pragmatism as well, since it was the language in which much business was transacted, not just in the baron's court but throughout everyday life.

Preservation of Gaelic Place-Names

Despite the penetration of English as the common language of lowland Scotland during the course of these centuries, Gaelic place-names still remained in use, even if they were often corrupted as Gaelic died out as a living language. Occasionally such place-names were translated directly into English, so that An t-Eilean Dubh became the Black Isle, while Ceannloch became Lochhead before it was renamed as Campbeltown in 1667. More usually only the sound of the original Gaelic was rendered into English so that the name itself lost any real meaning. There are literally thousands of such names throughout Scotland, as illustrated by Ben Lee for *Beinn Liath*, Sleat for *Sleibthe*, Rannoch for *Raineach*, Banff for *Banbh* and Drumnadrochit for *Drum na Drochaid*. Sometimes the Anglicised name ends in a curious and otherwise inexplicable -*s*, simply because the Gaelic place-name was originally in the plural. Examples are the Trossachs, derived from *Na Trosaichean*, or the 'Cross-Hills', Leuchars from *luachar*, or 'rushes', Largs from *learg* for a 'slope', and Foyers from the Gaelic *Fothair*, also meaning a 'slope'. Other etymologically meaningless place-names exist as tautologies, repeating the meaning of the original Gaelic elements, as in Point of Ardnamurchan, where *Ard* as the Gaelic word for a promontory has the same meaning as Point in English. Eilean Shona, Glenborrodale and Ardtornish Point are other examples, which all incorporate a Norse root with the same meaning as the Gaelic element, and indeed the last-mentioned place-name incorporates the English equivalent as well.

Coining of English Place-Names

Such Gaelic place-names typically exist alongside English place-names, especially in lowland Scotland, which were coined during these centuries for new settlements as well as natural features. Livingston, Winchburgh, Queensferry, Hawthornsyke, Newton, Blackness, Plewlands, Brownlaws, Cowhill and Foulshiels can all be cited as examples of such place-names from West Lothian, coined during the thirteenth and fourteenth centuries. They are all earlier than the later place-names of a distinctively Scottish character dating from the sixteenth century, likewise from West Lothian, such as Bankheid, Brigend, Braidmyre, Burnshot, Mylntown, Scottistown, Stanefauldhill, Gaitsyde, Quhitlaw and Meikle Brighouse, marking the emergence of Scots as a vernacular language akin to English. A 1452 charter from Fife displays much the same pattern of place-names. The majority of place-names mentioned were once Gaelic although spelt then according to Scottish conventions. They are sometimes qualified by English elements, often providing evidence for the division of land, such as Kynnaldy-*suthir* and Kinnaldy-*northir*, Balrymont-*Estyr* and Balrymont-*Westyr* or Malgask-*uvir* and Malgask-*nethir*, or giving the names of the propietors of such divided land, as with *Lambeis*lethin and *Priouris*lethin or *Priouris*-Kynmuk and *le Chawmeris*-Kynmuk. Only occasionally is there any reference to topographic features, as in Murecambosse, Levynnis-brig, Crag-fudy, Kirkland de Luchris, Muretone de Luchris and Cragroyihill. The remaining place-names are all English in derivation, some implying new settlements and farming activities, such as Newgrange, Newton and Newmyll, or new owners, such as Bonyngtoune, Gilmortoune, Wilkynstone, Greigstone and Freretoune. All the other non-Gaelic place-names describe natural features or settlement in less desirable localities, such as Byrehill, Fauside, Langraw, le Hache, Bynns, Urwell, Muretoune, Myretoune and Burchle.

The coining of such place-names by an English-speaking population argues strongly for the dividing up of earlier settlements, which occurred mostly through the partition and division of existing lands and only partly by the colonisation of wasteland. There is little or no evidence for the wholesale displacement of the native Gaelic-speaking population. Even if English-speaking incomers displaced individual Gaelic-speakers from their holdings, they still remained in sufficient numbers for Gaelic place-names now to be preserved throughout much of lowland Scotland. Only after a lengthy period of bilingualism did such Gaelic-speakers in the Scottish lowlands perhaps finally abandon their language for English, which by then had evolved into the distinctive dialect known as lowland Scots.

Anglicisation of Gaelic Place-Names

The loss of Gaelic as a living language in lowland Scotland often meant that the surviving Gaelic place-names took on corrupt forms of spelling and pronunciation, even as they were appropriated by Scots speakers, who eventually had no knowledge of Gaelic. Among these changes may be cited such Gaelic place-names as Balerno, Balmerino, Pitsligo, Aberlemno, Strathcathro and Cambo in which the original Gaelic suffix -*ach* was first altered into such forms as -*och*, -*auch* and -*augh*, as the vowel itself became more rounded during the fifteenth century and then was converted simply into the suffix -*o*, as the final consonant was lost in the sixteenth century. Such changes, which locally occurred very much earlier, were typical of the eastern counties of lowland Scotland. Farther north in the Grampian Highlands, where Gaelic was spoken for much longer, the final consonant was not lost in the same way, giving rise to such place-names as Badenoch, Garioch, Balloch, Tulloch and Rannoch, while Cabrach or Coigach preserve the original Gaelic. Elsewhere such forms as Dalgarnock or Balernock are found, especially in the west and south-west. Another variant affects the Gaelic place-name *Tulach*, meaning a 'hillock' or 'knoll', but more often a 'low smooth ridge', which changes into the prefix -*Tilly* or -*Tully*, giving rise to such place-names as Tillyfourie or Tullynessie. Similar changes affected Gaelic place-names ending in the suffix -*aich*, or its earlier form -*aigh*, seen in such place-names as Cairnie, Cluny, Crathie, Fyvie, Logie, Petty and Towie.

The anglicisation of Gaelic place-names beginning with *achadh*, meaning a 'field', which typically gave rise to such Scots place-names as Auchans, Auchendinny, Auchintoul and Auchnaclioch, has already been mentioned. Such place-names often passed through a half-way stage during this linguistic evolution, as illustrated by Achinclioch, for example, which had become Auchinclioch by the early seventeenth century. Much the same evolution is displayed by such place-names as Auchterarder, Auchterhouse or Auchter-muchty, as well as Ochtertyre, all starting with the Gaelic word *uachdar*, meaning an 'upland'. This Gaelic word evidently gave the early clerks or scribes great difficulty, since they variously rendered Auchterarder, for example, as *Uchterardour*, *Vchterardour*, *Ouchtyrardour* or *Wterardore*, before finally settling on the present spelling in the mid-sixteenth century.

Gaelic River-Names in English

The coining of English place-names in lowland Scotland rarely took account of existing Gaelic place-names except perhaps in the north-east of Scotland, where there is a quite distinctive set of stream names associated with the Scots word Burn, as discussed by W. F. H. Nicolaisen (1976). Derived from the Old English, and ultimately of Germanic origin, this word is normally placed after its qualifying element in such compound stream names as Braid Burn. Yet this order is quite often reversed in north-east Scotland, where stream names often adopt the distinctive form of Burn of Oldtown, or Water of Ailnack, as do other place-names, such as Mains of Auchindachy, Bridge of Nevis, Cotts of Newton or Boat of Garten. The earliest example of such a river-name is recorded from the mid-thirteenth century, when the Water of Esk was first mentioned, while the next century furnishes comparable examples in a Latinised or Frenchified context, such as *leBarre de Anewyth*, *Estirgrag de Gorgyn*, *vallis de Douglas*, *parci de Drum*, *lacus de leuyn*, and *grangia de Deruesey*. By the end of the fifteenth century such records become more commonplace, giving rise to such place-names as *Auldtoun de Knokinblew* or *Cotis de Lanbride*. Such names can hardly be the fanciful invention of English-speaking surveyors, mapping the country for the Ordnance Survey in the early nineteenth century, as long maintained as a delightful myth by its officers. Indeed they appear on the maps produced by William Roy when he undertook his Military Survey in the years after the 1745 Rebellion.

As argued by W. F. H. Nicolaisen (1976), it seems likely that such place-names were originally coined by speakers of lowland Scots. They apparently took the existing Gaelic stream names in particular and rendered their sound phonetically, often translating only *allt* into burn, so preserving their original word-order. Thus, *Allt an t-Sluic Leith*, meaning the 'Burn of the Grey Hollow' in Gaelic, became the Burn of Slock Lee. Sometimes the whole stream name was seemingly translated from the original Gaelic, giving rise to such examples as Burn of Oldtown or Burn of Blackpots, while later examples perhaps merely adopted this convention, giving rise to such examples as Burn of Berryhill, Burn of Cauldcotts or Burn of Davidston, where the second element in the name typically displays a variety of linguistic origins.

Often such streams were named after the country or terrain through which they flowed, as in Burn of Achlais (Gaelic: *achadh*, a field), Burn of Drumcairn (Gaelic: *druim*, a ridge) or Burn of the Boitain (Old Norse: *botn*, a valley). Others took the names of settlements, as in Burn of Birse, Burn of Houstry or Burn of Oldtown, or the names of valleys, hills or lochs, as in Burn of Crockadale, Burn of Melmannoch or Burn of Ola's Loch, while yet others simply incorporate the name of the stream itself, but in reversed order, as in Burn of Boyne or Burn of Turret. Such stream names are often shortened in ordinary speech, so that the Burn of Tervie simply becomes the Tervie.

These distinctive stream names could only have evolved where a Scots-speaking people came into contact over a lengthy period of bilingualism with native Gaelic speakers, even as Gaelic itself retreated as a living language. Indeed they were perhaps coined by Gaelic speakers themselves, especially if they gradually came to speak lowland Scots as a second language during this period. By literally translating such stream-names into lowland Scots it is more than likely that the distinctive word-order of the original Gaelic would be preserved. Such river names as Water of Buchat, and the names of river-crossings, like Bridge of Orchy and Boat of Garten, can likewise be explained as being translated directly from their Gaelic equivalents, even if these names have a rather wider distribution. Only settlement-names such as Mains of Callander do not appear linked in any way with equivalent place-names in Gaelic, and it may be that they simply imitate these other names.

Such an explanation cannot easily be applied to Orkney and Shetland nor to the north-east of Caithness, where many place-names have the same distinctive nature but where Gaelic was never spoken. Since the Norse language offers no such model for the construction of these place-names, it seems most likely they were introduced by immigrants from north-east Scotland, who had already adopted such a word-order in creating new place-names. Interestingly typical stream names such as Burn of Vacquoy, Burn of Aith and Burn of Setter are found along with a wide variety of other place-names exhibiting the same distinctive word-order, such as Hill of Wick, Point of Coppister, Wick of Collaster, Ness of Wadbister, Head of Mula, Taing of Noustigarth, Geo of Henken, Ward of Clugan, Keen of Hamar, Holm of Skaw, Lee of Saxavord and Breck of Newgarth. The plethora of such names and their Norse appearance suggest that the incoming Scots settlers undertook the wholesale adaption of what were once original Norse place-names and converted them according to their own conventions into Scots.

Changing Status of Gaelic

Even while all this evidence of place-names demonstrates that the Gaelic language was slowly disappearing from lowland Scotland during late medieval times, another even more momentous change affected its status. Up to the end of the fourteenth century, Latin documents consistently refer to Gaelic as *Scotice*, or *lingua Scotica*, while the Northern English of lowland

Scotland is termed *Anglice*. Fifty years later lowland Scots still called their language *Inglis*, but by the end of the fifteenth century, however, it was their lowland tongue that was increasingly known as *Scottis*, so reversing the convention of earlier centuries, while Gaelic became known somewhat disparagingly as Irish. Such a shift marked the gradual estrangement between the Gaelic-speaking Highlanders and the lowland Scots, which by this time was reflected in the satirical and often hostile references in early Scots literature, ridiculing the Gaelic language as a barbaric gibberish.

Chapter Three

PASSING OF THE ANCIENT EARLDOMS

The feudal settlement of Scotland started in the south and only later penetrated north of the Forth. This was predominantly the land of the Celtic
earldoms, occupying the heartland of the kingdom of the Scots. Their origins
are wreathed in obscurity since it is not until the twelfth century that they
first appear in the historical record. Even so the territorial outlines of nearly
all these earldoms seemingly match the earlier provinces of Pictland, or at
least their later sub-divisions. While three such provinces are named in the
Irish annals of the eighth and ninth centuries, they were only first described
in a manuscript dating from the twelfth century. Seven in number, they were
then known as Fib (Fife), Fidach (presumably Moray), Fotlaig (or Atholl),
Fortriu (Strathearn), Caitt (Caithness), Ce (Mar and Buchan) and Circinn
(Angus and Mearns). It is often assumed that these Pictish provinces were
ruled over by *mormaers*, or 'great stewards', first mentioned if only fleetingly
in the Irish annals of the tenth century, but rarely from Ireland itself. Such
sources nearly always describe them as leading the 'host', or provincial army
upon which the MacAlpin kings called for the defence of Alba, especially in
north-eastern Scotland. But they are hardly ever described in these sources
as ruling over the ancient provinces of Pictland, whose names mostly fell
into disuse. Instead they are nearly always associated with the later divisions
of these provinces, such as Moray, Strathearn, Mar, Buchan, Angus, Mearns,
and indeed Lennox, which apparently replaced the more ancient provinces
of Pictland.

Equally there is hardly any documentary evidence to suggest that the
ancient earldoms of Celtic Scotland were ever held by the direct descendants
of the Pictish *mormaers*. Indeed we do not even know if the office itself was
hereditary. The only evidence we have comes from the Celtic earldom of
Lennox. Alwin is named as its very first earl on record, late in the twelfth
century, admittedly in a charter dating from after his death. His ancestry is
obscure but a contemporary poem by Muredach Albanach and the ancient
Gaelic genealogies suggest that his father was Muredach and his grandfather
Maldouen, who were both called *mormaers* of Lennox in these sources.

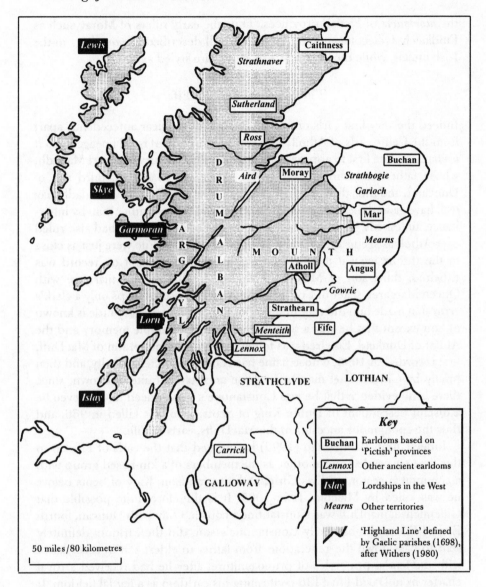

FIGURE 3.1 *Ancient provinces and earldoms of medieval Scotland (after Duncan)*

Otherwise only Gartnach and Ruadri as the very first earls of Buchan and Mar on record are called *mormaers* of their respective provinces in the Gaelic *notitae* of the twelfth century, inscribed on the blank pages of the Book of Deer. It is perhaps only that *mormaer* was rendered into Latin by the same word as used for earl, namely *comes*, so suggesting on quite spurious grounds that the Celtic earldoms of Scotland were once held by the *mormaers* of Pictish provinces. Thus the early rulers of Moray such as Findlaech, Gillecomgan and Macbeth are all described as *mormaers* in the Irish annals, while the later rulers of Moray are styled as earls.

The MacDuff Earls of Fife

Indeed the very first earls on record often have no clear antecedents, apart from the Celtic earls of Atholl, who were apparently of royal lineage or so it is claimed. The first to appear in the early twelfth century was Earl Madadh, whose father according to the Norse sagas was Maelmuir, third son of Duncan I, and thus the younger brother of Malcolm Canmore. Madadh may well have gained the earldom of Atholl by royal charter rather than by inheritance, unless his grandfather Crinan, lay-abbot of Dunkeld, had also ruled over Atholl as seems quite likely. The ancient earls of Fife were just as close to the throne even if it now seems unlikely that the first on record was Ethelred, third son of Malcolm Canmore by his second marriage with Queen Margaret, sister of Edgar the Aetheling. It was perhaps only a clerk's error that made him the very first Earl of Fife. Otherwise very little is known of him except that he was a true churchman of venerable memory and the Abbot of Dunkeld. Ethelred was followed by Constantine, son of MacDuff, first recorded in 1095, whose name has echoes of ancient royalty, and then briefly by Gillemichael macDuff, whose ancestry is quite unknown, since there is no evidence that he was Constantine's son. Indeed he may even be a distant descendant of Dubh, King of Scots, who was killed in 966, and thus the eponymous ancestor of the MacDuffs, earls of Fife.

Indeed John Bannerman (1993) has argued that the earls of Fife up to this time succeeded one another as the members of a kin-based group with a common ancestor, such as Giric, Dubh's grandson, King of Scots before he was killed by Malcolm II in 1005. It is therefore quite possible that Gillemicheal macDuff was Constantine's cousin. Only with Duncan, fourth Earl of Fife and most likely Constantine's son, did the earldom definitely start to pass down the generations from father to eldest son in accordance with the feudal principles of primogeniture, after he had received a royal charter from David I in 1136 confirming his earldom as a feudal fiefdom. It seems quite likely that Gillemichael's descendants then took the name of MacDuff and acted as leaders of their kindred whenever the Earl of Fife was a minor, just as a Highland clan in later times would appoint a Tutor at its head until its chief came of age.

Duncan and his successors were often given precedence over all the other earls of Scotland in witnessing royal charters, while the later earls of Fife certainly came to exercise the prerogative of enthroning the king himself at his inauguration. As John Bannerman (1993) argues, they were quite possibly accorded this status as a collateral branch of the MacAlpin dynasty, descended from Giric (997–1005), and his grandfather Dubh (962–6), after they had agreed to abandon their claim to the Scottish throne under the Celtic laws of succession. Indeed they may well have exercised this privilege even earlier at the inauguration of Malcolm Canmore as King of Scots, if MacDuff, Thane of Fife, is indeed a historical figure and not just an invention of such medieval chroniclers as Fordoun and Wyntoun in the fourteenth and fifteenth centuries. Foremost among all the subjects of the Canmore kings, they styled themselves in regal fashion as 'Earls of Fife by Grace of God'. Their kinsmen down to the ninth degree were able to claim an ancient right of sanctuary known as the Law of Clan MacDuff, escaping the normal penalties for murder, if they could reach MacDuff's Cross near the ancient Pictish capital of Abernethy in Fife. Indeed they still claimed that only the earls of Fife had jurisdiction over them, even after the male line of the ancient Earls of Fife had died out in 1353, after which the earldom passed to the Stewarts, Dukes of Albany.

The historical record casts little light on the ancestry of the other earldoms of Celtic Scotland. Even if we cannot be sure it seems quite likely that they first succeeded one another according to the Celtic laws of inheritance as the members of a kin-based society, making it difficult to determine exactly how they were all related to one another from the scanty records of the time. But just as the earls of Fife soon abandoned this practice in favour of the feudal principle of primogeniture, so did all the other earldoms in Celtic Scotland by the early decades of the thirteenth century at the very latest. Not long afterwards they started to marry off their sons to the daughters of the incoming Anglo-Norman nobility or even to their widows, even if it took several generations for some Celtic earldoms to adopt such a policy. Such marriages on occasion had the effect of giving the family lands in the south, which they then held of the English crown. Their further integration into the feudal system occurred whenever their daughters entered into marriage with the Anglo-Norman aristocracy. Often such marriages brought estates to their husbands, who then held them under feudal tenure from the Scottish Crown. But such marriages almost without exception had even more far-reaching consequences whenever these Celtic earldoms died out in the male line, allowing them to pass into the hands of an Anglo-Norman family.

The Comyn Earls of Buchan

The ancient earldom of Buchan was the very first to come by marriage into the possession of a powerful Anglo-Norman family, namely the Comyns, before it eventually passed to the Stewarts in the late fourteenth century. The ancient earls of Buchan first appear as historical figures in the mid-twelfth century. The first to be named was Gartnach, *mormaer* of Buchan, whose daughter married Colban, who became the Earl of Buchan in right of his wife. His son or grandson Fergus then became Earl of Buchan in the 1180s, but he died before 1214 leaving his daughter Marjorie as his sole heiress. Countess of Buchan in her own right, she carried the earldom of Buchan to the powerful Comyn family with their Anglo-Norman origins when she married William Comyn in the years before 1214.

The fortunes of the Comyn family in Scotland were laid nearly a century earlier by another William Comyn, a clerk in holy orders, whom David I made Chancellor of Scotland. He was a younger son of Robert Comyn, who it is said crossed the English Channel with William the Conqueror in 1066. Most likely only a nickname, the family name of Comyn is unlikely to come from the district of Comines in Normandy, never being written with a 'de' in the early Scottish records. Not long afterwards Robert Comyn was granted the earldom of Northumberland, before he was killed trying to possess his territories. His sons and grandsons then held lands in England, before his great-grandson Richard Comyn came north in the reign of David I, perhaps after his grand-uncle had been made Chancellor. He received the lands of West Linton and married Hextilda, who was the only grandchild of Donald *Ban*, last of the Celtic kings of Scotland. It gave their descendants the claim to the Scottish throne after the death of Margaret, Maid of Norway, in 1290, so fatal to their fortunes.

The eldest son of Richard Comyn and Hextilda to survive childhood was William Comyn, who had already been made Justiciar of Scotland north of the Forth, when he married Marjorie, Countess of Buchan in her own right. The marriage itself was quite evidently a political act by the Scottish crown which planted one of its most loyal servants in the unsettled lands of the north as the first of the 'Norman' earls of Celtic Scotland. After becoming Earl of Buchan by this marriage, William Comyn and his descendants, known as the Black Comyns from their heraldic colours, prospered greatly during the thirteenth century. They gained much power and influence in the service of the Scottish crown, helped by judicious marriages, which made them kinsmen to many of the most aristocratic families of the realm, including the earls of Fife, Dunbar, Strathearn, Angus, Mar and Ross.

The Comyn Lords of Badenoch

Just as powerful as the Comyn earls of Buchan in the thirteenth century were the Red Comyns of Badenoch, who were in fact the senior line. When William Comyn became the Earl of Buchan by right of his wife, he already had two sons by an earlier marriage. The younger son was Walter Comyn, who was made Lord of Badenoch by Alexander II around 1230, while he later became the Earl of Menteith by right of his wife Isabella, Countess of

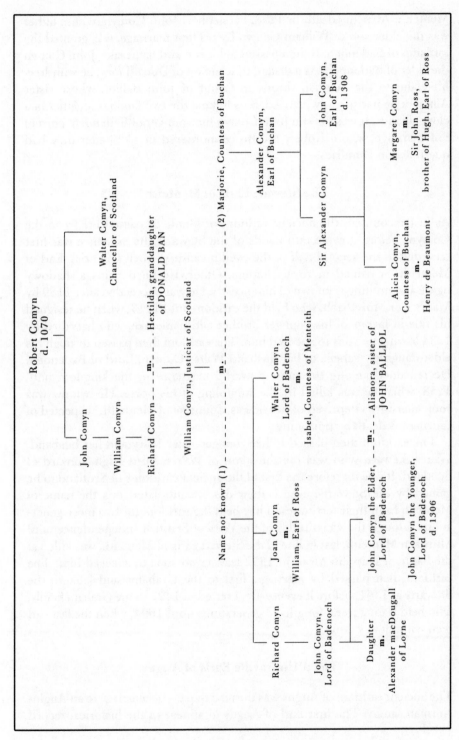

FIGURE 3.2 *The Comyns and their allies (after Duncan and the Scots peerage)*

Menteith. After his death in 1258, his nephew John Comyn, whose father was the elder son of William Comyn by his first marriage, was granted the lordship of Badenoch. It then passed to his son and namesake, John Comyn the elder of Badenoch. As a distant descendant of Donald *Ban*, he withdrew his claim to the Scottish throne in favour of John Balliol, whose sister Alianora he had already married, thus linking the two families together in a close alliance. It was his son John Comyn the younger of Badenoch, born of this marriage, whom Robert the Bruce murdered in 1306 after they had quarrelled in Dumfries.

The Stewart Earls of Menteith

As just recounted, the ancient earldom of Menteith passed briefly to the Comyns before it came into hands of the Stewarts. Its existence was first recorded in the second half of the twelfth century, when Gilchrist, Earl of Menteith, is named in royal charters. Otherwise he remains a shadowy figure and nothing is known of his ancestry. He was succeeded after 1189 by Maurice or Murethach, who held the earldom until 1213, when he resigned his title in favour of his younger brother and namesake, who had died by 1234 leaving no sons to succeed him. The earldom then passed through his elder daughter Isabella to her husband Walter Comyn, Lord of Badenoch. He remained among the most powerful magnates in the kingdom until 1258, when he was killed by the stumbling of his horse. His widow was soon afterwards deprived of her title as Countess of Menteith, suspected of causing his death by poisoning.

The earldom then passed to her younger sister Mary and her husband, Walter Stewart, who was the third son of Walter, third High Steward of Scotland. It was therefore the first of the ancient earldoms of Scotland to be gained by the Stewarts, even if their descendants later took the name of Menteith from their territories. They held the earldom for two more generations through the vicissitudes of the Wars of Scottish Independence until Murdach Menteith, last in line of the Stewart earls of Menteith, was killed at the battle of Dupplin Moor in 1332 leaving no sons to succeed him. The earldom then passed by marriage, first to the Grahams and later to the Stewarts in 1361, before it eventually reverted in 1427 to the Graham family, who held it for several long-lived generations until 1694, when the last earl died without any issue.

The d'Umfraville Earls of Angus

The ancient earldom of Angus was the next to pass by marriage to an Anglo-Norman family. The first Earl of Angus to appear in the historical record

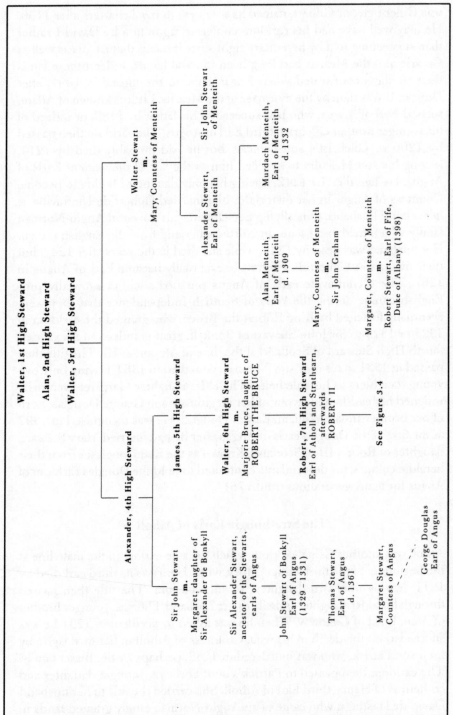

FIGURE 3.3 *Descent of the early Stewarts, earls of Angus and Menteith (after the Scots peerage)*

was Gillebrigte, or Gilbert, named as a witness to royal charters after 1150. He may well have had his earldom conferred upon him by David I rather than succeeding to it by hereditary right since it seems that Angus as well as Gowrie and the Mearns had long been in royal hands. Indeed these lands were perhaps confiscated when Edgar came to the throne in 1097, after Duncan II was slain by the mormaer of the Mearns. Little is known of Adam, second Earl of Angus, who had succeeded his father by 1189, or indeed of his younger brother Gilchrist, third Earl of Angus. The earldom then passed by 1206 to Gilchrist's son Duncan, but he had probably died by 1214, leaving his son Malcolm to succeed him as the last of the ancient Earls of Angus. He had died by 1242, leaving his only daughter Matilda to become Countess of Angus in her own right. She married Gilbert de Umfraville as her second husband, thus allying herself with this powerful Anglo-Norman family which held vast estates in Northumberland from the English crown. Her husband was dead by 1245, while she died in the years after 1247, but their infant son Gilbert de Umfraville eventually became Earl of Angus in 1267. The d'Umfraville earls of Angus pursued such an avowedly pro-English course during the Wars of Scottish Independence that they were eventually forfeited by King Robert the Bruce, who granted the earldom in 1328 or 1329 to Sir John Stewart of Bonkyll, great-grandson of Alexander, fourth High Steward of Scotland at the time of Alexander III. The title then passed in 1331 to his only son Thomas, who died in 1364, leaving only two young daughters as his sole heirs. The elder daughter Margaret eventually resigned her earldom in favour of her illegitimate son George Douglas, born of her brother-in-law William, Earl of Douglas. He was recognised in 1397 as the first of the Douglas earls of Angus after he had married Mary Stewart, daughter of Robert III of Scotland. Known as the Red Douglases from their heraldic colours, his descendants continued to hold the Douglas earldom of Angus for many generations until 1761.

The Strathbogie Earls of Atholl

Atholl was another Celtic earldom which became extinct in the male line at the beginning of the thirteenth century, when Henry as its third earl died by 1211, leaving only two daughters to succeed him. The title then passed through his elder daughter Isabella to her husband Thomas, younger brother of Alan, Lord of Galloway. When he was killed by accident in 1231 he was succeeded on the death of his wife, Countess of Atholl in her own right, by their son Patrick, who was murdered in 1242, perhaps by the Bisset family. The earldom then passed to Patrick's aunt Forflissa, younger daughter and co-heiress of Henry, third Earl of Atholl. She carried the title to her husband David de Hastings, who came of an Anglo-Norman family granted lands in

Angus during the reign of William the Lion. After his death without any sons in 1247 the earldom passed by marriage to John de Strathbogie, descendant of Duncan, fifth Earl of Fife, and after 1264 to their son David de Strathbogie and then to their grandson John de Strathbogie, who was executed by the English in 1306. Edward II of England then granted the earldom to David de Strathbogie, his son and heir, after it had been held briefly by Ralph de Monthermer, Earl of Gloucester. He was forfeited by King Robert the Bruce in 1314, and the earldom passed briefly to the Campbells and then to the Douglases, before it came into the hands of the Stewarts in 1342.

The Celtic Earls of Strathearn

The ancient line of the earls of Strathearn, who gave precedence only to the earls of Fife, lasted until 1344. The first to appear on record was Malise, who fought for David I at the Battle of the Standard in 1138. He was succeeded by Ferteth, possibly his son, who held the earldom in the 1160s, while his son Gilbert became the third Earl of Strathearn in 1171, marrying Maud d'Aubigny, who came from an Anglo-Norman family. After Robert, the eldest of his seven sons to survive his death in 1223, the earldom passed in succession from father to eldest son, each named in turn Malise from the Gaelic Maelisu, meaning the 'tonsured servant of Jesus'. The downfall of their line eventually occurred in 1344 when Malise, eighth and last Earl of Strathearn, was found guilty of surrendering his title to Edward Balliol in 1333, who had awarded it instead to John de Warenne, Earl of Surrey. David II then granted the earldom to Sir Maurice Moray, who was killed at the battle of Neville's Cross in 1346, leaving only a daughter who did not inherit his title. Meanwhile Malise as the last of the ancient earls of Strathearn had lost his earldom of Caithness as well, which he had gained by right of his great-grandmother Matilda, daughter of Gilbert, Earl of Caithness, after the Angus earls of Caithness and Orkney had died out in the male line in 1329. He then retired north to his earldom of Orkney, which he held of the Norwegian crown. When he died around 1350, he left five daughters by his two marriages as his co-heiresses, whose possessions in Caithness were a source of much conflict in later years.

The Ancient Earls of Mar

North of the Mounth, Ruadri as the very first Earl of Mar on record was known as well as its *mormaer*. He was succeeded by 1152 at the latest by Morgrund, perhaps related to the earls of Fife, and then in the years before 1183 by the mysterious figure of Earl Gilchrist, who held the earldom of

Mar until his own death in 1203. Even though he was survived by two sons, the earldom of Mar then remained vacant until it passed to Duncan as a younger son of Earl Morgrund, and then after his death in 1244 by his son William. He married Elizabeth, daughter of William Comyn, Earl of Buchan, so allying himself with the powerful Comyn family against the Durwards, who claimed the earldom of Mar for themselves. He was succeeded after 1276 by his son Donald, whose daughter Isabel married Robert the Bruce, Earl of Carrick, afterwards King of Scotland, probably in 1295. Captured at the battle of Dunbar in 1296, Donald probably died soon afterwards and certainly by 1305. His son Gartnait succeeded him but he too had died by 1305, leaving only his infant son Donald by Christain Bruce, sister of Robert the Bruce, as heir to the earldom of Mar. After spending many years in England he returned to Scotland in 1327, only to be killed in 1332 at the battle of Dupplin Moor while acting as the Regent of Scotland. His only son Thomas then became Earl of Mar while still an infant living in England. He eventually returned to Scotland but he died childless in 1374, so bringing the ancient earldom of Mar to an end in the male line. It afterwards passed by marriage briefly to the Douglases and then to the Stewarts in 1405, before it eventually passed in 1565 to the Erskines, who held it for several long-lived generations until 1716, when they were forfeited after the Jacobite Rebellion of 1715.

The Celtic Earls of Lennox

The Celtic earldom of Lennox only appears in the historical record late in the twelfth century but it survived until 1425 as the last of the ancient earldoms of Scotland. Alwin is named as its first earl, admittedly in a charter dating from after his death. It seems he had died by 1178 and soon afterwards the earldom was given by William the Lion, probably only in custody, to his younger brother David, Lord of Garioch and later Earl of Huntingdon. By 1199 the earldom had reverted to its ancient line when Alwin the younger, son and heir of the first Earl Alwin, was acknowledged as the Earl of Lennox. Despite this royal intrusion there is little evidence of Anglo-Norman settlement within the earldom, which resolutely retained its Celtic ambience to judge by the Christian names given to its earls and their descendants throughout the thirteenth century.

Earl Alwin the younger married the daughter of Gilchrist, Earl of Menteith, and by this marriage he apparently had nine sons in addition to his eldest son and heir, nearly all of whom married into local families with their native ancestry. Earl Alwin the younger was succeeded in 1214 by his eldest son Maldouen, who was granted a charter from Alexander II in 1238, confirming his possession of the earldom and all its lands apart from

Dumbarton Castle, which remained in the hands of the King. He possibly married a daughter of Walter, third High Steward of Scotland. The earldom passed to their grandson, who had died by 1305, and then to his son Malcolm, supporter of King Robert the Bruce after 1306, who was killed at the battle of Halidon Hill in 1333.

The next Earl of Lennox was Malcolm's son Donald, but little is known of him except that he was succeeded by his daughter and only child Margaret, who became Countess of Lennox in her own right around 1364. She married Walter of Faslane, who was a direct descendant of Aulay, fifth son of Earl Alwin the younger and the nearest heir-male to the earldom of Lennox. The ancient line thus continued even if her husband was mostly known as Walter, Lord of the earldom of Lennox. After they had resigned the whole earldom and lordship of Lennox into the hands of Robert II in 1385, it was granted out again to their son Sir Duncan of Lennox. It seems that his life was blameless and that he took little or no part in public affairs. He married Elen Campbell, daughter of Gilleasbuig Campbell of Lochawe and the widow of John, eldest son of John MacDonald, first Lord of the Isles. Their daughter Isabella then made a fateful marriage with Murdach Stewart, second Duke of Albany and Governor of Scotland until 1424, when James I returned from captivity in England intent on destroying his powerful family with their regal pretensions. Despite his great age Earl Duncan of Lennox suffered the same fate as his son-in-law when he was arrested, tried for treason and executed by beheading in May 1425. His death extinguished for ever the last of the ancient earldoms of Celtic Scotland.

Conflicts of Loyalty

Despite the slow but inexorable extinction of these ancient earldoms, they still remained a conservative force in the feudal society of Scotland until the outbreak of the Wars of Scottish Independence in 1296. Indeed their numbers were augmented during the early decades of the thirteenth century, when the ancient earldom of Carrick was first recognised and the feudal earldoms of Ross and Sutherland were created, just after the Norse earldom of Caithness and Orkney had passed into the possession of a family descended from the ancient earls of Angus. As already recounted, several earldoms then passed by marriage during the thirteenth century to such Anglo-Norman families as the Comyns of Buchan, the Stewarts of Menteith, the d'Umfravilles of Angus and the Bruces of Carrick, while the earldom of Atholl passed by marriage to David de Strathbogie, himself descended from a younger son of the Earls of Fife, after first passing through the hands of two sisters and their husbands, Thomas of Galloway and David de Hastings.

Even if their succession was sometimes challenged by other claimants, as happened with the earldoms of Menteith and Mar, and other earls occasionally met a violent end, it was not until the outbreak of the Wars of Scottish Independence in 1296 that these earldoms were threatened by upheaval. Indeed few individuals survived nearly twenty years of warfare, which ended with the Scottish victory at the battle of Bannockburn in 1314, even if most died of natural causes.

Apart from Duncan, Earl of Fife, still a minor in 1296, nearly all the Scottish earls supported the cause of John Balliol when faced by the invasion of their country by Edward I of England. Only Robert the Bruce, Earl of Carrick and the future king, joined the English army when it mustered at Wark, along with Patrick de Dunbar, Earl of March and Gilbert d'Umfraville, Earl of Angus. But once Edward I had conquered Scotland after the battle of Dunbar, they were all forced to swear fealty and homage to the English King as the overlord of Scotland. Many did not abandon their new allegiance even while the lesser barons and the common people were fighting to restore John Balliol as King of Scots under the leadership, first of William Wallace and Andrew de Moray, and then of John Comyn the younger of Badenoch in the years before 1306. Indeed they or their heirs mostly remained loyal to Edward I of England, even after Robert the Bruce had seized the Scottish throne in 1306. Then only John de Strathbogie, Earl of Atholl, along with Malcolm, Earl of Lennox and Alan, Earl of Menteith, rallied to his cause. Indeed when Malise, Earl of Strathearn, was forced under duress to render homage to King Robert the Bruce after his enthronement he objected, saying that he did not desire to be as frail as glass, as he would be to break his fealty to the King of England. Perhaps significantly only eight earls signed the so-called Declaration of Independence at Arbroath in 1320. Even so after King Robert the Bruce had triumphed at the battle of Bannockburn in 1314, he set about patiently restoring the ancient earldoms of Scotland by renewing their charters. While he forfeited the earldoms of Atholl and Angus to the Crown, he granted them out again to his own supporters, namely Sir John Campbell of Lochawe and Sir James Stewart of Bonkyll. Likewise while he suppressed the Comyn earldom of Buchan, its place was taken by the newly created earldom of Moray, granted in 1312 to Sir Thomas Randolph as his closest ally.

Rise of the Stewarts

All these earldoms had a very chequered history during the rest of the fourteenth century, so that they never really regained their former power and influence. Indeed their ranks were decimated in the early 1330s when the struggle for Scottish independence was renewed against the forces of

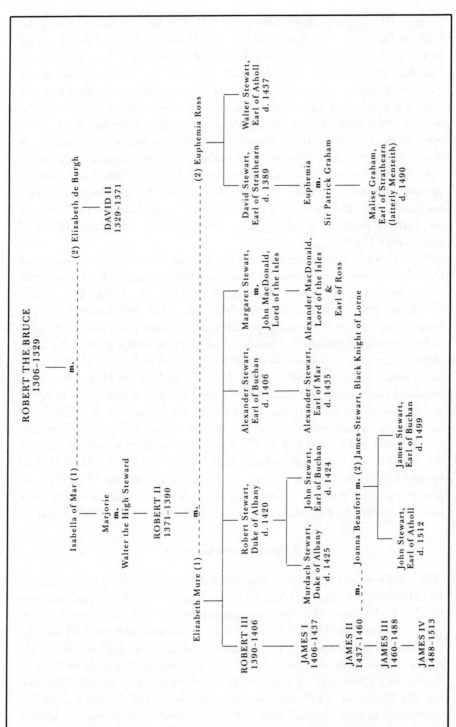

FIGURE 3.4 *Bruce and Stewart dynasties to 1513, showing selected earldoms (after Nicholson)*

Edward III and his protege, Edward Balliol. The brief success achieved by Edward Balliol after the battles of Dupplin Moor in 1332 and Halidon Hill in 1333, where seven earls were slain altogether, meant that they temporarily lost their estates to the 'Disinherited'. They suffered further losses at the battle of Neville's Cross in 1346, where two more earls were killed and several others captured. Even if they had sons to succeed them they were often minors at the time of their fathers' deaths, unable to influence the government of the country. Natural causes also took their toll, since several earls died without any male heirs to succeed them. Only the ancient earldoms of Lennox and Sutherland continued to be held during these years without passing by marriage to other families. Most of the other earldoms came into the hands of the Stewarts apart from the newly created earldom of Douglas, the Dunbar earldom of Moray after 1358, and the Douglas earldom of Angus after 1389.

The Stewarts were thus the one family that ultimately benefited most from the dynastic accidents and political misfortunes that befell the Scottish earldoms during the course of the fourteenth century. Unlike the Bruces, who were never prolific as a family, dying out in the male line in 1371, the Stewarts prospered remarkably, proliferating over the years until they came to hold nearly all the ancient earldoms of Scotland and a great many lordships towards the end of the fourteenth century, as well as the Crown itself. Long before he ascended the throne in 1371, Robert the High Steward of Scotland had gained the earldom of Atholl in 1342 when it was resigned in his favour by Sir William Douglas. Better known as the Knight of Liddesdale, he had come into the title after the death of Sir John Campbell at the battle of Halidon Hill in 1333, who left no heirs to succeed him as the first and only Campbell earl of Atholl. Then in 1357, after David II had returned to Scotland from captivity in England, Robert the High Steward was granted the earldom of Strathearn, which had remained vacant since 1346 when Sir Maurice Moray was killed at the battle of Neville's Cross.

Robert II and his Sons

When Robert the High Steward succeeded David II as King of Scotland in 1371 he already had several sons by his two marriages, who all vied with one another for honours. His eldest son John, born in 1337, and created Earl of Carrick in 1367, followed him in 1390 on the throne as Robert III after he had taken a more auspicious Christian name. Apart from the Earl of Carrick, Robert II had three other sons by his first marriage with Elizabeth Mure of Rowallane. Their second son was Walter Stewart, who in 1360 married Isabella, Countess of Fife, daughter and only heiress of the last Earl of Fife in the ancient line, who had died in 1353. He died soon afterwards, leaving his widow to resign her earldom to his younger brother Robert Stewart in 1371. The third son of Robert II by his first marriage, he first became the Earl of Menteith by his marriage in 1361 with Margaret Graham (Countess of Menteith in her own right after her mother's death in 1360 and already the widow of two other husbands and a divorcee), and then Earl of Fife. He was created Duke of Albany in 1398 and then became Governor of Scotland in the years after 1406, while James I was held captive in England, after he had served as its Regent during the reign of Robert III.

The fourth and youngest son of Robert II by his first marriage was Sir Alexander Stewart, better known as the 'Wolf of Badenoch'. He had the long-vacant earldom of Buchan conferred upon him in 1382 by his marriage with Euphemia Leslie, Countess of Ross in her own right after her father Hugh, last in line of the ancient earls of Ross, had died in 1372. After his death in 1405 without any lawful heirs, the earldom of Buchan then passed to his nephew John Stewart as the younger son of Robert Stewart, Duke of Albany, as did the earldom of Ross in 1417. It had previously been granted in 1372 to Sir Walter Leslie as the first husband of Euphemia Ross, and then after her death in 1395 to their son Alexander Leslie, who had died in 1402. John Stewart died without any issue in 1424, leaving the earldom of Buchan vacant until 1470, while the earldom of Ross passed in 1437 to Alexander MacDonald, third Lord of the Isles. Sir Alexander Stewart, Earl of Buchan and 'Wolf of Badenoch', had a natural son and namesake Sir Alexander Stewart, who became the Earl of Mar in 1404 when he abducted Isabel, Countess of Mar in her own right, and forced her into marriage. She had succeeded to her title around 1391 after the death of her mother Margaret, who held the earldom of Mar in her own right after the death in 1374 of her brother Thomas, last in line of the ancient earls of Mar.

The second marriage of Robert the High Steward took place around 1355 when he married Euphemia Ross, daughter of Hugh, fourth Earl of Ross and the widow of John Randolph, third Earl of Moray. David Stewart as the elder son born from this marriage first inherited his father's title to the earldom of Strathearn in 1371. A few years later he gained the earldom of Caithness as well, which had remained vacant ever since it was forfeited in 1344. He had died by 1389, when he was succeeded by his only daughter Euphemia Stewart, who became Countess of Strathearn in her own right. She resigned her earldom of Caithness in 1402 in favour of her uncle Walter Stewart, who was younger son of Robert the High Steward by his second marriage. He then became Earl of Atholl in 1404 after the title had been held first by John Stewart, afterwards Robert III of Scotland, and then by his eldest son David Stewart, Earl of Carrick, who died in mysterious circumstances while held captive by his uncle Robert Stewart, Duke of Albany, who briefly claimed the title for himself. Two years later the earldom of

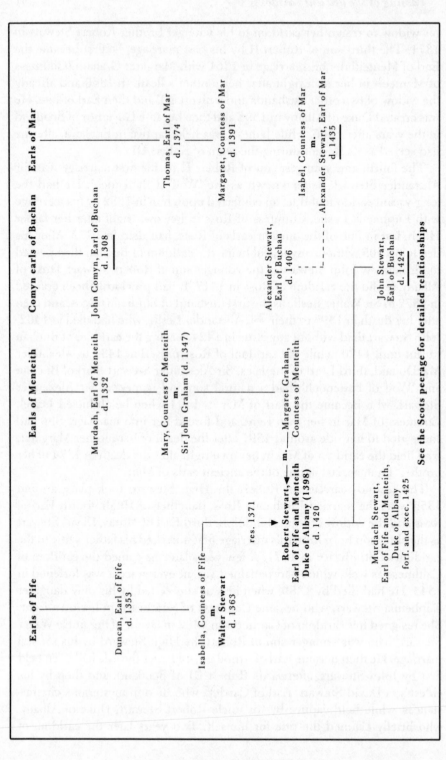

FIGURE 3.5 *Ancient earldoms of Scotland and Robert II's sons by his first marriage (shown in bold)*

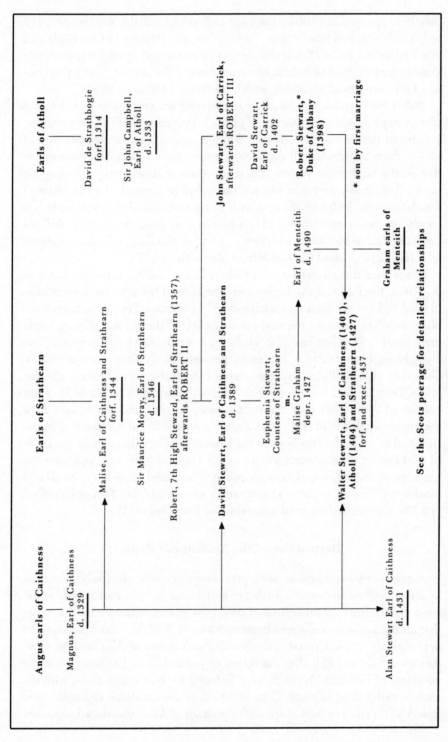

Angus earls of Caithness

Magnus, Earl of Caithness
d. 1329

Earls of Strathearn

Malise, Earl of Caithness and Strathearn
forf. 1344

Sir Maurice Moray, Earl of Strathearn
d. 1346

Robert, 7th High Steward, Earl of Strathearn (1357),
afterwards ROBERT II

David Stewart, Earl of Caithness and Strathearn
d. 1389

Euphemia Stewart,
Countess of Strathearn
m.

Malise Graham
depr. 1427

**Walter Stewart, Earl of Caithness (1401),
Atholl (1404) and Strathearn (1427)**
forf. and exec. 1437

Alan Stewart Earl of Caithness
d. 1431

Earl of Menteith
d. 1490

**Graham earls of
Menteith**

See the Scots peerage for detailed relationships

Earls of Atholl

David de Strathbogie
forf. 1314

Sir John Campbell,
Earl of Atholl
d. 1333

**John Stewart, Earl of Carrick,
afterwards ROBERT III**

David Stewart,
Earl of Carrick
d. 1402

**Robert Stewart,*
Duke of Albany
(1398)**

* son by first marriage

FIGURE 3.6 *Ancient earldoms of Scotland and Robert II's sons by his second marriage (shown in bold)*

Strathearn passed in 1406 by marriage to Patrick Graham, and then in 1413 to his only son and heir Malise Graham. He was deprived of his lands and title by James I in 1427, who conferred them instead upon his great-uncle Walter Stewart, Earl of Atholl, receiving instead the almost empty patrimony of the earldom of Menteith, which his family held until 1694.

Walter Stewart, Earl of Atholl, was executed ten years later in 1437 after he was implicated in the murder of James I. Indeed he had long entertained a claim to the throne of Scotland, arguing against a papal dispensation of 1347 which legitimised all the children then born to the first marriage of Robert the High Steward with Elizabeth Mure of Rowallane, including the future Robert III, who was himself the father of James I. The earldom of Strathearn was forfeited along with his other titles and it remained in the hands of the crown until 1631, when it was conferred upon William Graham, Earl of Menteith, who was a distant descendant of Malise Graham, who had been granted the earldom of Menteith in 1427.

It was thus during the reign of Robert II that the Stewarts first came to dominate the ranks of the higher nobility. Indeed his sons were eventually to hold eight of the fifteen earldoms then in existence. No doubt there were bitter rivalries between the various branches of the Stewart family, while there were other families that challenged such Stewart hegemony. The **Douglases** were perhaps the most powerful with their vast estates in Galloway, after William Douglas, nephew of Robert the Bruce's ally, Sir James Douglas, had been made Earl of Douglas in 1358 by David II. They continued to flourish over the next century as the Black Douglases until their eventual downfall and virtual destruction in 1455 at the hands of James II. Another powerful family were the **Lindsays**. They first gained the lands of Glenesk on the southern fringes of the Highlands by marriage with the Stirlings of Edzell, together with much other land in Angus. Sir David Lindsay of Glenesk in the next generation was created first Earl of Crawford in 1398 after he had married a daughter of King Robert II.

Destruction of the Ancient Earldoms

The hegemony exercised by such great magnates was effectively destroyed by the mid-fifteenth century. An Act of Parliament in 1401 had already weakened the territorial foundations of their power and influence by decreeing that all the baronies held within an earldom or lordship must in future be held directly of the Crown. Then the Stewart dukes of Albany were overthrown utterly in 1425 after the return of James I from England, when the earldoms of Fife and Menteith were forfeited to the Crown, along with the ancient earldom of Lennox. Even before then the earldoms of Buchan and Ross had reverted to the Crown with the death of Albany's second son at the battle of Verneuil in 1424. Then in 1429 the Dunbar earldom of Moray passed to the Crown after the last earl had died without any male issue. Several years later in 1435 the earldom of March was forfeited by the senior branch of the Dunbar family. Alexander Stewart, Earl of Mar, died in the same year without any heirs and this earldom then reverted to the Crown as well. Only two years later, after James I was murdered in 1437, the execution of Walter Stewart for high treason resulted in the forfeiture of his earldoms of Atholl, Caithness and Strathearn to the Crown. Finally the Black Douglases were forfeited in 1455.

By then nearly all the collateral branches of the Stewart family, and especially the sons and grandsons born of Robert II's second marriage with their dangerous pretensions to the Crown, had disappeared. Apart from the Douglas earls of Angus, only the earldoms of Crawford, Menteith and Sutherland still continued in existence, even if the earls of Menteith and Sutherland were held hostage in England for many years. However after the death of James I in 1437 the earldom of Ross was granted out to Alexander MacDonald, third Lord of the Isles, who thus became the territorial equal of the earls of Crawford and Douglas, and indeed entered into an alliance with them against the Scottish crown. By then the Crown itself held no fewer than nine of the ancient earldoms and eight of the lordships.

Although James II subsequently granted out some of these earldoms to his younger sons, while he created several new earldoms for his own supporters, the highest levels of late-medieval Scottish society had undergone a profound change and the earlier pattern of territorial earldoms and lordships was never restored. Faced with such a vacuum of political power and social status, Lords of Parliament were first created by a parliamentary Act of 1428, even if it was not until after 1445 that their institution became fully established. Their members were drawn from the land-owning ranks of the lesser nobility and particularly from those families who were now prominent in the service of the government. Especially noteworthy among these new families were the Campbell earls of Argyll and the Gordon earls of Huntly, who were to act as loyal servants of the Crown in the Highlands over the next two centuries.

Chapter Four

CONQUEST AND SETTLEMENT
IN THE NORTH

After Macbeth was killed by Malcolm Canmore in 1057, his stepson Lulach briefly ruled over Moray for a few months until he too was killed. He left a son Maelsnechtai, who perhaps came to terms with Malcolm Canmore, ruling over Moray as its *mormaer* under his authority, even if the Irish Annals gave him the title of *Ri* or 'King'. Nevertheless, Malcolm Canmore mounted an expedition north in 1078, when he captured Lulach's widow, Maelsnechtai's mother, but not Maelsnechtai himself. Afterwards it seems he entered clerical orders, dying in 1085. Thirty years later, during the reign of Alexander I, another royal expedition was apparently mounted in 1116 against Moray. It was made in retaliation for the murder of Lodmund, son of Donald, said to be a nephew of Alexander I. The rebels were pursued north by a cavalry force of mail-clad knights, which crossed the Spey and perhaps even penetrated farther north across the cattle ford of the Beauly River into Ross.

Rebellion in Moray

It was only in 1130 that a much more serious rebellion broke out in Moray, early in the reign of David I, when the Scottish King was abroad in the south of England. Angus, grandson of Lulach, had by then succeeded Maelsnechtai and perhaps his father Heth as *mormaer* of Moray. He evidently regarded himself as having a rightful claim to the Scottish throne by virtue of the ancient Celtic traditions of inheritance. He swept south across the Mounth at the head of a large army with his ally Malcolm macHeth, intent on seizing the whole kingdom for themselves. Even so their forces were no match for the armoured knights of the Anglo-Norman cavalry, hastily mustered to oppose the invasion by Edward, the King's Constable. The men of Moray were heavily defeated at the battle of Stracathro near Forfar. Angus himself was killed, together it was said with four thousand of his men, while the Scots lost a thousand men.

Malcolm macHeth escaped with his life, taking refuge in the Highlands before he was finally captured in 1134. Afterwards he was held prisoner for many years at Roxburgh Castle. When he was eventually released in 1157 by Malcolm IV he was granted the earldom of Ross, which may have been part of his ancestral lands. If he was not just held as a hostage for the good behaviour of his followers, the clemency shown to him after his capture and the eventual granting to him of the earldom of Ross may well suggest that he was of royal descent. Indeed the true ancestry of Malcolm macHeth remains a tantalising mystery in Scottish history, yet to be solved. His patronymic name implies that he was the son of Aed or Heth, who apparently ruled over Moray rather than Ross as its *mormaer* before Angus, at least according to the very scanty records of the time. It may be that Malcolm macHeth was Angus's brother. However it is sometimes argued that he was an illegitimate son of Alexander I, if not the eldest son of Ethelred, lay-abbot of Dunkeld and perhaps the first Earl of Fife, and thus the grandson of Malcolm Canmore, however unlikely this may seem.

The royal army in 1130 took full advantage of its victory at Stracathro apparently seizing all of Moray on behalf of David I. The earldom was forfeited by the Crown, and perhaps granted to the King's nephew William, son of Duncan II, and thus the grandson of Malcolm Canmore by his first wife Ingibjorg. Although he later married an Anglo-Norman heiress, Alice de Rumlli, who brought her husband the lordships of Craven and Coupland in the north of England, it is possible that William was previously married to a daughter of Maelsnechtai, son of Lulach, thus allying himself with the royal house of Moray. Indeed William himself may only have gained the earldom of Moray by right of his first wife rather than by royal decree since after her death and his subsequent marriage to Alice de Rumilli he was no longer known as the Earl of Moray.

The son of his first marriage and his descendants, known to history as the MacWilliams, later became troublesome contenders for the Scottish throne, often acting in alliance with the MacHeths. Indeed the next 100 years saw first the MacHeths and then the MacWilliams rebelling repeatedly against the Canmore kings, driven by their own claims to the Scottish throne. However, it may be argued that they were more intent on seizing their ancestral lands in Moray and Ross, hoping to stem the northern advance of the Canmore kings from their power base in the south. They perhaps saw themselves as ruling over Moray and Ross in virtual independence of the Canmore kings, just as the Celtic *mormaers* had done during the macAlpine dynasty.

David I perhaps had little authority over Moray itself, even after 1130. Indeed another rebellion broke out in 1142, led by the enigmatic and shadowy figure of Wimund the Bishop. He was a Savigniac monk at the

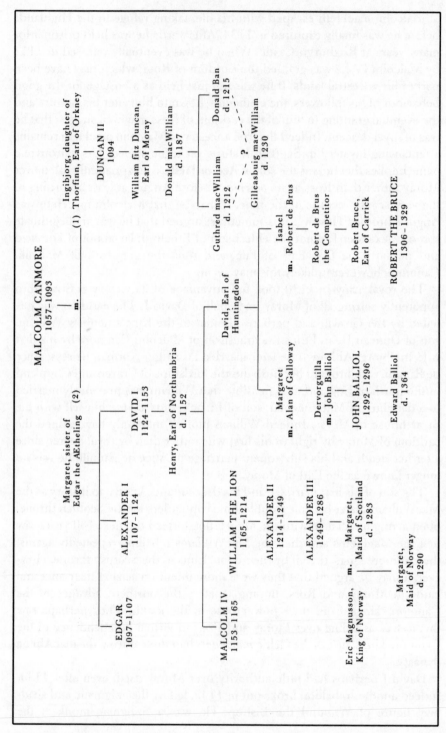

FIGURE 4.1 *The Canmore dynasty and the succession after 1290 (after Duncan)*

monastery of Furness in the north of England, who later moved to its daughter-house in the Isle of Man. There he found favour with Olav the Red, King of Man, who made him Bishop of the Isles around 1134. But he claimed to be the son of Earl Angus of Moray, which made him the great-grandson of Lulach, thus giving him a right to the Scottish throne according to the ancient Celtic laws of inheritance. This claim he pursued by waging a rebellion for several years against David I, supposedly from the mountainous fastness of the Highlands. After his eventual capture he was mutilated by blinding, ending his days at the Yorkshire abbey of Byland, where he regaled anyone who would listen to the heroic tales of his past exploits.

Settlement of Moray under David I

There is little evidence that David I was able to settle Moray widely with his own Anglo-Norman followers, since only a single grant of land is recorded from Moray during his reign. It was made to Freskyn, ancestor of the **Murrays**, who received the lands of Duffus lying between Elgin and the shores of the Moray Firth. His name suggests that he was Flemish, and he may be the same person as Freskyn, son of Ollec, who held lands in Pembroke from the Norman kings of England during the second quarter of the twelfth century. Who else settled Moray under feudal grant at this time is not known, but Freskyn must surely have had neighbours. Indeed he was followed north by Berowald the Fleming, who was granted the nearby barony of Innes and Nether Urquhart by Malcolm IV in 1160. His grandson founded the family known as the **Innesses** from their territories. Both families had already settled in West Lothian, where Freskyn held the lordship of Strathbrock, while Berowald's presence there is testified by the much truncated name of Bo'ness, originally Berowalds-toun-ness. Quite possibly Freskyn of Duffus was accompanied north by other Flemings when he settled in Moray, just as another group of Flemings had settled the upper reaches of the Clyde valley around the same time, leaving their names in such villages as Roberton, Lamington, Wiston, Symington and Thankerton. Otherwise we only know of the royal burghs established in Moray during the reign of David I at Forres and Elgin, perhaps with their own sheriffs, along with the sheriffdoms of Aberdeen, Banff, and Inverness, and the religious foundations of Urquhart and Kinloss.

Revolt of the macHeths

When David I died in 1153 he was succeeded by his young grandson Malcolm IV, since his only son and heir Henry, Earl of Northumberland, had died the previous year. Henry's death prompted David I to arrange that his grandson be conducted with a large army around all the provinces of Scotland by Duncan, Earl of Fife, proclaiming him to be the rightful heir to the throne. Nonetheless, the accession of Malcolm IV to the throne in 1153 almost immediately triggered a serious rebellion by the sons of Malcolm macHeth, who was still held prisoner at Roxburgh Castle. It was supported by his brother-in-law Somerled, self-styled King of Argyll and the Western Isles, whose sister Malcolm macHeth had married around 1130. We know hardly anything about this rebellion which broke out in November 1153 except that it 'disturbed and disquieted Scotland to a great extent'. It was probably triggered by the exclusion of a collateral branch of the royal family, as the MacHeths must have regarded themselves, and rightly so according to the ancient Celtic laws of succession, in favour of an heir who had not yet come of age. Indeed the need for a large army to accompany Malcolm as heir-designate around his kingdom in 1152 perhaps suggests much hostility to the prospect of his accession from amongst the Celtic earldoms.

Donald, the eldest son of Malcolm macHeth, was only captured at Whithorn by forces loyal to the throne in 1156, when he was imprisoned with his father in Roxburgh Castle. Even so Malcolm macHeth evidently reached an accommodation with Malcolm IV in 1157, when he was released from captivity and granted the earldom of Ross as recompense for his long years of imprisonment. Somerled himself turned to the conquest of the Western Isles around the same time, while making his peace with Malcolm IV in 1160, when the young King left Scotland for France in the service of Henry II of England. However the absence of Malcolm IV from his kingdom seems to have aroused much dissatisfaction for he was forced to return in the same year, when he was besieged for a time in his castle at Perth during the Revolt of the Six Earls. Four years later in 1164 Somerled led another rebellion against Malcolm IV, but it ended with his death, as recounted in the next chapter. Not long afterwards in 1168 Malcolm macHeth died as well, leaving a daughter Gormflaith, who married Harald Maddadson, Earl of Caithness and Orkney, as his second wife, as well as a son Donald. By then Malcolm IV had died in 1165 at the early age of twenty-five years. He was succeeded by his younger brother William, who later became known as William the Lion after reigning for nearly fifty years until his death in 1214.

The MacWilliams and their Rebellions

The torch of revolt in the north now passed to Donald mac William. He traced his ancestry through his father William, briefly Earl of Moray after 1130, to his grandfather Duncan II, thus giving him a legitimate claim to the Scottish throne under the Celtic laws of succession. The chronicles suggest that he had long been in revolt against the Scottish Crown, supported by a number of Scottish magnates, when William the Lion made his first expedition north with a large army to subdue Ross in 1179. The Scottish king built two new castles beyond Inverness to guard the northern approaches to Moray. The first was at Edirdour (or Redcastle) near the head of the Beauly Firth, protecting Moray from landward attack, while the second was farther north at Dunscaith, guarding the narrow entrance to the Cromarty Firth. Their siting makes little strategic sense unless they were built to contain the territorial ambitions of Harald Maddadson, Earl of Caithness and Orkney, rather than to guard Moray from any attack from the west by Donald mac William. Strategy might well have dictated the building of Urquhart Castle on Loch Ness to guard the south-western approaches to Moray along the Great Glen, even if it appears to date from the later reign of Alexander II.

Two years later Donald mac William launched another revolt against William the Lion, presumably fighting to reverse the advance of feudalism into Ross. Although little is known about the course of this rebellion, it evidently posed a real threat to the Scottish crown. Donald mac William may well have benefited from the widespread dissatisfaction within the kingdom which followed the capture of William the Lion at Alnwick in 1174 and his subsequent release by the English, bound by the Treaty of Falaise. Donald mac William held Ross for at least several years after his uprising in 1181 and the disturbances evidently spread as far south as Gowrie, where sixty insurgents led by Heth, perhaps the son of Donald macHeth, were trapped and killed at the abbey of Coupar Angus by Malcolm, Earl of Atholl. The King's authority over Moray was weakened as well when the royal castle at Auldearn was betrayed by Gillecolm, Marshal to the Earl of Strathearn, who surrendered it into the hands of Donald mac William.

It was only in 1187 that William the Lion was able to lead an army north to contain this rebellion, establishing his headquarters at the royal castle of Inverness, then at the limits of royal authority. Yet it was merest chance that brought the rebellion to an end. Disaffection was rife within the royal army and food supplies were running low when a foraging party of enthusiastic young knights under Roland, Lord of Galloway, came upon the forces of Donald mac William encamped upon the moor of Mam Garvia, somewhere to the west of Inverness. After a fierce fight he was slain and his severed head brought to William the Lion in triumph. Thereafter the rebellion itself collapsed, even if the MacWilliam claim to the Scottish Crown still remained a troublesome threat until 1230. After the events of 1187, however, William the Lion and his successors had full control over Moray, and what had once been a mighty province with its own royal house was eventually reduced to a small county marking the boundaries of the sheriffdoms of Forres and Elgin, as established in 1224.

Conflict with Harald Maddadson, Earl of Orkney

The failure of the MacWilliam revolt in 1187 brought the province of Caithness, which then extended as far south as the Dornoch Firth and the Kyle of Sutherland, much closer into contact with royal authority. This may well have prompted Harald Maddadson, Earl of Orkney under the Norwegian crown, to occupy Ross and possibly even Moray in 1196. He had been granted the earldom of Caithness by David I when only five years of age in 1139, while he later married Afreka, daughter of Duncan, Earl of Fife. Known to the chroniclers as 'a good and trusty man', there seemed little reason for him to turn against William the Lion, except that he had been fostered by Earl Rognvald of Orkney from an early age. Even so when Malcolm macHeth died in 1168 Harald Maddadson was no longer in dispute with his rivals for the Norse earldom of Orkney, whom he had already defeated in the Wars of the Three Earls. He evidently felt strong enough to set aside his first wife Afreka so that he could marry Gormflaith, daughter of Malcolm macHeth, Earl of Ross, thus perhaps laying a claim to the earldom for himself.

In fact Fordun tells us that Harald Maddadson was driven by the ambitions of his wife Gormflaith to recover her ancient inheritance in Ross, which was probably even then being settled by William the Lion with Anglo-Normans. Faced with this invasion William the Lion returned north with another large army in 1197, driving Harald Maddadson out of Ross, and forcing him to retreat north towards Thurso, where the royal army destroyed the earl's castle. Since stormy weather then prevented his escape across the Pentland Firth to safety in Orkney, Harald Maddadson was forced to submit to William the Lion. He only regained his freedom by giving up half his earldom of Caithness, which passed into the hands of his rival, Earl Harald the Younger, grandson of Earl Rognvald, who had already been favoured by the Scottish king. Harald Maddadson was also required to surrender Thorfinn, the eldest son by his second marriage with Gormflaith and thus an inheritor of the ancient MacHeth claim to the Scottish throne. Acting as a hostage evidently did not appeal to Thorfinn, since he appeared around this time with an army near Inverness, where he was defeated by forces loyal to the Scottish Crown. Indeed he only surrendered himself to the King's men after his father Harald Maddadson had been carried off in chains to Edinburgh in 1198 and imprisoned in Roxburgh Castle until Thorfinn agreed to take his place as a hostage.

After his release from captivity Harald Maddadson was faced by the territorial ambitions of Earl Harald the Younger, who in his absence had mounted a large invasion of Orkney, aided by forces loyal to him from Caithness and Norway. Roger de Hoveden, chaplain to Henry II of England, tells us that Harald Maddadson was forced to retreat to the Isle of Man after being defeated by Harald the Younger, but then returned north to annihilate his rival and all his army at a decisive battle fought in 1198, possibly at Clairdon near Thurso. Afterwards Harald Maddadson journeyed south under the safe conduct of the bishops of St Andrews and Rosemarkie to make his peace once more with William the Lion. Although he offered a large sum in silver and gold to redeem his lands in Caithness, it was refused unless he was prepared to repudiate his second wife Gormflaith, daughter of Malcolm macHeth, in favour of his first wife Afreka. By making Harald's son Thorfinn illegitimate, it weakened any claim that he might have entertained to the Scottish throne through his grandfather, Malcolm macHeth, Earl of Ross. Harald Maddadson resolutely refused to give up his second wife Gormflaith, or to surrender any further hostages, and it seems Caithness was given by William the Lion to his distant kinsman Rognvald Gudrodson, Norse king of Man.

Faced with this impasse, Harald Maddadson in 1201 evidently appealed to King John of England for help, although it is unlikely that he ever attended the English court in person. The Church now became involved in his struggles with the Scottish Crown. Already the bishops of Caithness appointed by the Scottish Crown had been confronted with much hostility, and this became especially acute during the reign of Bishop John (1185–1213). However a crisis was only reached in 1202, when Bishop John of Caithness learnt of the treasonable behaviour of Harald Maddadson in seeking the help of England against the Scottish Crown. He promptly reported the matter to the Scottish King, and Harald Maddadson reacted to this act of betrayal by invading Caithness with a large force from Orkney, intent on bringing the recalcitrant bishop to obedience. The affair then got out of hand when the Earl's men seized the bishop at Scrabster, blinding him and cutting out his tongue to show that he was a spy and an informer.

On hearing of the bishop's mutilation, which later underwent a miraculous cure or so it was said, William the Lion mounted yet another expedition north with a large army of several thousand men, reaching as far north as Ousdale, just beyond the Ord of Caithness. Harald Maddadson blocked his further advance with just as large a show of strength, while he had the support of England, so that the two armies did not engage one another. Instead he submitted once again to the Scottish King, who demanded of him 'every fourth penny', but otherwise allowed him to retain what was now the earldom of Caithness under the sovereignty of the Scottish Crown. His son Thorfinn suffered greatly for his father's intransigence, since he was blinded and castrated to remove any threat that he otherwise posed to the Scottish Crown, dying soon afterwards of his injuries at Roxburgh Castle. After the death of Harald Maddadson in 1206, the earldom of Caithness passed jointly to his other two sons by his second wife Gormflaith. They remained loyal to the Scottish Crown, evidently unwilling to share the fate of their brother Thorfinn.

Final Revolts in the North

Despite the death of Harald Maddadson in 1206, the north of Scotland still remained in an unsettled state. Although Donald mac William had been killed in 1187, he left a son Guthred macWilliam, who inherited his father's claim to the Scottish throne. Evidently Guthred was living as an exile in Ireland during the years before King John of England invaded the country in 1210. This invasion apparently resulted in Guthred's expulsion from Ireland, since he landed soon afterwards in Ross, where he gained the support of local magnates. By midsummer 1211 William the Lion had mustered an army of 4,000 men with contingents from Atholl, Buchan, Mar and Fife and marched north to rebuild the royal castles at Edirdour and Dunscaith. Sporadic fighting lasted until 1212, when the Scottish army was stiffened by mercenaries from Brabant, supplied by King John of England and the Earl of Winchester. Nevertheless the uprising only ended when Guthred macWilliam was betrayed by his own followers. Brought in fetters before William the Lion at Kincardine Castle, he was beheaded and his body hung upside down as a warning to other rebels. The Earl of Atholl invaded Ireland in the same year, laying waste to much of northern Donegal, presumably in reprisal for the support previously given by its inhabitants to the MacWilliams.

The death of William the Lion in 1214 and the accession to the Scottish throne of his son Alexander II, aged only seventeen years, caused yet another insurrection to break out in the north. Even so it was very nearly the last attempt by the house of Moray and its allies in Ross to regain their ancient Celtic inheritance. The rebellion was headed by Donald Ban, brother of Guthred macWilliam, acting in concert with Kenneth macHeth, who was possibly the son of Malcolm macHeth, if not his grandson. Sweeping south into Moray, they devastated the country with fire and sword. Significantly their rebellion was put down by the local Celtic aristocracy of Ross itself, acting in the person of Fearchair mac an t'sagairt, otherwise Farquhar macTaggart, son of the priest. He was most likely descended from the lay-abbots of the ancient Celtic monastery of Applecross in Wester Ross, if he did not belong to an hereditary line of lay-priests from the monastic foundation of St Duthac near Tain. Raising a powerful army from within his own territories, he was strong enough to defeat Donald Ban and his ally Kenneth macHeth, whereupon he brought their severed heads to the young King.

Alexander II rewarded him there and then with a knighthood and twenty years later granted him the earldom of Ross.

Afterwards there was peace in the north of Scotland until 1222, when a dispute arose between Adam, the Scottish bishop of Caithness, and the Norse inhabitants of his diocese over the payment of a butter teind. Acting with more zeal than discretion he had first doubled, and then trebled, the amount to be paid. The dispute had already reached the notice of Alexander II when the bishop was besieged in his residence at Halkirk by an angry mob of freeholders. Finding the house well defended, it was set alight and the unfortunate bishop burnt to death. On hearing of the bishop's murder, Alexander II mounted an expedition north in retaliation. Meeting no resistance, he reached Caithness and exacted a heavy penalty from the population. He fined John, son of Harald Maddadson and now Earl of Caithness, for his negligence in not coming to the bishop's rescue. Eighty men, said to be present at the riot, had their hands and feet cut off, and the freeholders had to pay a large fine to get back their forfeited lands. A chronicle recounts the killing of men, the castration of their sons and the banishment of their wives. Although praised fulsomely by the Pope for acting in defence of the Church, it is just as likely that Alexander II was intent upon strengthening his own authority over what was still a very remote part of his kingdom.

A final insurrection occurred against the Scottish Crown in the years after 1228, although the details are very confused. Its leader was Gilleasbuig of the 'race of MacWilliam', acting in alliance with Ruaraidh, who was almost certainly the eldest son of Reginald, King of the Isles and Somerled's grandson. They stormed the motte-and-bailey castle held for Alexander II at Abertarff near Fort Augustus by Thomas of Thirlestane and then burnt down much of Inverness, while plundering the surrounding countryside. The revolt was quelled by William Comyn, Earl of Buchan, whose son Walter was soon afterwards rewarded with the lordship of Badenoch. Determined to extinguish once and forever the threat posed by the Mac-William dynasty to the Scottish Crown, Alexander II ordered the judicial murder of the infant daughter of Gilleasbuig macWilliam, who was by then the last-surviving member of the MacWilliam family. She was slaughtered without any mercy in 1230 after a royal proclamation from the burgh crier by having her brains dashed out against the merchat-cross of Forfar. This barbaric act, described in the chronicles of Lanercost as somewhat too cruel a vengence, brought to an end those 'singular attempts to place a rival family on the throne of Scotland, which lasted . . . upwards of one hundred years, and which exhibit so extraordinary a proof of the tenacity and perseverance with which the Highlanders maintained their peculiar laws of succession, and the claims of hereditary title to the throne' (Skene 1886).

Feudal Settlement in Angus and Mar

Faced with the long-continued threat of rebellions in the years after 1130, especially in Moray and Ross, the Canmore kings attempted to bolster their power and authority by settling their own followers upon the land. Although this feudal settlement was begun by David I and Malcolm IV, it was William the Lion who virtually completed the feudalisation of Scotland north of the Forth. He granted lands in Fife, Gowrie, Angus and the Mearns in return for knight-service to such Anglo-Norman families as the Hays of Errol, who afterwards married into the Celtic house of Strathearn, gaining the earldom of Errol in the fifteenth century, and the Berkeleys of Inverkeilor, who later took the name of Barclay, together with the Mortimers, Melvilles, Giffords and Hastings among many others. The original Celtic earldoms started to be assimilated into the feudal system in Atholl and Strathearn, where royal grants of land were made in return for knight-service, especially to the younger sons of the native aristocracy and other landholders of lesser degree.

Farther north beyond the Mounth, William the Lion granted the lordship of Garioch to Earl David, his younger brother, in what was probably an attempt to curb the powers of the ancient earldom of Mar. After establishing his *caput* at Inverurie with its motte-and-bailey castle, known today as the Bass of Inverurie, Earl David remained as the lord of Garioch until his death in 1219, when his lands were divided between his three daughters and their husbands: Alan, Lord of Galloway, Robert de Brus, Lord of Annandale; and Henry de Hastings. Meanwhile Earl David had himself granted out his territories in a feudal fashion for knight-service, making smaller grants of land to various Anglo-Norman and Flemish families with their distinctive surnames.

Among the recipients was Malcolm, son of Bertoft the Fleming, whose ancestors supposedly reached Scotland in the retinue of Edgar the Ætheling in 1067. His descendants were the **Leslies**, Earls of Rothes, who took their territorial name from a place then known as Lesselyn in the Garioch, where they constructed a motte-and-bailey castle. Bartholf's grandson was afterwards appointed constable of the Earl David's castle at the Bass of Inverurie. The Leslies prospered greatly under the patronage of David II in the fourteenth century, when Sir Walter Leslie married Euphemia, Countess of Ross, and afterwards held the earldom of Ross by right of his wife. Later they distinguished themselves as professional soldiers in the seventeenth century. Sir Alexander Leslie, first Earl of Leven, took command of the Scottish army of the Covenant, defeating the royalist army of Charles I at Marston Moor in 1644, while David Leslie, grandson of the fifth Earl of Rothes, defeated Montrose at the battle of Philliphaugh in 1645.

Among the neighbours of the Leslies in the Garioch were other families, about whose origins we know very little, such as the **Forbeses**. Their name is territorial in origin, taken from the lands of Forbes on the banks of the River Don. It comes from the Gaelic *Forba*, meaning a field, coupled with the Pictish suffix *-ais* for a place-name. Their earliest record is a charter of Alexander III dating from around 1272, which simply confirmed Duncan de Forbes in possession of his lands, already held by the family. Their own traditions suggest that they were related to a Celtic family whose shadowy ancestor was Gilleoin of the Aird, claimed as an ancestor by several other Highland clans. The family itself and its many branches engaged in a protracted and very bitter feud with the Gordons of Huntly during the course of the fifteenth and sixteenth centuries, supported by their allies, the Keiths, Frasers, Crichtons and others, but opposed by their traditional enemies, the Leslies, as well as the Irvines and the Setons.

Garioch itself lay within the earldom of Mar, where Malcolm de Lundin received lands after he had married the daughter of Earl Gilchrist, founding the family known as the **Durwards**. Their son was Thomas de Lundin, who rose high in the service of William the Lion as his usher or door-ward, later taking the family name of Durward from this hereditary position. He attempted without any success to claim the earldom of Mar for himself before he died in 1231. He was granted instead a vast lordship lying between the Dee and the Don, comprising the greater part of the earldom itself, where he probably built as his *caput* the motte-and-bailey castle at the Peel of Lumphanan. These lands then passed to his son Alan Durward, who married Marjory, a natural daughter of Alexander II, and acted as Regent of Scotland during the minority of Alexander III after 1249. After his death in 1275 his lands were divided between his three daughters.

Among the neighbours of the Durwards were the **Bissets**, who were yet another Anglo-Norman family to settle around this time in Mar. The Bissets first came north with William the Lion in 1174, when the Scottish King was released from captivity in England under the Treaty of Falaise. Their name was originally French, derived from the diminutive of *bis*, meaning a 'rock-dove', so that there can be little doubt of their Anglo-Norman origins. On reaching Scotland they soon gained a foothold in the north, when Walter Bisset was granted the lordship of Aboyne by 1220, while his nephew John Bisset was granted the lands of the Aird near Beauly not long afterwards. The early motte-and-bailey castle of Walter Bisset at Aboyne was later converted into a great tower-house, built of stone, in the late thirteenth century. Despite such settlement the ancient Celtic earls of Mar still held much of upper Strathdon with their motte-and-bailey castle at the Doune of

Invernochty, perhaps constructed by the mysterious Earl Gilchrist in the late twelfth century.

Comyn Power in Buchan

North-east beyond Mar lay the earldom of Buchan with its *caput* at Ellon on the River Ythan. It was little affected by Anglo-Norman settlement during the reign of William the Lion. However towards the very end of his reign, as we have already seen, the earldom itself passed by marriage to the Anglo-Norman family of William Comyn, Justiciar of Scotland north of the Forth, when he married its sole surviving heiress Marjorie before 1214. When his son Alexander succeeded him in 1244, it seems that the *caput* of the earldom was then situated at the stone-built castle of Kingedward or Kineddar, north of Turriff, replacing their earlier motte of Ellon. It occupied a strategic site on top of a craig, protected by the Kingedward Burn to the west, but hardly anything now remains.

The later spread of Comyn power throughout Buchan and beyond its borders is witnessed by the scattered remains of their stone-built castles, all dating from the thirteenth century. Hardly any of these Comyn castles survived the Wars of Scottish Independence, except as ruins, which sometimes served as the foundations for later strongholds. Dundarg Castle was built in the thirteenth century on an imposing rock of red sandstone, looking out over the waters of the North Sea from the north coast of Buchan. Eight miles to its east are the ruins of Cairnbulg Castle, once known as Philorth Castle, and restored at the end of the nineteenth century. Its tower-house may be mid-thirteenth century in date. Farther south around the coast is the site of Rattray Castle, which was once a Comyn stronghold, as well as Inverugie Castle, perhaps originally held by the Cheynes even if its early history is obscure. Even farther south was the castle of Old Slaims, later held by the Hays, earls of Errol, but originally a Comyn stronghold.

The best preserved of all these Comyn castles is Balvenie, known originally as Mortlach, which occupies a strategic site near Dufftown, guarding the mouths of Glen Fiddich and Glen Rinnes, as well as the valleys running in various direction to Huntly, Keith, Cullen and Elgin. It was originally built as a large castle of enclosure with round towers projecting at the corners, which was first restored by the Earls of Douglas before their downfall in 1455, and then rebuilt as a Renaissance palace in the sixteenth century by a Stewart earl of Atholl, long after its destruction by King Robert the Bruce in 1308. It originally came into the hands of Alexander Comyn, second Earl of Buchan, by his marriage with Elizabeth, third daughter of Roger de Quincy, along with the hereditary office of High Constable of Scotland, which was resigned in his favour by her elder sister.

Kildrummy and the Lordship of Strathbogie

Stretching north-west from Mar lay the only route giving easy access to the lowlands of Moray. The lack of pasture along the high and barren passes of Minigaig and Drumochter farther west across the Mounth effectively precluded their use by large armies with cavalry in medieval times. Kildrummy Castle was later to guard this more easterly route into Moray. The 'noblest of northern castles' was built of stone in the early thirteenth century upon the site of a motte-and-bailey castle, dating from the twelfth century. Its construction is often attributed to Gilbert de Moravia, Archdeacon of Moray, and afterwards Bishop of Caithness, acting at the instigation of Alexander II, but it was most likely built by the Celtic earls of Mar, who occupied this imposing stronghold after they had abandoned their motte-and-bailey castle at Invernochty. They also built Migvie Castle near Aboyne.

Kildrummy Castle was built at first as a typical but very large castle of enclosure, with a pentagonal courtyard surrounded by a curtain wall. Round towers up to five storeys high were added later, projecting from the corners of the curtain wall, along with the flanking towers of a barbican guarding the gatehouse. Its design recalls Dirleton and Bothwell Castles farther south which were themselves influenced by the construction of Coucy Castle in France, built in the 1220s by the father-in-law of Alexander II. North-west of Kildrummy the remote and landlocked district of Strathbogie around Huntly lay astride the overland route from Mar north into Moray, where the River Bogie joins the Deveron, just upstream from Huntly. Its strategic importance was recognised when its lands were granted to David, younger son of Duncan, fifth Earl of Fife, and ancestor of the later Earls of Atholl, late in the reign of William the Lion. He established his *caput* at the motte-and-bailey castle at Strathbogie, or Huntly as it is now known, where the Gordons later built their own stronghold in 1374.

The Morays and their Neighbours

Beyond Strathbogie few details are known of the early settlement of Moray itself, apart from the grant of Duffus to Freskyn by David I and the later grants to Berowald the Fleming by Malcolm IV. Around a hundred years later in 1242 the descendants of Freskyn of Duffus held a great many estates scattered along the coastal lowlands of the Laich of Moray, stretching from Fochabers to Inverness and along the lower reaches of such rivers as the Spey, the Findhorn and the Nairn as this family rapidly grew in strength and influence. It was his grandsons Hugh de Moravia, ancestor of the earls of Sutherland, and William de Moravia, ancestor of the Murrays of Bothwell, who first adopted the territorial designation *de Moravia* for their family name around 1200. It later became the well-known surname of Moray, now usually spelt as Murray. Most likely it was only adopted with royal permission, once this powerful and influential family had taken the place of the Celtic earls of Moray, who had proved so troublesome to the crown. Even so the Crown may still have held estates around the upper reaches of the Findhorn and the Spey, while royal burghs were well established along the coastal fringe by 1214, when they could be found at Banff, Cullen, Elgin, Forres, Auldearn, Nairn and Inverness, together with the sheriffdoms at Banff and Inverness. Much of the land around these burghs was royal forest, created by William the Lion as hunting reserves.

Nevertheless, a number of ancient Celtic families still survived in Moray, holding the thanages of Rathenach, Brodie, Dyke, Moyness, Cawdor and Kinmylie, among whom nowadays only the **Brodies** still retain a distinct identity. Their name is most likely territorial in origin, derived from the Gaelic word *brothaig*, meaning a 'ditch', unless it is a corruption of the old Pictish name 'Brude'. Their seat was Brodie Castle, occupied by the family in one form or another since the twelfth century, although the present building dates from 1567. Neighbours of the Brodies were the **Roses** of Kilravock, who trace their origins to the lordship of Ros in Normandy, whence they take their name. Despite statements to the contrary they are not connected in any way to the ancient Celtic family of Ross. Instead they were closely related to two other Anglo-Norman families, namely the Boscos and the Bissets. According to their traditions they all crossed the English Channel with William the Conqueror in 1066, perhaps in the retinue of his half-brother Odo, Bishop of Bayeux. After settling in England their descendants apparently came north in the mid-thirteenth century, when all three families are found holding lands around the shores of the Moray Firth. The Roses of Kilravock first became established when Elizabeth de Bisset married Andrew de Bosco, and their daughter Marie married Hugh de Ros around 1290, bringing with her the Bisset lands of Kilravock near Inverness which have remained in the hands of their descendants ever since.

Another Anglo-Norman family closely related by marriage to the Bissets were the **Grants**, whose name comes from the French word *grand*, meaning 'great'. After settling in Northamptonshire with the Bissets as their neighbours they eventually appeared in Scotland during the thirteenth century. Then William le Grand acquired the lands of Stratherrick to the south of Loch Ness by marrying Mary, daughter of Sir John Bisset of the Aird. His son Sir Laurence le Grand became Sheriff of Inverness in 1258. After the Wars of Scottish Independence the family acquired the lands of Glen Urquhart and Glen Moriston. It was only later in 1434 that they settled in Strathspey, after Sir Iain Grant had married the heiress of the ancient family of Glencairnie, descendants of the ancient earls of Strathearn. Their lands were erected into the free barony of Freuchie in 1493. By then the Grants had come to think of themselves as a Highland clan, taking on the Celtic traditions of their surroundings, and eventually referring to themselves as such in a written document of 1538.

The Bissets themselves fell from favour in 1242 after they were implicated in the murder of Patrick, Earl of Atholl. He was the only son of Thomas, younger brother of Alan, Lord of Galloway, and Isabel, Countess of Atholl in her own right. Walter Bisset of Aboyne was Patrick's uncle by marriage and he perhaps entertained a claim to the estates which would be inherited by his nephew when he came of age. Whatever the truth of the matter John Bisset of the Airds, nephew of Walter Bisset of Aboyne, betrayed his guilt by fleeing soon afterwards to Ireland, where it seems he received lands in the Glens of Antrim from Henry III of England, whose service he had entered. Walter Bisset was himself exiled to England after his lands had been attacked by the Comyns, but he was restored to favour in 1248 after he had been captured at Dunaverty Castle which he had seized on behalf of the English king.

Settlement of Badenoch and Strathspey

Farther inland the Canmore kings attempted to subdue the hinterland of Moray by establishing lordships and baronies in the upland regions of Strathspey and Badenoch, starting near the Laich of Moray and extending slowly inland, as Professor Barrow (1975) has shown. William the Lion first favoured Gilbert, Earl of Strathearn, whom he granted the lands of Kinveachy in Strathspey, perhaps as a reward for helping William the Lion to suppress the rebellion of Donald mac William after 1179. Gilbert afterwards gained further lands in the north by his second marriage to Ysenda, who brought him her inheritance of Glencairney in Strathspey. Their descendants still held these lands in the fourteenth century before they passed by marriage to the Grants. The earls of Fife were also granted lands in Strathspey after Duncan, fifth Earl of Fife, was appointed Justiciar of Scotland, north of the Forth, in the years before 1178. They gained the lordships of Cromdale and Stratha'an in the Spey valley towards the end of his reign, probably after his son Malcolm had become the sixth Earl of Fife after his father's death in 1204.

Apart from William Comyn, soon to become Earl of Buchan by his marriage to Margaret, Countess of Buchan, there were other powerful supporters of William the Lion in the north. They included Thomas Durward, as well as Malcolm, eldest son of Earl Morgrund of Mar, who acted in concert with one another in putting down the MacWilliam revolt of 1212, despite their competing claims to the earldom of Mar itself. Not long afterwards these magnates and their dependants were greatly rewarded for their support of the Crown. Thomas Durward was appointed sheriff of Inverness by 1226, while a few years later his son Alan was granted the lordship of Urquhart on the western shores of Loch Ness. He may have built the very earliest part of Castle Urquhart still surviving. Occupying a strategic site high above the waters of Loch Ness and defended from landward attack by a deep ditch, it was only a small enclosure at first, built upon the site of an earlier motte and an even older vitrified fort. The castle later passed to the Comyns, Lords of Badenoch, who most likely built the irregular curtain-wall that formed its outer defences, when the original enclosure was converted into a inner citadel. The great tower-house of Urquhart Castle is much later in date, since its upper storeys at least were probably built by the Grants of Freuchie after 1509, after they had received the lordship of Urquhart from James IV. The stronghold played a prominent role in the Wars of Scottish Independence, while later it became a royal castle when it was often threatened and sometimes captured in the fifteenth and sixteenth centuries by the MacDonalds, Lords of the Isles, in their struggles with the Crown.

Gilbert Durward, as yet another member of the Durward family, received the lordship of Boleskin on the eastern shores of Loch Ness around the same time as Alan Durward was granted Urquhart. The remote lordship of Abertarff at the very head of Loch Ness was granted to Thomas of Thirlestane, who had connections with the Durward family as a vassal of Alan, lord of Galloway, who was himself the brother of Earl Thomas of Atholl. He constructed the motte-and-bailey castle at Abertarff, destroyed in the uprising of 1228. Another feudal grant was given to Walter Bisset of Aboyne, who received the upland district of Stratherrick, lying to the south of Inverness. Evidently all these grants were intended to safeguard the approaches to lowland Moray from along the Great Glen.

Further grants to safeguard the south-westerly approach to Moray by way of Glen Spean and the Spey valley were made, particularly in the years after 1230, once the final MacWilliam revolt had been suppressed. Already the lordship of Abernethy in mid-Strathspey had been granted in 1226 to James, son of Earl Morgrund of Mar and the brother of Malcolm, who had played an active role in putting down the earlier MacWilliam revolt of 1215. Nonetheless when danger again threatened after 1228, it was William Comyn, Earl of Buchan and Justiciar of Scotland north of Forth, whom Alexander II appointed despite his advanced years as the warden of Moray to defend the province from attack by Gilleasbuig macWilliam.

Comyn Lords of Badenoch

Soon after the defeat of Gilleasbuig macWilliam, Alexander II granted the lordship of Badenoch, not to William Comyn, Earl of Buchan, who died in 1233, but to his younger son Walter by his first marriage, who was himself Earl of Menteith by right of his wife Isabella, Countess of Menteith. After his death in 1258 without any sons to succeed him, the lordship of Badenoch passed to John Comyn, eldest son of Walter's elder brother Richard, and then after he died in 1278 it passed to his descendants, known as the Red Comyns from their heraldic colours. The family itself became enormously powerful in Badenoch and Strathspey, perhaps first governing the country from their *caput* at Ruthven near Kingussie, where it seems they constructed an exceptionally large motte without a bailey. Later it was possibly converted into a stonebuilt castle, whose foundations are now hidden by the Hanoverian barracks built after the 1715 Rebellion.

Elsewhere in Strathspey the Comyns held the thirteenth-century stronghold of Lochindorb, built on a small island in the centre of the loch, while Castle Roy belonged to the Lords of Abernethy as the descendants of the Earls of Mar. Both were stone-built castles of enclosure with square outlines, but only Lochindorb had small towers placed at its four corners. It resembles Inverlochy Castle, situated much farther west in Lochaber at the head of Loch Linnhe and held by the Comyns of Badenoch in the late thirteenth century. It is a nearly square castle of enclosure with round towers projecting from each corner, one of which was built larger than the others to serve as a donjon or keep. The Comyns of Badenoch even made their presence felt farther south in Atholl, where the earliest part of Blair Castle, still known as Cummings Tower, was built by John Comyn the Elder in 1269, much to the annoyance of the Earl of Atholl who was then absent in England. It was presumably intended to guard the southern approaches to the various passes across the Mounth, which not only gave access to Strathspey by way of Drumochter and the more easterly pass of Minigaig between Glen Bruar and Glen Tromie, but also to the province of Mar by way of Glen Tilt.

Feudal Settlement of Ross

Farther west beyond Moray the rebellion of Harald Maddadson in 1196 was most likely directed against the feudal settlement of Ross by William the Lion, which followed the earlier collapse of the MacWilliam revolt in 1187. However we only learn much later of the Bisset lordship of the Aird, lying around Beauly but perhaps originally centred upon the royal castle of Edirdour, and the Mowat lordship of Cromarty, most likely first established around the royal castle of Dunscaith, and both settled by Anglo-Norman families. It was John Bisset of the Aird who founded the Valliscaulian priory of Beauly in 1230. He died without a male heir in 1258, when it seems his lands of the Aird were divided among his three daughters and their husbands, if indeed they had not been forfeited in 1242 for his part in the murder of Patrick, Earl of Atholl. The lands of Lovat, east of the Beauly river, passed by marriage with a Bisset heiress, first to Sir David de Graham and then after his death almost certainly to Sir Simon Fraser, ancestor of the Frasers of Lovat.

The **Frasers** are an Anglo-Norman family who proudly trace their ancestors to Anjou in France, where they gave their original name of Frezel to the lordship of La Frezeliere. It later became corrupted into Frassier, perhaps after they adopted the *fraisse* or strawberry as their emblem. Simon Fraser was the first on record to appear in Scotland around 1160, when he held lands at Keith in East Lothian. Five generations later his namesake and direct descendant Sir Simon Fraser was a staunch supporter of Scottish independence, winning the battle of Roslin in 1303, only to be executed with great cruelty after he had been captured by Edward I of England in 1306. His kinsman Sir Alexander Fraser became the Chamberlain of Scotland in the years after the battle of Bannockburn, where he had acquitted himself with great honour. He married Mary, sister of King Robert the Bruce, and their grandson married Joanna, daughter of the Earl of Ross, who brought to her husband the lands of Philorth in Buchan with its castle at Cairnbulg in 1375. Several generations later Alexander Fraser of Philorth married the heiress of Lord Saltoun, and the latter-day chiefs of Clan Fraser have borne this title ever since.

Meanwhile the Frasers of Lovat had established themselves in the Bisset lands of the Aird, where they are first recorded in a charter of 1367. Then in 1416 they secured more of the Bisset lands in the Aird when Hugh Fraser married Janet Fenton, who was descended from Sir William Fenton who had earlier married another Bisset heiress. Not long afterwards they gained lands in Stratherrick, south of Inverness, and one third of Glenelg, perhaps from the Earl of Moray. They were raised to the peerage under the title of the Lords Fraser of Lovat in the mid-fifteenth century. Well before then they had taken on all the trapping of a Highland clan, whose chief was known to his Gaelic-speaking followers as *MacShimidh*, son of Simon. Their eponymous founder can be none other than Sir Simon Fraser, younger brother of Sir Alexander Fraser, Chamberlain of Scotland, who had gained a third part of the Bisset lands of the Aird by marriage with an heiress of Sir David de Graham. Until very recently the family occupied Beaufort Castle just south of Beauly, built in the eighteenth century on much the same site as their earlier stronghold of Castle Dounie.

Close neighbours of the Frasers of Lovat were the **Chisholms**, who were a Border family of uncertain origin. The first to appear in the north was Robert de Chesholme, who was appointed by David II as the constable of Urquhart Castle in 1359 in succession to his maternal grandfather, Sir Robert Lauder of the Bass, and afterwards as Justiciar of the North and Sheriff of Inverness. His eldest son Alexander Chisholm laid the foundations for the family's future prosperity in the north when he acquired wide estates by marrying Margaret, daughter of Weland of the Aird. Her lands included Strathglass with its castle at Erchless, which remained the seat of Clan Chisholm until 1887.

Ross evidently remained in a very unsettled state until Fearchar macTaggart brought the MacWilliam rebellion of 1215 to an end. Only knighted at first by Alexander II, he was afterwards granted the earldom of Ross, perhaps in 1235 if not earlier, after helping the Scottish King to subdue yet another rebellion in Galloway. Traditionally Fearchar mac Taggart traced his antecedents back to the O'Beolains, who were the hereditary lay-abbots of Applecross, originally founded by St Maelrubha in the seventh century, and supposedly descended from the Irish high-king Niall of the Nine Hostages. The last of the O'Beolain Earls of Ross died in 1372, when the title passed by marriage first to the Leslies, then the Stewarts and finally the MacDonalds, Lords of the Isles, before it was forfeited to the Crown in 1476. Meanwhile the junior branch of the family continued as the **Rosses** of Balnagowan.

The Earldom of Sutherland

North of Ross, the ancient Norse province of Cait once stretched as far south as Strathoykel and the Kyle of Sutherland. However after his successful expedition north to Caithness in retaliation for the murder of Bishop Adam in 1222, when Earl John, son of Harald Maddadson, was forced to submit, Alexander II may well have separated Sutherland from the earldom of Caithness, if indeed this had not happened earlier after Harald Maddadson had rebelled against William the Lion. Perhaps as late as 1235 Sutherland was itself erected into a separate earldom for William de Moravia, great-grandson of the first Freskyn of Duffus, after his family had established a powerful presence north of the River Oykel. By then they held virtually all of present-day Sutherland, except for the district of Strathnaver in the far north, which then consisted of the present-day parishes of Farr, Tongue, Durness and Eddrachillis, stretching as far west as the western seaboard of the Scottish mainland, south of Cape Wrath. No doubt the Freskyns of Duffus had played their part during the reign of William the Lion in bringing the rebellions of Harald Maddadson to an end. It is likely that they were rewarded with lands in Sutherland, which had perhaps come into the hands of the Scottish Crown after the death in 1198 of Earl Harald the Younger without any heirs to succeed him.

Certainly by 1211 Hugh de Moravia, grandson of the first Freskyn of Duffus, occupied a large tract of land in Sutherland within the parishes of Dornoch and Creich. He afterwards granted Skelbo and the lands of Invershin to his kinsman Gilbert de Moravia, then archdeacon of Moray. Gilbert was later appointed by Alexander II as the bishop of Caithness after the murder of Bishop Adam in 1222. He was instrumental in moving the bishopric south from its exposed and dangerous position at Halkirk to the ancient ecclesiastical site of Dornoch in 1223, where David I had much earlier established a community of Benedictine monks. There it came under the protection of William de Moravia, eldest son and heir of Hugh de Moravia, who had died by 1222.

The Earldom of Caithness

William de Moravia most likely received the earldom of Sutherland in 1235 around the same time as Farquhar macTaggart was created Earl of Ross. Farther north the Norse earldom of Orkney and Caithness had already ended in 1231, when Earl John Haraldson, son of Harald Maddadson, was killed in a dynastic quarrel, leaving no male heirs. Caithness as well as Orkney then passed to the mysterious figure of Magnus, kinsman to the earls of Angus, after the earldom had briefly been held by Malcolm, last of the ancient earls of Angus, and then by Walter Comyn, Earl of Menteith. Earl Magnus held Caithness under the sovereignty of the Scottish Crown, while he still owed allegiance as Earl of Orkney to the kings of Norway. Alexander II could therefore only grant Caithness to a claimant whom the kings of Norway were willing to recognise as the Earl of Orkney.

Following the arguments of Barbara Crawford (1985), we can only speculate why the earldom of Angus should have furnished such a person, since the identity of Earl Magnus's father is not known with any certainty. According to one chronicle, Earl John Haraldson, last of the Norse earls of Caithness and Orkney and the son of Harald Maddadson, had a daughter whom he surrendered as a hostage to William the Lion at the very end of his reign. Alexander II may well have married her off, quite possibly to a younger son of the Angus family. Earl Magnus was perhaps the eldest son of this marriage, especially as his name suggests that his mother was of Norse ancestry. Magnus apparently succeeded to the earldom of Caithness and Orkney with the evident agreement of both kingdoms, presumably after he had come of age in 1235, given that his maternal grandfather was Harald Maddadson.

Joanna de Strathnaver

Earl Magnus died four years later in 1239, when his successor Earl Gilbert inherited only half the earldom of Caithness, while the other half went to a mysterious heiress known to us only as 'Joanna de Strathnaver'. Historians have speculated wildly about her identity and why she should have received only half a share in the lands belonging to the earldom of Caithness. Virtually all that is known of her is that she was married to Freskyn de Moravia who was a nephew of William de Moravia, first Earl of Sutherland. However she is traditionally regarded as a daughter of the Moddan family of the Dales who were related by marriage to Harald Maddadson, Earl of Caithness and Orkney.

Although Moddan of Dale himself was killed by an ally of Thorfinn the Mighty in 1040, his descendants apparently inhabited the Dales of Caithness, as Strathnaver and its neighbouring valleys were then known to the saga-writers, living in harmony with their Norse neighbours. Indeed Earl Hakon Paulsson, grandson of Thorfinn the Mighty, married a daughter of the Moddan family, and among their descendants were many of the later earls of Orkney and Caithness, including Harald Maddadson. They also had a daughter Ingibjorg, who was married to Olav the Red, King of Man and the Isles, and a granddaughter Ragnhild from this union was married in her turn to Somerled, King of Argyll and the Isles. So clearly they were a family of consequence.

While Joanna de Strathnaver may well have been an heiress of the Moddan family, it is just as likely that she was a daughter of the earls of Angus, as Barbara Crawford (1985) has suggested. Certainly she had a sister called Matilda, sometimes identified as Matilda, daughter of Malcolm, last in line of the ancient earls of Angus. If Joanna's sister Matilda and Malcolm's daughter Matilda were one and the same person, she would then be the same Matilda who became the Countess of Angus in her own right after her father's death in the years before 1242. As already mentioned Matilda, Countess of Angus, married Sir Gilbert d'Umfraville in 1243, who thus became the first of the d'Umfraville earls of Angus. Accordingly Joanna and Matilda would have shared not only the inheritance of their father Malcolm, last of the ancient earls of Angus, but also the inheritance of their kinsman Magnus, Earl of Caithness and Orkney, since both men died without leaving any sons.

It is quite plausible that the Scottish Crown granted Matilda the earldom of Angus, while Joanna herself received a half-share in the earldom of Caithness, which included lands mostly in the north of the present-day county. Why she received only half her natural inheritance is best explained by the Norse laws of inheritance, which prevented an heiress from succeeding to a title in her own right. Indeed it seems likely that Earl Gilbert, who succeeded Earl Magnus in 1239, was granted the other half of Caithness, while he also received the whole of Orkney from the King of Norway. His descendants held the two earldoms for three more generations until 1329 when Malise, Earl of Strathearn, succeeded the last of the Angus earls of Orkney and Caithness, who had died without issue, as already noted.

The Cheynes in Caithness

After the death of Joanna de Strathnaver in the years before 1269 without any male heirs, her half-share in the lands of Caithness were divided between her two daughters. Mary married Reginald Cheyne, bringing him a quarter-share in these lands. His family were Norman in their origins but it is unlikely that their name came originally from the district of Quesnay in Normandy, as often stated. As Professor Barrow has emphasised (personal communication), the surname is always written with the definite article as *le Cheyne*, never as *de Cheyne*, so it can only mean literally 'the dog' in French. He notes a Rainaldus Canis recorded before 1182 as beneficiary of Sauvigny in land in Creuilly near Caen in the department of Calvados who as Renaud le Chen or Reginald la Cheyne must be ancestor to the Reginald Cheynes in Scotland.

Appearing in Scotland only at the very beginning of the thirteenth century, the **Cheynes** gained rapidly in power and influence. Sir Reginald le Chein, nephew of John Comyn of Badenoch, was Sheriff of Kincardine before he was appointed to the office of Chamberlain of Scotland between 1267 and 1269, when he held the lands of Inverugie near Peterhead. He was followed by his son and namesake Sir Reginald le Chein who married Mary, daughter of Joanna de Strathnaver by her marriage with Freskyn de Moravia. Her quarter-share in the lands of Caithness passed to their son Sir Reginald Chein, who received the other quarter-share in the lands of Caithness from his maternal aunt, who had no children of her own. He left two co-heiresses at his death in 1341, so that the Cheyne lands in Caithness then passed by marriage in the mid-fourteenth century to the Keiths of Inverugie and to the Sutherlands of Duffus.

Chapter Five

KINGS OF THE WESTERN ISLES

The strategy of feudalisation that had been so successful in establishing the authority of the Canmore kings throughout the north of Scotland was also pursued farther west in Argyll and the Western Isles, but ultimately to much less effect. The treaty seemingly imposed upon Edgar, King of Scots, by Magnus 'Barelegs' of Norway after his great expedition of 1098 meant that only Argyll itself came under the sovereignty of the Scottish Crown, if it could be exercised, while all the Western Isles were held by Norway, together with the Northern Isles of Orkney and Shetland. Magnus 'Barelegs' had mounted his expedition in 1098 soon after the death of Godred Crovan in 1095, intending to force his son and successor Lagmann to recognise the suzerainty of Norway over his kingdom of Man and the Western Isles. A year after Lagmann died in 1102, Magnus 'Barelegs' was himself killed during the course of another great expedition to the Western Isles. The history of the kingdom of Man remains very obscure for the next few years until Olav the Red began his long rule, probably during the second decade of the twelfth century. He evidently held all the Western Isles as well as Man itself, while rendering tribute to the kings of Norway as his overlords. However they were too preoccupied with their own dynastic struggles in Norway after 1130 to exert any real authority over their overseas possessions.

Somerled, King of the Isles

Nevertheless the Scottish Crown was apparently quite unable to impose its own rule over Argyll and the western seaboard of the Scottish mainland around this time, let alone the Western Isles. It was Somerled, King of the Isles and Lord of Argyll, who stepped into this vacuum of political power, carving out a petty kingdom for himself in Argyll and the Western Isles, not just by means of his powerful fleet of sea-going galleys but by judicious marriages as well. He eventually came to rule over Argyll and all its offshore islands in virtual independence of the Scottish kings.

Somerled was the progenitor of two great and very early clans in the history of the Scottish Highlands, namely the MacDonalds and the Mac-Dougalls. Even so his name is Norse, meaning 'summer voyager or warrior'. It most likely refers to the Viking tradition of going on raiding parties during the summer, given the treacherous waters of the Minch in winter. He was known to the Irish annalists as *Ri Innse Gall* or 'King of the Isles of the Strangers', as the Hebrides were then called. Tradition suggests that he was of Celtic descent, since his father Gillebrigte and his grandfather Gilladomnain both had Gaelic names. Indeed the histories of Clan Donald trace his ancestry back to Godfrey mac Fergus, King of Argyll and the Hebrides, whom the Annals of the Four Masters describe as an ally of Kenneth mac Alpin in 843. However the very existence of Godfrey mac Fergus has recently been doubted. The Annals of the Four Masters were compiled only in the seventeenth century and while his name appears in the many pedigrees of Clan Donald, dating from the late fourteenth century at the earliest, he is never mentioned in earlier annals or chronicles. According to the traditions of Clan Donald, many generations before Godfrey mac Fergus was his distant ancestor Colla Uais, who was the semi-legendary king of Airgialla in the fourth century AD, from whom Clan Donald claim descent. Possibly Somerled belonged to the mixed race of Viking and Gael, known as the *Gall–Ghaidheal*, which the scant records of the time suggest then inhabited the Western Isles of Scotland, if not Galloway, given that his mother may well have been Norse.

The rise of the *Gall–Ghaidheal*, or 'foreign Gaels' as they were known in the Irish Annals, first occurred in the ninth century. As piratical raiders with a reputation for barbaric savagery it seems the leaders of the *Gall–Ghaidheal* were men of Norse descent like Ketil Flatnose, who took refuge in the Hebrides after being driven from his homeland in western Norway. The Viking sagas record their exploits, suggesting that they wielded a great deal of military power, while the Annals of Ulster mention them as leading large war-parties in attacks against Ireland, Strathclyde and the Pictish province of Fortrui during the middle decades of the ninth century. Later the descendants of Ketil Flatnose were to sail north to the Faroes and Iceland, which they settled in the second half of the ninth century. It seems they left behind a mixed population, known as the *Gall–Ghaidheal*, after the Viking invaders had first married into the local Gaelic-speaking population of the Hebrides.

The early history of Somerled or Somhairle mac Gillebrigte, to give him his Gaelic name, is a matter of myth and legend. It is said by the seanachies of Clan Donald that Somerled's father Gillebrigte, or his grandfather Gilladomnain, escaped to Fermanagh after they had been expelled from their ancestral lands of Dalriada by the Norse kings of Man, which they had held perhaps ever since the time of Godfrey mac Fergus. They returned later with Somerled, who then recovered his ancestral lands by force of arms. But it is perhaps more likely that Somerled's family only settled in Ardgour and Morvern after leaving Ireland for the very first time in the decades before 1130. There is little evidence that they ever lived in Dalriada before then, unless Godfrey mac Fergus was indeed their ancestor and King of the Isles, before his supposed death in 853. Quite possibly they had more in common with other families from Ireland, who settled in Argyll around this time, whose ancestry has been elucidated by W. D. H. Sellar (1971).

Among these families the MacSweens, the Lamonts and the MacLachlans all trace their ancestry back to Amrothan, grandson of Flaithbhertach, King of Ailech in northern Ireland, who died in 1036 as the distant descendant of the semi-legendary Niall of the Nine Hostages. Perhaps fleeing from the northerly advance of the Ui Neill in Ireland, Amrothan himself settled in Cowal or Knapdale during the second half of the eleventh century and married a daughter of a 'king of the Scots'. Perhaps the king in question was even Donald *Ban*. He had sought refuge in the Western Isles after Macbeth had seized the Scottish throne in 1040, when he possibly returned to his ancestral lands of the *Cenel nGabrain* in Dalriada, even if he did not go to Ireland. After Donald *Ban* was finally overthrown in 1097 his lands in Dalriada were quite possibly settled by Amrothan's descendants, who founded the families of the MacSweens of Knapdale, the Lamonts of Cowal and the MacLachlans of Loch Fyne during the late twelfth and early thirteenth centuries. Faced by dynastic pressures in Ireland Somerled's family perhaps had much the same history, crossing from Ireland in the late eleventh century and then settling in Ardgour and Morvern in the early twelfth century, as tradition would have it.

Sea-Power in the Western Isles

Much of Somerled's strength rested on his sea-going fleet of war-galleys. Given the ease of travel throughout the Highlands nowadays, it is now difficult to appreciate just how important were the sea-lanes of the Western Isles in such remote times. The sea was not then a barrier to communication but a highway, allowing the rapid deployment of forces by galley throughout the islands and deep into the Highland hinterland along the many sea-lochs. Galleys provided easy access across the North Channel to Gaelic Ulster and especially to Antrim, and indeed there were many links between the two countries, then and later.

The use of galleys rather than the old skin-covered boats or currachs of the Celts was clearly a result of Norse influence. Long before before the defeat of King Hakon at the battle of Largs in 1263, the Gaels had adopted the Norse style of shipbuilding, which had earlier allowed the Vikings to

establish their authority from Orkney and Shetland to the Irish Sea, domi-
nating all of the Western Isles and the adjacent seaboard of the Scottish
Highlands. Later, galleys were carved as a symbol of naval power on numer-
ous Highland tombstones and Celtic crosses in medieval times, while the
Black Galley of Man is a prominent feature on the coats of arms of the
MacDonald and the MacDougall families, who claim descent from
Somerled. Their success at sea was celebrated in many Gaelic poems of the
period.

Like the beautiful but awesome longships of the Vikings, galleys or birlinns were clinker-built boats, constructed from overlapping planks of wood
held together with bent nails. They had single masts and square sails, as well
as banks of oars, but their more upright stems and sterns lacked the raking
lines of the Viking longships. Such galleys could be rowed as well as sailed,
which proved a strategic advantage over sailing ships in calm weather. By
the fourteenth century at the very latest, Highland birlinns were fitted with
rudders instead of the single oar previously used for steering, making them
much easier to manoeuvre. Such galleys remained the foundation of Gaelic
power over the Western Isles and the adjacent mainland of the Scottish
Highlands for nearly five centuries, until the Union of the Crowns in 1603
allowed James VI of Scotland access to the English navy with its powerful
fleet of warships.

Somerled's Rise to Power

We might well discount as apocryphal the ancient story of Clan Donald that
Somerled was drawn one day from a life of obscurity by his Celtic clansmen
of Morvern and Ardgour, who called upon him to resist a Viking raid by
Olaf the Red, Norse King of Man. Apparently he only agreed if he were to
catch a particularly elusive salmon that very day. Fortunately his day's fishing
was successful and the salmon is even now displayed on the arms of Clan
Donald. Faced by much greater forces, Somerled adopted the tactic of
marching and counter-marching his own men from behind a hill in a variety
of different guises. The invaders were so deceived regarding his true
strength that they were routed after a spirited charge and driven back to
their galleys with much loss of life. It was supposedly from such humble
beginnings that Somerled first established his rule as King of the ancient
province of Argyll, which then stretched north to Wester Ross, in the early
decades of the twelfth century.

Despite his antagonism with Olaf the Red, who then held the Isle of
Man and all the Western Isles for Norway, Somerled made an advantageous
marriage in 1140 with the King's natural daughter Ragnhild. This he

supposedly achieved by a crafty stratagem. Rejected as a suitor, Somerled waited until he encountered Olaf the Red anchored with his galleys off Ardnamur-chan. A shipwright in Somerled's crew swam across to Olaf's galley under cover of darkness and drilled several holes in its keel, which he sealed with tallow. Setting sail the next day for Skye, Olaf's galley soon sprang a leak as the tallow gave way in a rising sea. Forced to seek Somerled's help, Olaf was refused any assistance until he agreed to Somerled marrying his daughter. Tradition holds that the MacIntyres are the descendants of the shipwright who performed such a signal service for Somerled.

Olav the Red was murdered by his nephews in 1153, bringing his long and successful reign of four decades to an end. He was succeeded by his son Godred the Black, whose tyrannical manner alienated many of his Hebridean chieftains. Their leader Thorfinn turned to Somerled for support, requesting that Somerled's eldest son Dugall be proclaimed King of the Isles while still a boy. Learning of this challenge to his power, Godred the Black set sail in January 1156 with a large war-fleet to attack Somerled and his allies. After a bloody but indecisive encounter off the north-west coast of Islay, a treaty was agreed whereby Godred ceded to the sons of Somerled the islands south of Ardnamurchan Point, while he himself retained sovereignty to the north over Skye and the Outer Hebrides, which he continued to rule from the Isle of Man.

This treaty effectively extended Somerled's influence over what was once the ancient Celtic kingdom of Dalriada. The islands of Islay, Jura, Colonsay, Mull, Tiree and Coll were all added to his mainland possessions, which then stretched from Kintyre through modern-day Argyll and beyond to Ardnamurchan. Such a division of the Western Isles apparently lasted for more than a hundred years until the great expedition of King Hakon of Norway to the Western Isles in 1263 ended with his defeat at the battle of Largs. Two years later in 1158 Somerled launched a ferocious attack against the Isle of Man with a force of more than fifty galleys, laying waste to the whole island after he had defeated Godred the Black in battle. Since Godred then fled to Norway, remaining there until after Somerled's death in 1164, it seems likely that Somerled had succeeded in establishing his rule as *Ri Innse Gall* over all the Western Isles by this time, including Skye and the Outer Hebrides.

Somerled and the Scottish Crown

As far as we know Somerled remained at peace with David I of Scotland until the latter's death in 1153. Contemporary sources mostly refer to

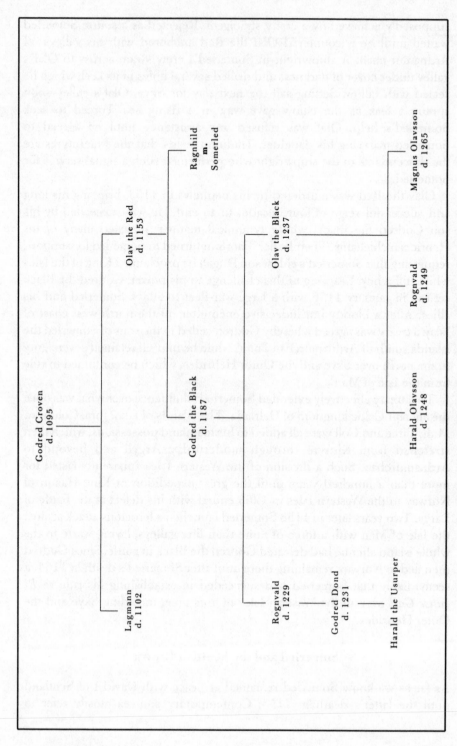

FIGURE 5.1 *Norse kings of Man (after Duncan and Brown)*

Godred Croven
d. 1095

Lagmann
d. 1102

Olav the Red
d. 1153

Ragnhild
m.
Somerled

Godred the Black
d. 1187

Rognvald
d. 1229

Godred Dond
d. 1231

Harald the Usurper

Olav the Black
d. 1237

Harald Olavsson
d. 1248

Rognvald
d. 1249

Magnus Olavsson
d. 1265

Somerled as *Regulus* of Argyll, which suggests that he held his mainland territories of Argyll in the Celtic manner, governing them in near-independence but perhaps acknowledging the King of the Scots as his overlord or high-king. There is no evidence that Somerled ever considered himself a feudal vassal of David I. Instead he most likely rendered tribute to David I by virtue of the time-honoured Celtic system of cain. This may be why David I, even while he claimed the right to revenues and tribute in kind from Argyll and Kintyre, evidently did not expect that he would be paid every year, since cain was normally only paid every two or three years. Likewise the chronicles assert that men from Argyll and the Western Isles fought in England on behalf of David I at the battle of the Standard in 1138, along with contingents from Orkney and elsewhere, and Somerled may even have been their leader. The raising of such forces could be regarded as part of the tribute he owed to the Scottish King under the Celtic custom of hosting, quite outwith the feudal system, even if they were not simply fighting as mercenaries.

After David I had died in 1153, Malcolm IV succeeded his grandfather on the Scottish throne when he was only twelve years of age. It was perhaps the extreme youth of the new king which prompted a revival of the old Celtic laws of succession, which again favoured claimants from the house of Moray. Already, in the years before 1134, Somerled's sister had married Malcolm macHeth. It was a marriage that testifies to the status of Somerled's family, even before he had himself gained any great power over Argyll and the Western Isles. Quite apart from his Celtic ancestry, Somerled was almost bound to support his brother-in-law Malcolm macHeth, still held captive at Roxburgh after his earlier rebellion against David I in 1130.

Accordingly, for whatever reason, Somerled rebelled in January 1154 against Malcolm IV with the support of his two nephews, the sons of Malcolm macHeth, as already recounted. Although Donald macHeth was captured at Whithorn in 1156, Somerled's power over Argyll and the Western Isles after his defeat of Godred the Black apparently enabled him to force an accommodation upon Malcom IV, who released father and son in 1157, elevating the elder Malcolm macHeth to the earldom of Ross. Somerled himself became reconciled to Malcolm IV in 1160, after the Scottish king had journeyed to France in support of Henry II of England and perhaps needed peace at home after the Revolt of the Six Earls at Perth. Afterwards Somerled visited the Scottish court in Perth at Christmas, where he acquired his nickname of 'Sit-by-the-King'. Their reconciliation was so important to the Scottish Crown that it marked an event that was subsequently used to date a royal charter. Even so it seems possible that Somerled abandoned it when Malcolm IV attempted to deprive Malcolm macHeth of the earldom of Ross in favour of Florence, Count of Holland, who had married the King's sister Ada in 1161.

Death of Somerled

Indeed only three years later Somerled launched a powerful attack in 1164 upon the Scottish mainland. Raising an army from all his possessions, with contingents from Argyll, Kintyre, the Western Isles, Ireland, and perhaps Galloway and Orkney as well, he sailed up the Firth of Clyde with a powerful fleet of 160 galleys, landing his forces near Renfrew. Although he may have been intent upon seizing the throne of Scotland for himself, or perhaps engaged in carving out a wholly independent kingdom for himself in Argyll, neither explanation seems very likely. As MacDonald and MacLean (1992) have argued, it seems likely that it was essentially an attempt to stem the westerly advance of feudal power under Malcolm IV, which Somerled could well have regarded as a threat to his own possessions in Argyll and the Western Isles. Already David I had settled Walter fitzAlan as the High Steward of Scotland on great estates around Renfrew and farther south, while Malcolm IV had granted David Olifard, who founded the Anglo-Norman family of Oliphant, together with several Flemings, lands around Bothwell and further inland in upper Clydesdale. In striking at Renfrew, the *caput* of Walter fitzAlan, Somerled quite likely hoped to destroy the power of these powerful Anglo-Norman barons and their knights.

Somerled was apparently slain during the ensuing battle, along with his son Gillecallum, even if it is said that he was opposed by only a very inferior force of Scots, led in all probability by Walter fitzAlan, the High Steward of Scotland. Somerled's fighting prowess, almost unmatched at sea, possibly did not stand him in good stead in a land-battle, faced by the mounted might of Anglo-Norman knights clad in armour. However tradition holds that he was assassinated in his tent before the battle, betrayed by his own nephew. Such a tradition often emerges to explain the death of a heroic figure, thought by later generations as invincible in battle. Afterwards it is said that his body was carried to Iona where he was buried, upon the orders of Malcolm IV. Again it now seems more likely that his body was laid to rest at Saddell in Kintyre, where a Cistercian monastery was later founded by his son Reginald, if indeed he himself was not its founder.

Norway and the Western Isles

After Somerled's death fighting the forces of the Scottish Crown in 1164, Godred the Black evidently returned from Norway to reclaim his territories. He ruled in person over the Isle of Man until his death in 1187, while appointing his elder son Rognvald to take charge of the island of Lewis. After his death the Isle of Man was held by Rognvald as its King, even if he was born out of wedlock, while his younger brother Olav the Black ruled

Lewis under him. Finding Lewis 'almost totally unfit for cultivation', it being rocky and mountainous, Olav the Black eventually petitioned his brother Rognvald for somewhere else to live, whereupon he was seized and carried away to Scotland to be held prisoner by William the Lion, probably in 1207. It followed the brief attempt by the Scottish King to grant Caithness to Rognvald Gudredsson, as he was known in the Norse sagas, during the rebellion of Harald Maddadson against the Scottish Crown.

Two or three years after 1207 an expedition was launched from Norway, intending most likely to overthrow Rognvald in favour of Olav the Black and prompted by Rognvald's lack of allegiance to the Norwegian crown, which he had thrown off soon after becoming King in 1187. It was led by Uspak, said in the sagas to be Somerled's grandson. However the expedition deteriorated into little more than a raiding party, riven by internal quarrels. Olav the Black was eventually released from captivity after the accession of Alexander II to the Scottish throne in 1214 and, returning to the Isle of Man, he evidently made his peace with his elder brother Rognvald. Nonetheless their quarrel still remained, especially after he was forced to renounce his first wife, and he finally deposed Rognvald in 1226.

Somerled's Descendants and their Territories

Meanwhile Somerled's territories had been divided among his three surviving sons by Ragnhild after his death in 1164. The exact nature of this division remains quite uncertain, given the lack of any contemporary records. We can only speculate from what we know of the territories held later by their descendants in the thirteenth and fourteenth centuries. Somerled's eldest son was almost certainly Dugald, who was made King of the Isles in 1156, although his seniority has been disputed. He probably gained Somerled's mainland territories of Lorn, if not Morvern and Ardnamurchan as well, along with the islands of Mull, Coll, Tiree and the northern half of Jura. Nothing is known of his life after 1175 and it is not even known when he died. Despite the claims of MacDonald historians, he was almost certainly the eponymous founder of Clan Dougall. His son Duncan lived during the first half of the thirteenth century, when he founded the Valliscaulian Priory of Ardchattan in 1230 on the northern shore of Loch Etive, while his grandson Ewen macDougall succeeded him as 'King John' in 1248. The family first used the appellation *de Ergadia* before they became known as the MacDougalls of Argyll in the mid-thirteenth century.

Somerled's second son Reginald may well have received Islay and Kintyre, together with Colonsay and the southern half of Jura, lying at the heart of his dominions. His seal described him as 'King of the Isles' and 'Lord of Argyll and Kintyre', perhaps suggesting that he laid claim to other territories on the mainland, north of Kintyre, which otherwise came within Dugald's sphere of influence. These lands of Knapdale and Glassary were probably held by equally ancient Celtic families by then, such as the MacSweens, who built the stone castle of Castle Sween in Knapdale at an early date, together with the Lamonts and MacLachlans farther east in Cowal. Reginald himself was the founder and benefactor of several religious houses. They included the Benedictine monastery and an Augustinian nunnery on the island of Iona, and probably the Cistercian monastery at Saddell in the north of Kintyre, most likely founded with his father Somerled. He also made benefactions to Paisley Abbey, where he is thought to have ended his days, dying perhaps as late as 1227. His double-sided seal, reminiscent in itself of royalty, depicted a galley filled with men at arms on one side, as testimony to his power as 'King of the Western Isles'. Surprisingly enough the other side apparently depicted him as a mounted knight in armour, carrying a drawn sword in one hand, so that the Gaelic society of the Western Isles was not immune to the chivalric ideals of Anglo-Norman knighthood even at this early date.

What territories Somerled's youngest son Angus held is subject to much debate. There is no evidence that he ever received Bute, as often stated, which was almost certainly held by the Stewart family by 1204. Indeed Bute and perhaps even Arran was quite likely seized by the Scottish Crown in the aftermath of Somerled's defeat in 1164. Even if the Chronicle of Man asserts that Reginald was defeated in a battle with Angus in 1192, there is no reason to suppose that it was fought over the possession of Arran, as commonly thought. Equally there is little or no evidence that Angus ever held Garmoran, as the districts of Moidart and Knoydart lying between Ardnamurchan and Glenelg were then known, along with its offshore islands of Rhum, Eigg and the Uists.

According to the Chronicle of Man while Angus was victorious over his brother Reginald in 1192, he was eventually killed with his three sons fighting the 'Men of Skye' in 1210, leaving no male heirs. His death was probably connected with the Norse expedition of the same year under Uspak, his own nephew and the son of Dugald. Reginald himself had two sons, Donald and Ruairi, who might well have benefited from their uncle Angus's death in 1210, perhaps receiving his territories. They had attacked Skye in 1209, while they raided the north of Ireland in 1212 and 1214. The elder son Donald evidently succeeded to his father's possessions in Islay and Kintyre. He was the founding father of Clan Donald and its many branches, such as the MacDonnells and the MacConnells. Chief among these families were the MacDonalds of Islay, who later held the powerful lordship of the Isles as the descendants of Somerled, inherited from the MacRuaris. Reginald's other son Ruairi somehow came into possession of

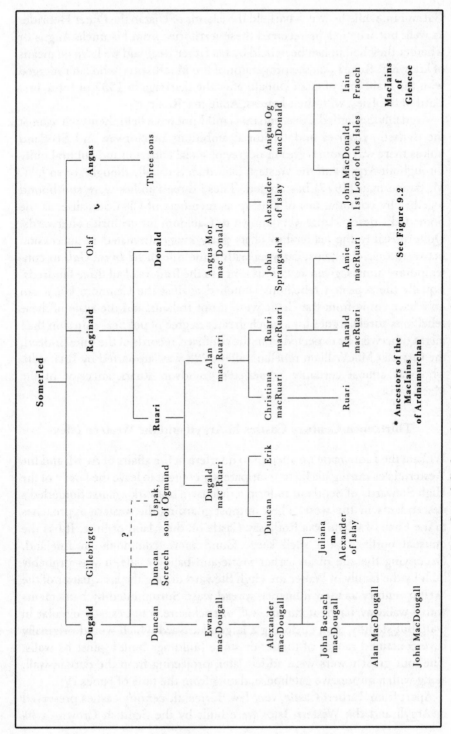

FIGURE 5.2 *Somerled's descendants (after Duncan and Brown, and Munro and Munro)*

Garmoran, while he may have held the islands of Uist in the Outer Hebrides as well, but whether he received these territories from his uncle Angus or whether they had in fact been held by his father Reginald we have no means of knowing. Ruairi was the progenitor of the MacRuairis, who later merged with the main line of Clan Donald after the marriage in 1337 of John, first Lord of the Isles, with their heiress, Amie macRuairi.

Arguably Somerled's descendants could not have held their own against the dynastic rivalries and territorial ambitions of Norway and Scotland unless there was a much greater degree of social cohesion and cultural unity throughout Argyll and the Western Isles than is usually thought, or so J. W. M. Bannerman (1977) has argued. These three families were still bound together by common ties of kinship as members of Clan Somairle, as the Somerled's descendants were known to Gaeldom for centuries afterwards. Quite possibly the leadership of its petty kings alternated in succession between their chieftains, carrying with it the title of *Ri Innse Gall* in contemporary annals, given at various times to the leaders of all three kindreds. Equally the repeated rebellions launched against the Canmore kings can only have come from the Celtic west, if not Ireland, and the scale of these rebellions surely argues for a much greater degree of political cohesion than might otherwise be expected from the confused records of the time. Indeed, the very last MacWilliam rebellion after 1228 was supported by Ruaraidh, who was almost certainly Somerled's grandson Ruari, ancestor of the MacRuaris.

Thirteenth-Century Castles in Argyll and the Western Isles

William the Lion made no attempt to interfere in the affairs of Argyll and the Western Isles during his lifetime, apparently content to leave the family of the High Stewards of Scotland to form a defensive bulwark against Somerled's descendants in the west. Their outpost guarding the western approaches to the Firth of Clyde was Rothesay Castle on the island of Bute. It has the unusual outlines of a shell keep, found more commonly in England. Occupying the site of an earlier motte-and-bailey castle, it was probably built by the family of Walter the High Steward during the last quarter of the twelfth century as their influence spread west. Surmounted by battlements with a walkway, its great curtain-wall of enclosure is not exactly circular in plan, but slightly oval, enclosing a large courtyard which would originally have contained ranges of timber or stone buildings built against its walls. The four great towers were added later, projecting from the curtain-wall, along with a impressive gatehouse, dating from the time of James IV.

Apart from Tarbert Castle, very few thirteenth-century castles preserved in Argyll and the Western Isles were built by the Scottish Crown or its agents as an expression of royal authority. Nearly all these castles it seems were built by independent Gaelic-speaking magnates. Almost without exception, they built their strongholds on islands and other sea-girt rocks. Especially favoured sites were on top of rocky craigs by the seashore, close to a shelving beach, where fleets of galleys could be landed. Often still preserved as romantic ruins, their brooding presence in the Highland landscape remains as a dramatic testimony to the great power of the 'Barons of Argyll and the Isles' during these years. Indeed these castles 'constitute a unique monument of private fortification, indisputably the most remarkable collection of 13th-century lords' strongholds to be found in any single region of Britain', to quote the words of Professor Barrow (1981).

The oldest stone-built castle on the Scottish mainland south of Caithness is often reputed to be Castle Sween on the shores of Knapdale, even if its early history is virtually unknown. It was most likely built towards the very end of the twelfth century by Suibhne, Lord of Knapdale and progenitor of the MacSweens, if not slightly later by his son Dugald mac Suibhne. Rather than being a great Norman keep with spacious floors, as often described, it was probably built as a simple castle of enclosure, roughly oblong in plan, with flat buttresses at its four corners and also set midway along its four walls. The same Dugald mac Suibhne may well have built the earliest parts of Skipness Castle, facing Arran across the Kilbrannan Sound from the north-east of Kintyre, which consist of a rectangular hall-house with a chapel. These buildings were later incorporated into the curtain-walls of a great castle of enclosure, built after the 1260s by Walter Stewart, Earl of Menteith, who by then held Knapdale on behalf of the Scottish Crown. The remains of another hall-house is found at Lochranza on Arran, possibly built by Dugald mac Suibhne as well, unless it is later in date.

Farther south only the last vestiges of Dunaverty Castle now overlook the waters of the North Channel between Scotland and Ireland from the southern tip of the Mull of Kintyre. It was clearly in existence as a stone-built castle by the mid-thirteenth century since it was stormed in 1248 by Alan, natural son of Thomas of Galloway, after it had been seized by Walter Bisset. He had started to fortify it against the Scots, encouraged by Henry III of England. Since Donald, son of Reginald, apparently held Kintyre during the first half of the thirteenth century, he was most likely responsible for its construction. What other castles he might have built elsewhere within his territories, and especially on Islay, remains a mystery. Clan Donald as his descendants made their *caput* at Finlaggan in the very heart of Islay, where it is said by Dean Monro in 1549 that they had a residence 'well-built in palace-work according to their old fashion', and a chapel, occupying a small island known as Eilean Mor, lying just offshore in Loch Finlaggan and reached by a causeway. Recent excavations have identified both these buildings among more than a dozen others of medieval date on Eilean Mor, which was itself defended around its perimeter by a stout timber palisade, backed by a wooden walkway. More surprisingly the flattened remains of lime-mortared walls were uncovered on the even smaller Eilean na Comhairle, or Isle of the Council, lying slightly farther offshore beyond Eilean Mor, and traditionally identified as the meeting-place of the Council of the Isles. Apparently demolished deliberately in the fourteenth century, they are perhaps all that remains of a fortified hall-house or stone-built castle of enclosure, dating from the thirteenth century. Elsewhere on Islay only the now ruinous castles of Dunnyvaig and Loch Gorm are built of stone, but their date is equally an enigma.

North of Knapdale the barony of Lochawe was probably held by the ancestors of the Campbells in the thirteenth century, even if they do not appear in the historical record until its very end. It is said that they built Duntrune Castle as a small castle of enclosure in the late thirteenth century. It stands on a rocky promontory jutting out into the waters of Loch Crinan, guarding the narrow isthmus between Loch Fyne and the Sound of Jura. However their stronghold was situated farther north at Innischonnel Castle, occupying the small island of the same name, surrounded by the waters of Loch Awe. Built as a rectangular castle of enclosure in the thirteenth century, its flat buttresses are reminiscent of Castle Sween. Other islands in Loch Awe served a similar defensive purpose, including Fraoch Eilean, where a fortified hall-house was built by Gilchrist macNaughton, after he had been granted a charter to act as its keeper by Alexander III in 1267.

North of Loch Awe, the great power of the MacDougalls, Lords of Lorn, before their downfall in the Wars of Scottish Independence is reflected in the castles of enclosure that they built during the course of the thirteenth century. Chief of these fortresses is Dunstaffnage Castle, guarding the southern head-land at the entrance to Loch Etive and overlooking the sheltered anchorage of Dunstaffnage Bay to its east. Perched on top of a rocky craig, its plan is quadrangular, following the contours of the rock, so that its lofty walls of enclosure surround a central courtyard, making up the flat top of the craig itself. Round towers project slightly at two corners, while a larger tower with rounded outlines at another corner was later modified to form a gatehouse. It was probably first built by Duncan mac Dugald, Somerled's grandson, who founded Ardchattan Priory in 1230, or his son Ewen, who held the lordship of Lorn after his father's death in 1248.

Several other castles were built to defend the island territories of the MacDougalls in the thirteenth century. Duart Castle on the island of Mull occupies a very stategic position, overlooking the entrance to the Sound of Mull from the Firth of Lorne. Built originally as a square castle of enclosure in the thirteenth century, and later greatly modified and enlarged as a tower-house, it came into the hands of the MacLeans of Duart in the fourteenth century. Other thirteenth-century castles attributed to the MacDougalls are the rock-girt castles of Cairnaburg in the Treshnish Isles, guarding the approaches to Coll and Tiree from the island of Mull, and the equally remote castle of Dunchonnell in the Garvellachs, guarding the sea-lanes south from Dunstaffnage to the island of Jura. The MacDougalls also built a thirteenth-century hall-house at Coeffin on the island of Lismore, while the medieval bishops of Argyll constructed the episcopal castle of Achadun at the southern end of the island early in the thirteenth century. The MacDougalls may also have built Mingary Castle, which occupies a strategic position on the southern coast of the Ardnamurchan peninsula, overlooking the northern entrance to the Sound of Mull. It was built in the thirteenth century as a small castle of enclosure with hexagonal outlines, as determined by the shape of the rocky outcrop on which it stands, close to the shore.

Farther north beyond Ardnamurchan lay the lands of Garmoran and the Uists, held by the MacRuaris. Their stronghold was apparently Castle Tioram, built on an island in Loch Moidart near the mouth of Loch Shiel. Accessible only at low tide, it has much the same plan and distinctive appearance as Mingary Castle, except that its outlines are pentagonal, shaped around the contours of the underlying rock. Its early history is obscure, but it was held around 1320 by Christian macRuari and then in the 1350s by her niece Amie macRuari, first wife of John MacDonald of Islay, first Lord of the Isles. It was most likely built by the MacRuaris, perhaps a century earlier. Whether they built any other castles to guard their island territories remains a mystery. Only Kisimul Castle on the island of Barra has been attributed to the thirteenth century, but it was probably built by the MacNeils of Barra in the fifteenth century.

Two other castles north of the ancient province of Argyll may well date from the thirteenth century. Dunvegan Castle in the far north-west of Skye was the ancient stronghold of the MacLeods of Harris and Dunvegan and, much altered and restored, it still remains their family residence. Although a great tower was built during the fourteenth century and further buildings were added in later centuries its main defence is an irregular wall of enclosure, which follows the rocky contours of the ground in a manner typical of other thirteenth-century castles in the western Highlands. Dunvegan Castle may thus date from the time of Leod, progenitor of the MacLeods, who it is thought lived in the thirteenth century. Likewise the very earliest parts of Eilean Donan Castle, built on an offshore island where Loch Duich passes into Loch Alsh near Dornie, may well be thirteenth century in date, making up a small castle of enclosure with rectangular outlines. Often attributed to Alexander II on very little evidence, it was later held by the MacKenzies of

Kintail, perhaps as the vassals of the ancient earls of Ross, who received a grant of the lordship of Skye and Lewis from Alexander III in 1264.

Alexander II and the Western Isles

After Alexander II ascended the throne in 1214 he soon turned his attention to subjugating the west. He certainly launched one expedition against Argyll, most likely in 1222, if not an earlier one mentioned by Fordun as occurring in the previous year, which it seems was driven back to Glasgow by a storm, long before he embarked on his ill-fated expedition of 1249. We know very little about the course of this 1222 expedition, which it seems lasted only a few weeks, but it may well have been directed more towards Kintyre and Knapdale than the north of Argyll. Apparently it brought the country into submission without any military engagement, whereupon Alexander II rewarded his followers and loyal Argyllsmen with the lands that had been confiscated. Walter the High Steward was possibly granted Cowal at this time and a stone-built castle constructed at Dunoon. This 1222 expedition followed an earlier one made by Alexander II in the autumn of 1221 to put down a rebellion in the north by Donald MacNeill, of whom we otherwise know nothing. Conceivably he was an ally of Ruari, Lord of Garmoran, Somerled's grandson, and it may well be that the expedition in 1222 was intended to seize Ruari's lands which he held by charter in Kintyre. Twenty years later Alexander II granted the burgesses of Glasgow the right to trade through Argyll and Lennox.

Afterwards the authority of the Scottish Crown was perhaps reinforced by the building of Tarbert Castle, guarding the strategic isthmus between Knapdale and Kintyre, which gave easy access by porterage to the sea-lanes of the Inner Hebrides from the Firth of Clyde. It was originally built as a simple castle of enclosure with rectangular outlines, containing four ranges of stone buildings within its courtyard, of which only the foundations now remain. Although its construction is often attributed to King Robert the Bruce in the 1320s, it shows features in common with other royal castles like Kincardine and Kinclaven, which were almost certainly built during the reigns of William the Lion or Alexander II.

The Western Isles evidently remained in an unsettled state until 1229 when Duncan and Dugald Screech, sons of Dugald mac Somerled, greatly disturbed the peace, much to the displeasure of King Hakon of Norway, perhaps suggesting that Alexander II was behind their actions. Meanwhile Olav the Black had already made himself King of Man and the Isles in 1226 when he deposed his elder half-brother Rognvald after a long struggle. He thus regained his rightful inheritance as originally decreed by his father Godred the Black before he died in 1187. Even after 1226, however, the quarrel continued between the two brothers, only to end when Rognvald was killed by the treachery of Olav's men in 1229, thus leaving Olav the Black to rule over the kingdom of Man without any opposition. Even so the Isle of Man was still threatened with invasion by Alan of Galloway, who had long been an ally of Rognvald, acting in virtual independence of Alexander II of Scotland and holding considerable estates in Ulster from the English Crown. Olav the Black therefore sailed to Norway to seek assistance in 1230, only to find that King Hakon was about to launch an expedition to bring the Western Isles back under his own control.

Norse Expedition of 1230 to the Western Isles

Like the earlier foray of 1209 or 1210, this expedition set sail under Uspak, whom King Hakon had already appointed as King of the Hebrides, and perhaps Argyll and Kintyre as well, reigning under the sovereignty of Norway. Indeed Uspak took the name of Hakon in honour of his royal patron: his original name of Uspak was apparently a Norse attempt at the Gaelic name Gilleasbuig. He is sometimes described as the son of Ogmund, which may be an attempt to render Somerled's lineage name of MacGilleadhomhmain into Norse. He is known from elsewhere in the Norse sagas as the brother of Duncan and Dugald Screech, themselves the sons of Dugald mac Somerled, thus strengthening the view that he was descended from Somerled himself.

The expedition under Uspak sailed west by way of Orkney and the Isle of Skye until it reached the Sound of Islay, where its leaders met up with Duncan and Dugald Screech, and their cousin Somerled, representing it seems the interests of the Scottish Crown. Although an attempt was made to reach an amicable agreement, hostilities broke out and Somerled was killed. Nevertheless Uspak allowed Duncan to escape, while Dugald Screech was carried off a prisoner under his protection and nothing more was heard of him. The expedition, now consisting of eighty ships, rounded the Mull of Kintyre, so avoiding the royal castle at Tarbert, and sailed up the Firth of Clyde to the island of Bute, where the castle at Rothesay was garrisoned by the Scots. Laying siege to the castle, it was taken after three days, but with the loss of 360 men. Then hearing that Alan fitzRonald, Lord of Galloway, had set sail with a fleet of 200 galleys, the expedition withdrew towards the south of Kintyre.

Uspak died in Kintyre of his injuries, received earlier when a stone was dropped from the battlements during the siege of Rothesay Castle, thus depriving the expedition of its leader. Command then passed to Olav the Black who had accompanied the expedition from Norway. He ordered the Norse fleet to sail to the Isle of Man, which he afterwards ruled over as a faithful vassal of King Hakon of Norway, while he entrusted the Hebrides to his nephew Godred Dond, son of Rognvald. Godred Dond was killed soon afterwards in Lewis and the descendants of Somerled apparently regained their island possessions in the Outer Hebrides, if indeed they had ever been lost.

Scottish Claim to Sovereignty

When Olav the Black died in 1237 his son Harald Olavsson succeeded him as King of Man. At first Harald Olavsson refused to do homage to King Hakon for his territories, even if he made his peace with the Norwegian King in 1240, attending the court in Norway before returning to the Isle of Man in 1242. However by 1244 Alexander II was actively petitioning King Hakon of Norway for the return of the Western Isles, which he was prepared to buy outright, but to no avail. The Scottish King no doubt felt threatened in the west by the English settlement of Antrim, which had been aided and abetted by the Norse kings of Man. Indeed he could only trust the allegiance of Duncan mac Dugald, Lord of Lorne. When he died in 1248, his son Ewen macDougall succeeded to his father's territories as 'King Ewen', only to abandon any allegiance to Alexander II in favour of King Hakon of Norway.

Ewen macDougall, King of the Isles

Faced with the demands of Alexander II for sovereignty over the Western Isles, King Hakon of Norway tried to strengthen his own position. This he did in 1248 by marrying his daughter Cecilia to Harald Olavsson, King of Man and the Isles, who had travelled to Norway in 1247 in order to renew his oath of allegiance to the Norwegian King. Shortly after the wedding Ewen macDougall, Lord of Lorn, and his kinsman Dugall macRuari, Lord of Garmoran, arrived as well at the Norwegian court, evidently intent on pressing their competing claims to the Western Isles. In fact both were apparently favoured by King Hakon, who granted them each the title of King over their island possessions. Shortly afterwards Harald Olavsson set sail with his royal bride on the return voyage to the Isle of Man, but they were both drowned when their ship foundered in stormy weather, caught in the tidal race of Sumburgh Roost, just south of Shetland. News of the tragedy did not reach Norway until the spring of 1249, when King Hakon ordered Ewen macDougall to sail west as quickly as possible and rule over all the Western Isles, perhaps even including the Isle of Man, until another strategy could be devised.

When Alexander II learnt of the wide if temporary commission given by King Hakon to Ewen macDougall, he abandoned any attempt to purchase the Western Isles from Norway, planning instead to conquer them by force of arms. However Ewen macDougall first received a safe conduct from four Scottish earls so that he could met Alexander II to explain his actions. The Scottish King now demanded of Ewen that he surrender Cairnaburg and three other castles, which probably included Dunstaffnage and Dunchonnel, as well as the dominions that the King of Norway had assigned to him. This Ewen macDougall resolutely refused to do, despite the offer of much larger territories in Scotland as recompense, arguing that he could remain loyal to both the kings of Scotland and Norway for the lands he held separately of them.

It was after this refusal that Alexander II embarked on his ill-fated expedition of 1249 against Ewen macDougall. He assembled a large fleet of ships in the Firth of Clyde and then presumably sailed round the Mull of Kintyre and northwards into the Firth of Lorne, probably intending to seize Dunstaffnage Castle. But the expedition ended in disaster when the Scottish King suddenly fell ill of a fever while at anchor in Oban Bay. He died soon afterwards on the island of Kerrera, leaving his eight-year old son to rule Scotland as Alexander III. The Celtic ceremonials at his inauguration, if not just a relic of earlier rituals, were evidently intended to stress the historic claim of the Scottish Crown to Argyll, and more especially the Western Isles, where the Canmore kings had their ancestral roots in the Scots kingdom of Dalriada, dating back to the time of Kenneth mac Alpin.

Final Years of Norse Sovereignty

News that King Harald Olavsson and his bride were dead only reached the Isle of Man in the spring of 1249. He was succeeded as King of Man by his brother Rognvald, who however only reigned for twenty-seven days before he was slain, and Harald, son of Godred Dond, made himself King. Next year he was summoned to Norway by King Hakon. There he was detained as a usurper, since the rightful heir to the Manx kingdom was Magnus Olavsson, brother of Harald Olavsson, and the son-in-law of Ewen macDougall. Perhaps for this reason Magnus Olavsson now allied himself with Ewen macDougall, who had earlier fled to Lewis when threatened by Alexander II and his fleet. Together they embarked in 1250 on a futile attempt to seize the Isle of Man. They were repulsed with much loss of life when the native Manxmen objected to Ewen macDougall still styling himself as King of the Isles when he addressed them, instead of Magnus Olavsson, whom they considered the rightful heir. Ewen macDougall evidently went to Norway after this setback, since he is said to have accompanied King Hakon on an expedition against the Danes in 1253. Magnus Olavsson returned to the Isle of Man in 1252, where he was welcomed by the people, and two years later he was appointed by King Hakon of Norway to rule as King over his island territories.

Although Alexander II had died on Kerrera, his expedition west in 1249 did not fail completely, for we learn in 1250 of a royal bailiff in Argyll, perhaps administering the lordship of Lorn. However Ewen macDougall was restored to his mainland territories as Lord of Argyll in 1255 through the good offices of Henry III of England, who now interfered in the affairs of Scotland to protect the interests of his young daughter Margaret, married if only in name to the young Alexander III. By coming under the protection of the English King, Ewen macDougall was the first to enter into what later became an important series of alliances between the MacDonald lords of the Isles and the English monarchy during the fourteenth and fifteenth centuries. Meanwhile he agreed with the royal council then ruling over Scotland during the minority of Alexander III to make an annual payment of sixty merks to the Scottish Crown for his lands, guaranteed by the earls of Mar, Fife and Atholl. Thereafter he acted as the loyal liege of Alexander III, at least for his mainland territories, while his daughter married the Earl of Strathearn. Whether or not he ever severed his links with King Hakon is not clear, despite his failure to gain the kingship of Man and the Western Isles under the sovereignty of Norway. Even so he was expected to defend his territories on the mainland of Scotland from any invasion by a 'foreign prince', who could have been none other than King Hakon of Norway. Ewen macDougall must have realised that a renewed assault by the Scots on the Western Isles was only a matter of time, perhaps when Alexander III came of age, and that it was then likely to succeed.

Indeed soon after Alexander III started to rule in his own right in 1261, he sent two envoys to Norway, once again demanding that the Western Isles be returned to Scotland. King Hakon detained them over the winter, suspicious that they had tried to slip away without permission. Meanwhile Alexander III had granted the islands of Skye and Lewis to William, now Earl of Ross after the death of his father Fearchar macTaggart, probably around 1251. He mounted a savage attack upon Skye in 1262, committing the most barbarous acts, burning churches and houses, killing men and women, and impaling young children upon spears, or so it was reported to King Hakon of Norway by Dugald mac Ruari, great-grandson of Somerled. It was then that King Hakon decided to embark on his great expedition of 1263, which finally ended with the loss of the Western Isles to Scotland.

King Hakon's Expedition of 1263

After assembling a large fleet in Norway, consisting perhaps of 150 long-ships, which he commanded from a great flagship with a golden prow, King

Hakon of Norway set sail in the summer of 1263 for Scotland. He landed first in Shetland, where his fleet lay in Bressay Sound for two weeks, and then sailed south to Orkney. Hardly anything is known of Orkney in the years before 1263, except that Earl Magnus had died in 1239, only to be succeeded by Earl Gilbert. After his death in 1256 Magnus Gilbertsson as the next Earl of Orkney and Caithness was caught between Scotland and Norway in their struggle for sovereignty over the Western Isles, since he owed allegiance to both kingdoms for his earldoms. At first he favoured Norway, obeying a summons to visit King Hakon before the great armada set sail from Bergen in the summer of 1263. Indeed he could hardly have done otherwise since Orkney was the base from which King Hakon intended to set sail for the Western Isles. Upon reaching Orkney Earl Magnus was dispatched by King Hakon to Caithness, apparently to collect payments from its inhabitants, even although they had previously been forced to give up hostages to Alexander III as a guarantee of their loyalty to Scotland. Thereafter he was expected to catch up with King Hakon as he moved south, but nothing more is heard of him until 1267.

King Hakon himself left Orkney with his fleet on 10 August, already very late in the season. Rounding Cape Wrath, he sailed first to Lewis and then across the Minch past the islands of Rona and Raasay to the Sound of Skye, where he was joined by Magnus Olavsson, King of Man. The armada continued south through the Sound of Mull, where King Hakon was met by Dugald mac Ruari, King of Garmoran. On reaching the island of Kerrera, Hakon dispatched fifty ships to raid the peninsula of Kintyre, south of Tarbert, under the command of Dugald mac Ruari and Magnus Olavsson, King of Man, together with five Norse leaders. Another fifteen ships were dispatched to Bute, where they captured the Stewart castle of Rothesay. Hakon himself sailed south with the rest of his fleet to the island of Gigha.

There Ewen macDougall, Lord of Argyll, came aboard Hakon's flagship to ask that he be released from his obligations to the Norwegian crown, since he now held even greater territories from the King of Scotland. Although he offered to surrender his island possessions, King Hakon detained Ewen on board his ship, hoping for a change in heart. King Hakon also summoned into his presence Angus Mor mac Donald, Lord of Islay and the great-grandson of Somerled by his son Reginald, who now held his island territories from the Norwegian King. But he too had divided loyalties since he held Kintyre from Alexander III, even if this was a matter of dispute with Norway, given the original claim by Magnus 'Barelegs' to the peninsula. Greatly impressed by the strength of the Norse fleet, which had ravaged his lands in Kintyre, he reluctantly agreed to join King Hakon, surrendering hostages as a pledge of his own good faith and paying a levy of a thousand cattle according to *Hakon's Saga*. Hakon for his part agreed to protect the interests of Angus Mor mac Donald in any treaty that might be reached with Alexander III.

King Hakon now sailed around the Mull of Kintyre, sacking the castle at Dunaverty at its southern tip, and then north to the anchorage of Lamlash on the eastern coast of Arran. There, negotiations were set in train with Alexander III, who was by then in Ayr, where he could guard the coast of Carrick from the Norse. They made little progress. Even if the Scottish King was perhaps prepared to accept Norwegian sovereignty over the Western Hebrides, he certainly was not prepared to surrender Arran, Bute and the Cumbraes to Norway, as demanded of him. Even the release of Ewen macDougall to act as an envoy to Alexander III made no difference. King Hakon came to suspect that the Scots were playing for time, hoping that the Norse fleet would be forced to retreat at the onset of winter. He therefore issued a formal challenge to Alexander III that they should join battle if peace could not reached, judging that his fleet was far superior to any sea-going force commanded by the Scots.

When this challenge was ignored Hakon ordered another forty ships to join a raiding party on Loch Long, commanded by Magnus Olavsson, King of Man, alongwith Dugald mac Ruari, King of Garmoran, and Angus Mor macDonald, Lord of Islay. The expedition crossed the narrow isthmus at Tarbert by porterage to reach Loch Lomond, plundering several islands there, and even penetrating far inland towards Stirling. It was most likely directed, not just against the earldom of Lennox, still held by its ancient family, but against the Stewart earldom of Menteith. Although apparently just a diversion, this expedition evidently had the serious intent of attacking the Stewart territories around the Firth of Clyde.

Indeed Earl Maldouen of Lennox was married to Elizabeth, daughter of Walter the High Steward, while her brother was Walter Stewart, who held the earldom of Menteith by his marriage with Mary, Countess of Menteith in her own right. Already he had apparently gained the lands of Skipness in what was then the south of Knapdale from Dugald mac Suibhne in 1262. Other members of the Stewart family, if not Alexander the High Steward himself, most likely held the contested islands of Bute, Arran and the Cumbraes by this time. Evidently attempting to retain his sovereignty over the Western Isles, Hakon pursued a strategy that directed his forces against the ancient Stewart lordship in the west of Scotland, just as Somerled had done nearly a century earlier.

Norse Defeat at Largs

Faced by the masterly inactivity of the Scots, Hakon's expedition finally came to grief after he had moved his fleet in late September, first to an anchorage off the island of Bute and then into the lee of the Cumbrae islands, just off Largs. An autumnal gale sprang up during the night of 30 September and several ships dragged their anchors, only to be driven ashore on the Scottish mainland near Largs. The next day saw a skirmish between their crews and the local inhabitants, evidently intent on looting the Norse ships. They however fled when more Norwegians landed. The storm abated the following day, when King Hakon himself came ashore with a larger force, perhaps numbering several hundred men, intent upon retrieving the more valuable stores, as one beached ship was evidently a merchantman. They were interrupted by the arrival of a Scottish army, most likely under the command of Alexander the High Steward and perhaps accompanied by Walter Stewart, Earl of Menteith, who was then Sheriff of Ayr. The writer of Hakon's saga put its strength at six hundred knights on horse-back, augmented by a large number of foot-soldiers well armed with bows and battle-axes. King Hakon was persuaded back on board his flagship as the Norwegian forces fought a rearguard action against the Scots. How the battle ended is not clear, even if it is unlikely that the Scottish forces were ever routed as claimed by *Hakon's saga*. More likely an uneasy truce was reached which allowed the Norwegians to come ashore the next day to carry off their dead, who it seems were later buried on Bute. The Norwegian fleet evidently remained off the Cumbraes for the next two days, after which it sailed away to Lamlash, having burned the boats stranded on the beach at Largs.

The so-called battle of Largs was perhaps not much more than a skirmish but it was decisive in ending nearly five centuries of Norse supremacy over the Western Isles. Indeed King Hakon still had sufficient strength to con-template going to Ireland to aid the native Irish in expelling the English settlers, but his lieutenants resolutely refused, given a serious lack of provi-sions. Sailing around the Mull of Kintyre, he reached the Sound of Islay where he demanded a tribute of 360 cattle from Islay or its equivalent value in meal and cheese. Continuing north to Kerrera, where he took shelter from another storm, he vainly summoned Ewen macDougall to his presence, only to learn that Ewen's men had plundered the Isle of Mull. King Hakon now sailed through the Sound of Mull, dropping anchor near Tobermory. There he deprived Ewen macDougall of all his island territories, awarding them instead to Dugald mac Ruari, King of Garmoran, while he granted the islands of Bute and Arran to Dugald's brothers, even if these actions were now just empty gestures. He then sailed north past Skye, where he was forced to take shelter fron another storm in Loch Snizort, and then rounding Cape Wrath he was becalmed off Durness, so that he only reached Orkney at the very end of October. He decided to winter in Orkney, although most of his fleet had already sailed back to Norway. He was taken ill while staying in the Bishop's Palace at Kirkwall and died several weeks later, ending his life on 16 December 1263.

Seizure of the Western Isles by Scotland

The aftermath of King Hakon's expedition showed that Norwegian hegemony over the Isle of Man and the Western Isles of Scotland had been broken for ever. Only Dugald mac Ruari and his brother Alan still remained loyal to Norway, now ruled by King Magnus as Hakon's son and heir. As soon as Alexander III heard of the death of King Hakon, he promptly made plans to invade the kingdom of Man. They proved superfluous when Magnus Olavsson came to Dumfries, intent on doing homage to the Scottish king for his kingdom of Man. He promised the service of five galleys of twenty-four oars, as well as five galleys of twelve oars, if he were to be protected against any assault by Norway. Magnus Olavsson died in 1265 and the island was then governed for the next ten years by royal bailiffs. A serious revolt broke out in 1275 against their administration, led by Godfrey, the illegitimate son of Magnus Olavsson, the last king of Man, which was put down by Alexander III with great severity. Thereafter two parties emerged, differing in their adherence to the Scottish Crown. It was no doubt the party favouring independence that later sought the help of Edward I of England to free themselves from Scottish rule, only to succumb finally to English suzerainty after the conquest of the island by Edward III in the fourteenth century.

Meanwhile another expedition went north in 1264 under the command of Alexander Comyn, Earl of Buchan and Alan Durward, directed towards the subjugation of Ross, Sutherland and Caithness. Fines were extracted from the local people and hostages were taken from Caithness and the Isle of Skye. William macTaggart, second Earl of Ross, was granted the lordship of Skye and Lewis, and it is possible that these islands were threatened or attacked and perhaps even occupied at this time. The Orkneys were evidently threatened by the Scots army as well but the threat came to nothing, perhaps because they were too well defended. Then even before Norway could sue for peace the Western Isles were brought under Scottish rule during the course of a major campaign in 1264, led by William, Earl of Mar. The expedition probably departed from Ayr, where the sheriff had ordered ships to be built for the king. Although some Hebrideans opposed it violently, they were killed or put to flight, while prisoners were taken hostage and their lands laid waste. Almost without exception the descendants of Somerled abandoned their previous allegiance to Norway for their island territories, submitting instead to the authority of Alexander III. Angus Mor mac Donald, Lord of Islay, surrendered his young son Alexander as a hostage for his own good behaviour. Perhaps at this time, if not nearly fifty years later during the Wars of Scottish Independence, the barons of Argyll bound themselves to rise against the Lord of Islay under pain of forfeiture if he did not do the king's will, suggesting that his lands in Islay and Kintyre had not been forfeited.

Even if Dugald mac Ruari never submitted to the Scottish King before his death in 1268, his brother Alan mac Ruari now acknowledged his allegiance to Alexander III. He received full possession of the lands of Garmoran, which then included Knoydart, Moidart, Arisaig and Morar, as well as a grant of all the islands of the Outer Hebrides, apart for Lewis. Ewen macDougall had already declared himself subject to the Scottish Crown when he had refused to join King Hakon in 1263. After his death in the years before 1275, his son Alexander macDougall evidently became a loyal supporter of Alexander III for he was given 'care and custody' of Kintyre, Argyll and Lorn. We find him leading the Scottish expedition which suppressed the Manx revolt of 1275, along with Alan, brother of Dugald mac Ruari, Lord of Garmoran, and several other magnates.

Only the MacSweens of Knapdale suffered forfeiture for their support of King Hakon of Norway during his great expedition of 1263. Holding all their territories on the Scottish mainland without being subject to Norway, they did not come under the terms of the Treaty of Perth in 1266. In fact they had apparently already been ousted from their lands by Walter Stewart, Earl of Menteith, even before King Hakon's expedition actually set sail, since they were forced to grant him all their lands of Skipness in the north of Kintyre in 1262, perhaps as their feudal superior. They had every incentive therefore to support King Hakon of Norway in 1263, only to suffer the consequences after his defeat at the battle of Largs. Over fifty years later the MacSweens were to fight on the losing side during the Wars of Scottish Independence, when they lost all their remaining lands in Scotland and, emigrating to Ireland as the captains of Highland galloglasses or mercenary soldiers, became permanently resident there as the Mac-Sweeneys or Sweenys.

Treaty of Perth

Faced with the military supremacy gained by the Scots over the Isle of Man and the Western Isles, King Magnus of Norway had little choice but to make peace with Scotland. After prolonged negotiations the Treaty of Perth signed between the two countries in 1266 was surprisingly generous, setting the seal upon the good relations that afterwards existed between the two countries. Norway agreed to renounce her claim to the territories that Magnus 'Barelegs' had gained in 1098 in return for an initial payment of

4,000 merks of silver in four annual instalments, together with further payments of 100 merks each year, to be made in perpetuity. This the Chronicle
of Melrose asserts was intended to mark an act of homage by Alexander III
to the King of Norway. Known as the 'Annual of Norway', it was paid each
year at Kirkwall Cathedral with only occasional lapses until the custom itself
died out nearly a hundred years later. It was further agreed that the inhabitants
of the Western Isles should become the loyal subjects of Scotland, but if they
did not wish to live under its laws and customs they were free to take their
goods and leave in peace. King Magnus of Norway sent a document, releasing
his subjects in the Western Isles from any allegiance to the Norwegian
crown. Nevertheless the metropolitan archbishop of Trondheim retained
his ecclesiastical jurisdiction over Man and the Western Isles.

Only Orkney and Shetland remained under the sovereignty of Norway
for another two centuries, until these islands were forfeited to Scotland in
default of a dowry promised by the King of Denmark and Norway to James
III. Magnus Gilbertsson only reappeared on the scene in 1267, a year after
the Treaty of Perth was signed, when he went to Norway to renew his pledge
of loyalty to King Magnus Hakonsson, whereupon he received back his
earldom of Orkney. Thereafter it seems that the Earl of Orkney and his
immediate descendants remained as loyal vassals of the Norwegian crown
and indeed became the premier earls of this kingdom, while they still held
Caithness from the Scottish Crown.

Chapter Six

EDWARD I, HAMMER OF THE SCOTS

Alexander III was killed by accident in 1286 when he fell from his horse near Kinghorn in Fife, returning late at night from Edinburgh to the company of his second wife Yolande, daughter of Robert, Count of Dreux. His death marked the end of what was later regarded as a Golden Age, when Scotland enjoyed long-lasting peace, stability and prosperity. He had two sons and a daughter born to him by his first wife Margaret, eldest daughter of Henry III of England, but they were already dead. The sole surviving heir to the Scottish throne was his granddaughter Margaret, born of his daughter's marriage with Erik Magnusson, King of Norway. Only three years of age at the time of her grandfather's death, and always weak and sickly, she was known as the 'Maid of Norway'. Alexander III had already persuaded a parliament of leading magnates at Scone in 1284 to recognise her as his heir. Among their number were Alexander macDougall, Lord of Argyll, Angus Mor mac Donald, Lord of Islay and Alan mac Ruari, Lord of Garmoran, all firmly entrenched as members of what came to be known as the community of the Scottish realm.

After the death of Alexander III Scotland was ruled by six 'Guardians' on behalf of the young heir to the Scottish throne, who was still living in Norway. They rather unwisely negotiated the Treaty of Birgham-on-Tweed in 1290 with Edward I of England, who agreed that the 'Maid of Norway' should marry Edward's son and heir, thus making it possible that any son born of their union would come to rule as the king of both countries. Soon afterwards Margaret left Norway to claim her inheritance, but she died in Orkney without even setting foot upon her kingdom. Her death left Scotland without a direct heir to the throne from the last three generations of Canmore kings. Edward I of England ruthlessly exploited this constitutional crisis, intent on bringing Scotland under the suzerainty of his own kingdom, just as he had recently conquered Wales.

The Great Cause

Thirteen 'Competitors' now presented themselves as contenders for the Scottish throne. Nearly all were descended from the great Anglo-Norman families whose grandfathers or great-grandfathers had married daughters of the Canmore dynasty and more especially the daughters of Earl David of Huntingdon, younger brother of William the Lion. They agreed with the four surviving 'Guardians' of Scotland that Edward I of England should act as the adjudicator of their claims in what became known as the 'Great Cause'. The English king only agreed to do so if the Scots magnates accepted him as their overlord, thus renewing the claims of the English Crown to sovereignty over Scotland.

Several of the 'Competitors' could only argue that they were descended from the illegitimate children of William the Lion or his son Alexander II, so that their claims were quickly rejected. Margaret's father Eric Magnusson of Norway was likewise rejected, as was Floris, Count of Holland, who could not produce any documents to support his claim. This left only three 'Competitors' of any standing, who all claimed descent from the great-granddaughters of David I of Scotland by his grandson David, Earl of Huntingdon. Among their number was Robert Bruce the 'Competitor', grandfather of the future king, whose father had married Isabella, second daughter of Earl David of Huntingdon. His claim was much strengthened by his brief designation in 1238 as heir-apparent to Alexander II, before his son Alexander was born in 1241.

Yet it was John Balliol who had perhaps the strongest claim to the Scottish throne, since he was able to claim seniority of descent from David I's eldest great-granddaughter Margaret through her marriage with his grandfather Alan fitz Roland, Lord of Galloway. Even so it passed through the female line by the marriage of his mother Devorguilla, daughter of Alan of Galloway, with his father John Balliol the Elder, who held his lands at Barnard Castle and Bywell from the English Crown. It was this marriage that brought the lordship of Galloway to the Balliol family and, after the death of his mother Devorguilla in 1290, John Balliol the 'Competitor' inherited this lordship. Favouring seniority of descent over closeness of degree as the essence of primogeniture, Edward I of England eventually declared himself in favour of John Balliol. Even if it was a decision later repudiated by the Scots, who argued that it had been made under duress, there is little doubt that the due processes of medieval law were followed. It was a decision accepted by nearly three-quarters of Bruce's own supporters in the royal council set up to consider the matter, even if Robert Wishart, Bishop of Glasgow, and James the High Steward voiced their own doubts.

Robert Bruce the 'Competitor' reacted to the decision even before it was made by resigning his own claim to the Scottish throne in favour of his eldest son. Robert Bruce the Elder was already the Earl of Carrick by right of his wife Marjorie, eldest daughter and heiress of the Earl of Carrick. She had seized his person and forced him into marriage in 1271, after she had herself been widowed while still a child. Refusing to do homage to John Balliol if he became king, Robert Bruce the Elder then resigned his earldom in favour of his own son, Robert the Bruce, the future king. He thus became the Earl of Carrick in his own right, only two days after his grandfather had resigned his claim to the Scottish throne. No doubt Robert the Bruce considered that he had inherited his grandfather's claim at the same time as his earldom.

John Balliol, King of Scots

John Balliol was enthroned as King of Scots at Scone on 30 November 1292 and not long afterwards he swore allegiance to Edward I of England in an act of homage for his kingdom of Scotland. But the English King then reneged on his promise that the laws and customs of Scotland would be respected, stating that it had only applied while the country was without a king. He took it upon himself to review the judgments made by the Scottish courts, while Balliol was even forced to appear in person at Westminister to answer for decisions made under his jurisdiction. Worse followed when Edward I demanded the Scots support him as his vassals in waging war against Philip IV of France. Faced with these indignities a council of twelve leading magnates, now consisting of four bishops, four earls and four barons, took the government out of Balliol's hands in 1295 and entered into a military alliance with the French, who were now at war with England. Not surprisingly Edward I regarded this early manifestion of what later became known as the Auld Alliance as an act of rebellion against him as the overlord of Scotland. Nonetheless it was the Scots who struck the first blow in the ensuing hostilities, which marked the very start of the Wars of Scottish Independence, by mounting an abortive attempt to seize the castle of Carlisle at the end of March 1296.

Edward I retaliated by invading Scotland at the head of a powerful army, consisting it is said of four thousand knights on horseback and twenty-five thousand foot-soldiers. He first sacked Berwick-upon-Tweed early in April 1296, putting nearly all its burgesses and lesser men to the sword with the utmost brutality. Soon afterwards Balliol renounced his allegiance to Edward I, while the English army utterly defeated the Scots who had gathered at Dunbar to oppose its northward advance. Now faced with hardly any resistance Edward I advanced to Edinburgh, where he captured the castle after a siege of eight days, and then by way of Linlithgow to Stirling Castle, which he found abandoned by the Scots. He continued without any opposition to Perth, where he learnt that Balliol, said to be hiding with only a few of his Comyn allies in the Glens of Angus, if not Badenoch, was now intent on suing for peace.

The erstwhile King of Scotland surrendered to Edward I and renounced his kingdom, after which he was stripped of his crown, sword and sceptre, as well as his tabard or surcoat, hood and knightly girdle. Even the royal arms emblazoned on his surcoat were torn off, so that he became known to later generations of Scots as 'Toom Tabard', or empty surcoat. It was a ceremony of ritual humiliation more usually suffered by a knight found guilty of treason than by the king of an independent country, forced to abdicate. The judgement of Edward I was even more contemptuous when he supposedly remarked, 'a man does good business when he rids himself of a turd'. John Balliol was escorted south to captivity in the Tower of London, before he was allowed to live in relative comfort with his son Edward near Hertford. Three years later they both left England to live as exiles on their family estates in Picardy.

Edward I and his First Expedition North

Meanwhile Edward I continued his northward progress in triumph, taking possession of what was now a conquered country and receiving the submissions of its leading inhabitants. He first crossed into Deeside over the eastern flanks of the Mounth from Montrose amd Kincardine, stayed in Aberdeen for five days and then marched north to Banff by way of Kintore and Fyvie. No doubt he was intent upon subduing the territories of the powerful Comyn family in Buchan and Mar as the close allies of John Balliol. Turning west along the coast and stopping overnight at Cullen he reached Elgin after two more days on the march, camping out overnight. After three nights spent at Elgin he turned inland to Rothes, where he dispatched a force into the Comyn lordship of Badenoch. Other detachments were sent west where they occupied the royal castles of Nairn, Forres, Urquhart, Dingwall and Cromarty. The Bishop of Durham had accompanied Edward I as far north as Rothes, but he was now sent south with his own army to Kindrochit, or Braemar as it is now known, possibly marching there by way of Stratha'an and the Lecht. Edward I himself then crossed the mountains by Cabrach and the headwaters of the Deveron to reach Kildrummy Castle and Kincardine O'Neil, before returning over the Cairn O'Mount to Brechin and Arbroath.

Edward I then continued on his southward progress to Scone, where he ordered the removal of the Stone of Destiny to Westminister Abbey. Marching from Perth through Fife to St Andrews and Dunfermline, and then to

Stirling and Edinburgh, he carried off the Scottish regalia and nearly all the documentary records of the Scottish Crown, along with a fragment of the True Cross, first brought to Scotland by St Margaret, queen of Malcolm Canmore. On reaching Berwick he called a parliament on 28 August 1296, which proceeded to take oaths of loyalty from his conquered subjects in Scotland. No fewer than fifteen hundred Scottish names were appended with their seals to what later became known as the 'Ragman Rolls', as the great magnates and high officers of the Church made their submission to Edward I, along with noblemen, prelates and many other men of lesser degree.

Scotland was now subject to a military occupation by the English forces. Edward I could have appointed another 'Competitor' as King of Scotland to rule under him, and it might have been the wiser course. Even if Robert Bruce the 'Competitor' had died the previous year, his son and grandson had joined Edward I of England at Wark before he had even entered Scotland, professing that they were still faithful to the English King. After the Scottish defeat at Dunbar, the elder Bruce had asked Edward I to install him as King of Scotland, only to be met with a contemptuous refusal. Instead Scotland was to be reduced like Wales to a mere principality of England.

Rebellion against the English Occupation

Minor uprisings and insurrections now soon spread throughout nearly the whole country, except for the Lothians. Such open hostility to England was perhaps fostered by the Church, fearing for its own independence. After only a few months William Wallace and Sir Andrew de Moray emerged as the foremost leaders of the rebellion against the English occupation, operating in different parts of the country. Wallace was the second son of Sir Malcolm Wallace of Elderslie, near Paisley, who was himself a vassal of James, fifth High Steward of Scotland. Rallying the forces of resistance to his banner, and perhaps aided in secret by Robert Wishart, Bishop of Glasgow, and his feudal superior James the fifth High Steward, William Wallace joined Sir William Douglas in May 1297. Together they attacked William Ormesby when he was holding court at Scone as the Justiciar of Scotland and he barely escaped with his life. Their success in putting Ormesby to flight encouraged the Scottish nobility to rebel against the English occupation of their country.

Chief among these great nobles was Robert the Bruce, Earl of Carrick. Even if he had given a solemn undertaking at Carlisle that he would remain loyal to Edward I, he now recruited his own vassals from his lands in Carrick, saying that his oath to the English King had been extracted from him under duress. He was joined by Robert Wishart, Bishop of Glasgow, Sir William Douglas and James the High Steward, among several other barons. But while the other magnates were fighting for the restoration of John Balliol as the lawful King of Scotland, Robert the Bruce was clearly more interested in pursuing his own claim to the throne, inherited from his father and grandfather. Such dissension within the Scottish camp so weakened their resolve that they sought to make their own peace with the English forces, which they had encountered at Irvine, fearful that they might lose their lands.

William Wallace himself took advantage of the protracted negotiations with the English by escaping to the sanctuary of Selkirk forest. Thereafter he drew his strength from the common people who joined his struggle in resisting the English occupation. His tactics were those of a guerilla leader, avoiding pitched battles against the English cavalry, but who moved instead with great speed and mobility through the countryside to strike at the English garrisons when least expected, inflicting casualties and spreading alarm. He was so successful that Wallace had already crossed the Tay to besiege the English garrison in the castle of Dundee by August 1297, intent upon joining up with a northern uprising under the leadership of Andrew de Moray.

Andrew de Moray was a descendant of the ancient Flemish family first established in the north by Freskyn of Duffus. Captured at the battle of Dunbar in 1296, he had managed to escape from imprisonment at Chester. Returning north by May 1297, he first attacked Castle Urquhart along with the burgesses of Inverness, which was then held for the English by William de Warenne. The later course of this uprising in the north is not known in any detail, but Gartnait, son and heir of the Earl of Mar, and the Countess of Ross both wrote to Edward I informing him of the help they had given to the English forces in the north. By June 1297 matters were so serious that Edward I ordered John Comyn, Earl of Buchan, and his kinsman John Comyn the younger of Badenoch, north to quell the uprising, where they were joined by Henry Cheyne, Bishop of Aberdeen. However the royal castle of Inverness, held by Sir Reginald Cheyne for Edward I as the Guardian of Moray, as well as the castles of Elgin, Banff and Aberdeen, were most likely seized by the rebels. Early in September 1297 a sizeable body of foot-soldiers under Andrew de Moray were masters of the whole country north of the Tay. Not long afterwards, they joined the forces of William Wallace at Dundee and marched south to gather in strength on the high ground just north of Stirling. There they faced an English army which had belatedly set out from Berwick to suppress the Scottish revolt. Commanded by John de Warenne, Earl of Surrey, and Hugh de Cressingham it probably numbered around 300 cavalry and 10,000 foot-soldiers.

Battle of Stirling Bridge

Perhaps learning from their mistakes at the battle of Dunbar, where the Scots had abandoned the high ground only to be slaughtered in large numbers, Wallace and Moray massed their troops on the south-facing slopes of Abbey Craig just a mile north of Stirling Bridge. This wooden bridge was then the only means of crossing the marshy flood-plain of the River Forth, which had not yet been drained. It could only be crossed at best by horsemen riding two abreast. After two false starts the English army began to cross the bridge on 11 September 1297. The Scots commanders allowed the vanguard to reach the northern bank before they released their own foot-soldiers, mostly archers and spearmen, who charged downhill to overwhelm the enemy. Trapped by the marshy ground along the river, Cressingham was slain along with a hundred of his knights and perhaps half the English foot-soldiers lost their lives as well. The Earl of Surrey fled south to Berwick, where he took ship for England, while the Scots displayed strips of skin, flayed from Cressingham's body, as a token of their famous victory at various places around the country.

Andrew de Moray was mortally wounded in the battle, dying within two months of his injuries. This left William Wallace in supreme command of the rebellion against England. Knighted by a Scottish earl, he was made Guardian of the kingdom over which he now ruled in Balliol's name. He spent the next few months raising a conscript army throughout the land, subject to rigid discipline, and threatening anyone who did not answer the call to arms with the gallows. Significantly the leading Scottish magnates took no part in mustering their vassals for military service. Wallace then launched a punitive raid into the north of England in November 1297 where his new army laid waste to the countryside with utmost savagery, bent on retribution for the ills done to Scotland.

Scottish Defeat at Falkirk

Edward I was back in England by March 1298 after his campaigns in Flanders and he started to prepare for a new assault across the Border. He assembled an army of more than 2,000 cavalry and 12,000 foot-soldiers, mostly Welsh archers, which reached Roxburgh at the beginning of July and then marched north to Edinburgh under his personal command. Beset with difficulties in obtaining supplies by sea, which arrived as wine not much-needed food, and facing unrest from the Welsh archers after they had drunk the wine on empty stomachs, Edward I was close to retreat when he learnt that William Wallace was encamped with his army near Falkirk.

William Wallace now allowed himself to be drawn into a pitched battle with the English forces on 22 July 1298. He first drew his much smaller army into a defensive position, enclosing his forces in a palisade of wooden stakes, bound together by rope. Within this enclosure he closely packed his spearmen into four or five great *schiltrons*, perhaps of fifteen hundred men apiece, looking very much like giant hedgehogs bristling with spears, slanting out on all sides against the enemy. Between them he placed archers from Ettrick forest, while nearly a thousand cavalry lay in the rear under the command of the Scottish nobility. They were to play no part in the ensuing battle of Falkirk.

After some argument among his commanders Edward I attacked at first with his heavy cavalry, which was repulsed when it broke against the Scots army with its massed spearmen. He then brought forward his Welsh archers with their longbows, who rained streams of arrows with deadly effect upon the stationary *schiltrons*. Even though the Scottish foot-soldiers stood firm with dogged resistance as their ranks were decimated, eventually they were overwhelmed and broken by repeated charges of the English cavalry. The Scots foot-soldiers 'fell like blossoms in an orchard when the fruit has ripened'. Meanwhile the Scots cavalry had faded away as soon as battle was joined, leaving several thousand of their own countrymen to die upon the field of battle. Even if Wallace himself escaped with his life, his authority was shattered and he resigned as Guardian of Scotland after reaching the banks of the Forth.

Edward I in the Ascendant

Edward I made a less than triumphant progress through the lowlands of Scotland after his victory at Falkirk, since his army was soon faced with star-vation. He did not mount another expedition to subdue Scotland until 1300, when he invaded Galloway, first capturing Caerlaverock Castle and then putting a Scottish force to flight near the River Cree. By then the Scots had the support of Pope Boniface, who issued a papal bull, challenging Edward I to furnish proof that he had a rightful claim to Scotland as its overlord. This impasse forced him to agree a truce with the Scots which lasted until May 1301. Edward I then invaded Scotland once again but his campaign ended inconclusively with yet another truce, early in 1302, forced upon him by the French, who were now threatening to install John Balliol as King of Scotland by force of arms.

The Scots under John Comyn the younger of Badenoch then went on the offensive when the truce ended in November 1302. He and Simon Fraser defeated the English forces of occupation in a surprise attack at Roslin in

February 1303. But Edward I was now free to mount another full-scale invasion of Scotland, after the French defeat by the Flemings at the battle of Courtrai. He mustered a powerful army at Roxburgh and marched north to Edinburgh without encountering any opposition, determined to subdue the whole country, south and north. Mindful of the English defeat at Stirling Bridge in 1297, he had already arranged for three pontoon bridges to be built in prefabricated sections and shipped north from King's Lynn. Avoiding Stirling Castle his army of 7,000 men crossed the River Forth using these pontoons, once they had been placed in position.

Edward I and his Second Expedition North

Edward I then marched north to Perth, where he stayed for more than three weeks at the end of June 1303. He then continued north through Coupar Angus and past Dundee to Brechin where the English forces laid siege to the castle. After it fell Edward I marched north to Aberdeen and then by way of Inverurie, Banff and Cullen to Elgin and Kinloss, following much the same route as in 1296. Turning inland towards the Comyn fortress of Lochindorb Castle, he stayed there for several days in late September 1303 while he took the submission of the leading magnates in the north. He then returned south, marching first to Castle Roy near Boat of Garten and then down the Spey valley to Mortlach (now Balvenie) Castle, before he continued south through Strathbogie and past Kildrummy Castle to Deeside. After crossing the Mounth by way of Cairn O'Mount to Arbroath and Dundee, he marched south to Stirling, where the castle was still held by the Scots, and then to Dunfermline where he spent the winter in the company of his queen.

Faced with the victorious progress of Edward I throughout the country, nearly all the leading magnates once again hastened to make their peace with the English King, who offered them lenient terms if they would submit by 2 February 1304. A week after this date envoys from Edward I came to parley with John Comyn the younger of Badenoch and his council at Strathord near Perth. Even if they strove to preserve the laws, customs and privileges of the country, they had little choice but to accept the dictates of Edward I. The castles and strongholds of Scotland were to be surrendered into the hands of the English. Given a promise that their lives, liberties and lands would be preserved, but fined for their actions as thought fit by Edward I, John Comyn and his fellow Scots were forced to capitulate. Only William Wallace was finally excluded from the peace imposed upon Scotland by Edward I of England. Soon afterwards he was declared an outlaw at a parliament held at St Andrews, attended by the leading Scottish magnates as well as the English barons.

Martyrdom of William Wallace

Thus it was only William Wallace who suffered a martyr's death in Scotland's cause, after he was captured over a year later in August 1305, when any further resistance to the English occupation came to an end. After the Scottish defeat at the battle of Falkirk in 1298 and his resignation as Guardian of Scotland he had acted as a roving ambassador for Scotland, leaving the country for France and possibly Norway. He returned soon after the Scottish victory at the battle of Roslin in February 1303, only to find that the tide had turned once more against the Scots. Remaining at liberty for the next two years he was eventually captured in 1305 near Glasgow. He was handed over to the English by Sir John Stewart of Menteith, keeper of Dunbarton Castle, who despite later condemnation was honour bound to do so.

William Wallace was tried summarily at Westminister as an outlaw and a traitor. Found guilty of high treason after what was a travesty of a trial, since he had never taken an oath of allegiance to Edward I, he was drawn through the streets on a hurdle to Smithfield where he was hanged. While still alive his body was cut down from the gallows and disembowelled. His head was impaled upon a stake above London Bridge and the four quarters of his dismembered body were sent north for public display at Newcastle, Berwick, Perth and Stirling (or perhaps Aberdeen). Thus died arguably the greatest of all Scottish patriots, whose deep attachment to his country lay quite outside the loyalties more typical of a feudal society and whose actions were never tarnished by self-interest. Fiery and impetuous, and capable of savage atrocities, he was a born leader who had inspired the common people of Scotland with a fierce determination to resist the English occupation of their country.

Government by Edward I

Even if he had once again crushed Scotland Edward I still had to pacify the country and install an effective government. Unable to subdue the country by sheer force, he needed the collaboration of the leading Scottish magnates. Ten of their number were chosen by the Scots to attend an English parliament at Westminister in September 1305, just a month after Wallace's execution, which drafted an ordinance for governing Scotland in the manner of Ireland. Although the chief offices of the crown were intended for Englishmen, the King's council did include some Scots. Many Scottish magnates had their lands restored to them after the payment of heavy fines, which went to pay for Edward I's expenses in conquering Scotland for a second time, and the local government of the country was placed in their hands, wherever they were appointed as sheriffs and keepers of the royal castles. Yet within six months, Edward I of England was faced with a new and quite unexpected crisis when Robert the Bruce murdered John Comyn the younger of Badenoch within the sacred precincts of Greyfriars church of Dumfries on 10 February 1206. This undeniably squalid act with its sacrilegious overtones was nonetheless a momentous event in Scottish history. It marked the start of yet another prolonged struggle for Scottish independence, which ended with Robert the Bruce ruling over an independent country as King Robert I of Scotland.

Actions of Robert the Bruce

Even if Robert the Bruce had played an active role in the early struggles against Edward I, expediency rather than principle evidently governed his actions throughout these years. Indeed it was hardly in his own interest to support the restoration of John Balliol as King of Scotland, given the claim that he himself entertained to the Scottish throne. Neither Robert the Bruce nor his father had taken any part in the campaign against Edward I in 1296, which ended with the Scottish deafeat at the battle of Dunbar. Indeed they had joined the English army at Wark, after first defending the castle of Carlisle against a Scottish attack, among whose leaders was John Comyn the younger of Badenoch. However Robert the Bruce changed sides in the early summer of 1297 and after the Scottish defeat at the battle of Falkirk in 1298 he was elected jointly with John Comyn the younger of Badenoch as a Guardian of the realm, ruling over Scotland on behalf of John Balliol. But ousted from this position in 1300, and faced with the likely prospect that John Balliol might soon regain the throne with French help, Robert the Bruce was the very first of the Scottish magnates when he submitted to Edward I of England in February 1302.

Thereafter he sided with the English King, claiming his estates in England after the death of his father in 1304, and marrying as his second wife Elizabeth, daughter of the Earl of Ulster, who was foremost amongst Edward's Anglo-Irish supporters. Appointed by Edward I as sheriff of Ayr, he contributed 1,000 foot-soldiers to the English army which invaded Scotland in May 1303, and even took part in an English raid into south-east Scotland early in 1304, directed against the forces of William Wallace. Evidently he hoped by such means to persuade Edward I to look more favourably upon his own claim to the Scottish throne. Yet it seems that he was playing a double game. During the siege of Stirling Castle in June 1304 he signed a secret bond with Bishop Lamberton of St Andrews, perhaps despairing of any preference from Edward I. It bound them to assist one another if threatened by 'any persons whatsoever', and it further required them not to attempt any 'arduous business' without first consulting one another. Even if the language was obscure, and no doubt deliberately so, it soon became clear that they planned nothing less than an attempt to place Robert the Bruce upon the Scottish throne.

Bruce's Murder of John Comyn

There can be no doubt that John Comyn the younger of Badenoch would have opposed such a plan, given his close ties with the Balliol family and his own claim to the Scottish throne. Indeed if John Balliol were to die without any heirs he would be the next in line as his nephew to the Scottish Crown. Most likely Robert the Bruce had arranged to meet his rival at Dumfries in February 1306, seeking to gain Comyn's support for his own plans. Tradition asserts that Robert the Bruce offered to support Comyn's claim to the Scottish throne if he were granted the Comyn lands, even if Comyn would not support his own claim in return for the Bruce lands. Yet while Edward I was apparently unaware of the secret pact made with Bishop Lamberton it may well have come to the notice of John Comyn. Even so Scottish patriotism could well have embellished the strict facts of history when contemporary and later sources suggest that they quarrelled after Comyn threatened to betray Robert the Bruce to the English King, or that he had even done so. More likely Comyn refused his support for Robert the Bruce and the two men came to blows. John Comyn fell wounded in front of the high altar, only to be dispatched by one of Bruce's companions. It is hardly likely that the famous conversation ever took place, when Robert the Bruce supposedly said 'I doubt I have slain the Red Comyn' to Kirkpatrick, who responded by declaring 'I'll mak siccar [sure]'. They would surely have talked in Norman French, rather than using the local vernacular of Lowland Scotland.

Whatever prompted the fatal blow it was impetuous and foolhardy, since it put at risk any slight chance that Robert the Bruce might have of success. No doubt the two men had agreed to meet within the sanctuary of the church, and so the death of John Comyn meant that Robert the Bruce had committed not just murder but sacrilege as well. Soon afterwards he was excommunicated by the Pope in Rome, prompted by the wrath of Edward I. Even more serious was the blood-feud engendered by the murder with the powerful Comyn family and its Balliol allies, scattered far and wide throughout nearly all of Scotland, but especially in the north. By striking the fatal blow Robert the Bruce had challenged the power and influence of the Comyn family, who were deeply entrenched within the community of the realm. The bitter struggles of the next few years thus took on the nature of a civil conflict between these opposing factions, before the hostilities eventually turned into a patriotic war of national independence against the English. By then a great deal of damage had been done to the feudal structure of the country, particularly in the Highlands, which it took centuries to repair. The verdict of history would surely have been harsh if King Robert the Bruce had not ultimately proved successful in establishing Scotland as a free and independent nation.

Robert the Bruce, King of Scots

No sooner had he killed John Comyn the younger of Badenoch than Robert the Bruce was forced into hasty and quite unpremeditated action. Driven by desperation rather than his own ambitions, he had little choice but to seize the throne of Scotland before the full retribution of Edward I fell upon his shoulders. Acting with boldness and decision he seized Dumfries and other castles in the south-west. He then rode north to Glasgow where he could count on the enthusiastic support of its bishop, Robert Wishart. Joined by only a small retinue of knights he then hurried to Scone, where he was installed on 25 March 1306 as the King of Scotland, six weeks after the murder of John Comyn. Two days later a simple ceremony was performed by Isabella, Countess of Buchan, aunt of the Earl of Fife, whose family had traditionally installed the kings of Scotland upon the Stone of Destiny, even though she was married to John Comyn, Earl of Buchan. Present at this ceremony were his four brothers Edward, Nigel, Thomas and Alexander and his step-nephew Thomas Randolph, later created Earl of Moray. Others present were the bishops Robert Wishart of Glasgow, William Lamberton of St Andrews and David de Moray, together with the Earls of Atholl, Menteith and Lennox, and a few other barons, among whom were James Douglas, later known as the 'Good Sir James', the son of Sir William Douglas, who had been among the first to join William Wallace in 1297, as well as Neil Campbell and Gilbert de la Hay.

Defeat at Methven, and the Skirmish at Dalrigh

Even if the newly crowned King of Scotland was a usurper who had seized the Scottish throne by force, many soon rallied to his standard. They came not just from his own lands of Carrick and Annandale, but more especially from beyond the Forth, always the heartland of Scottish resistance to the English. But disaster soon struck. Reacting incredulously to the news from Scotland, Edward I sent the Earl of Pembroke north, charged with suppressing the insurrection without mercy. Yet by June 1306 Robert the Bruce evidently felt strong enough to approach Perth, now occupied by English forces. Challenged to give battle outside the town walls, the Earl of Pembroke declined to fight given the lateness of the hour, only to attack the unwary

Scots after they had camped for the night at Methven, just west of the town. What followed was more a rout than a battle, since the Scots were overwhelmed. Even if Robert the Bruce escaped with his life, along with the Earl of Atholl and James Douglas, many of his leading supporters were killed or captured, while the common soldiers lost their trust in him as a leader, and deserted his cause. It was but a small remnant of his forces which afterwards sought refuge in the mountains of Atholl.

Now faced with the spectre of defeat and pursued by the English cavalry, Robert the Bruce retreated west from Atholl towards Argyll and the Isles. The extreme danger of his position soon became apparent when he encountered the hostile forces of the MacDougalls at Dalrigh, or the King's Field, just south of Tyndrum, only a few weeks after the defeat at Methven. Their chief was now Alexander macDougall of Lorne, son of Ewen macDougall, Lord of Argyll. He was a close kinsman of the murdered Comyn, who was his nephew by marriage. As the terrain was unsuitable for cavalry, Robert the Bruce and his mounted knights were forced to retreat when they were attacked by a thousand foot-soldiers under Alexander macDougall. The day was only saved by a fierce rearguard action fought in desperation by Robert the Bruce himself. Tradition asserts that he was wearing the 'Brooch of Lorn', still in the possession of the MacDougalls, which was plucked from his person during the struggle, although it is more likely to belong to the sixteenth century.

Sanctuary in the North

After the skirmish at Dalrigh, Bruce's queen Elizabeth, his daughter Marjory by his first marriage and his sisters Mary and Christina were all sent for safety to Kildrummy Castle under the escort of Nigel Bruce and the Earl of Atholl. There they came under the protection of Bruce's sister Christina, widow of the Earl of Mar, and his own sister-in-law, since he himself had been married to Isabella, sister of the very same Earl of Mar. Finding themselves still in danger the party then escaped north to Ross, accompanied by the Earl of Atholl, eventually taking refuge in the sanctuary of St Duthac's Chapel at Tain. Even if they had hoped to reach Orkney, they were seized by William, Earl of Ross. All the knights in their company were executed without trial, while the Earl of Atholl was carried off to London, where he was executed on a gallows built thirty feet higher than usual as a mocking tribute to his royal ancestry.

Meanwhile Kildrummy Castle was besieged by Edward, Prince of Wales, and the Earl of Pembroke. When it was compelled to surrender by a traitor within its walls, who set fire to a grain-store, Neil Bruce was taken prisoner. Transported south to Newcastle he too was executed as a traitor, along with sixteen other Scots loyal to Robert the Bruce, denied even the right to speak in their own defence. The royal ladies were kept in close confinement after their capture, while the Countess of Buchan, who had the effrontery in Edward I's eyes to officiate at the enthronement of Robert the Bruce at Scone, was kept imprisoned for four years in a cage built of lattice-work within a tower of Berwick Castle. A similar fate befell Mary Bruce, sister of Robert the Bruce, imprisoned likewise in a cage at Roxburgh Castle.

Role of the Campbells

Fighting for Robert the Bruce during his encounter with the MacDougalls at Dalrigh was Sir Neil Campbell, who with the aid of the Earl of Lennox probably helped the future King of Scotland to escape through the mountains of Lennox and then across Loch Lomond before he reached the safety of Kintyre. Unlike many other Highland clans, the **Campbells** do not have an ancient pedigree that can be traced back to some distant if half-legendary ancestor, like Niall of the Nine Hostages. Yet their long rise to power and influence in the Western Highlands extends back to the reign of Alexander III, when Sir Colin Campbell or his father was appointed as the royal baillie of Lochawe and Ardscotnish, comprising nearly all of mid-Argyll between Lorn and Loch Fyne, apart from Glassary and Craignish. Farther north were the territories of the MacDougalls, who held the stronghold of Dunstaffnage under their chieftain Alexander macDougall of Lorn. During the reign of John Balliol a territorial dispute evidently broke out between the Campbells and the MacDougalls, culminating in a battle that was fought in 1294 at the String of Lorn, which forms a narrow pass of low-lying country separating Loch Avich from Glen Scammadale to the north of Loch Awe. Sir Colin Campbell was killed and his son Neil succeeded him. The death of his father at the hands of the MacDougalls may well have prompted Sir Neil Campbell to join Robert the Bruce in his fight against the Comyns, to whom the MacDougalls were closely related by marriage.

Clan Donald and its Divided Allegiance

Once Robert the Bruce and his party had reached Kintyre they came under the protection of Angus Og mac Donald. He now held the lordship of Kintyre following the death of his father Angus Mor mac Donald around 1300, if not earlier. His elder brother was Alexander macDonald of the Isles, Lord of Islay. Their father had long been an adherent of Robert Bruce the 'Competitor', attending a meeting at Turnberry with his son Alexander in 1286 which was intended to place Robert the Bruce's grandfather upon the Scottish throne, rather than the Maid of Norway. Even after Balliol had been placed by Edward I upon the Scottish throne in 1292, Angus Mor mac Donald continued steadfast in his support of the Bruce family, even refusing to answer the summons of Alexander MacDougall as the newly appointed sheriff of Argyll to do homage to John Balliol as the King of Scotland in 1293. However he died around 1296 and his eldest son Alexander macDonald succeeded him.

Alexander macDonald of Islay had already sworn allegiance to Edward I in 1291 and thereafter he was steadfast in his support of the English interest during the troubled years leading up to the events of 1306, and indeed afterwards. Despite his marriage with Juliana, daughter of Alexander macDougall of Lorn, he had previously been engaged in a bitter dispute over land with his father-in-law, which came before Edward I in 1292 over the head of John Balliol. He received a grant of land for services rendered to the English Crown in 1296, when the Scottish nobility were forced to render an oath of loyalty to Edward I after the battle of Dunbar. Indeed, he was so trusted by the English King that he was made Admiral of the Western Isles. This office was evidently no sinecure since he was faced with the hostility of Alexander macDougall of Lorn, his father-in-law, now presumably acting in the Balliol interest against England. Even though he had renewed his pledge of loyalty to Edward I in July 1296, after the English conquest of Scotland, only two months later Alexander Stewart, Earl of Menteith, had received a commission from the English King to take possession of all the MacDougall castles, fortresses, islands and lands.

Alexander macDougall of Lorn was himself imprisoned in Berwick Castle for nearly a year, until he was released in May 1297. Almost immediately however he attacked the territories of Alexander MacDonald of Islay, while it seems likely that he also encouraged the illegitimate sons of Alan mac Ruari, Lord of Garmoran and the Uists, to attack Skye and Lewis, which were still held by William, Earl of Ross. It was reported to Edward I that the MacRuaris had committed great outrages, laying waste to the land and burning all the ships engaged there in the service of the English. Alexander MacDonald of Islay had to write to Edward I asking him to instruct all the magnates of Argyll and Ross to help him keep the peace. Despite repeated threats the insurrection apparently continued for several years until Ruari MacRuari, the eldest son of Alan mac Ruari, was finally captured by Alexander MacDonald of Islay and his two brothers, Angus Og and John Spranach.

Alexander macDougall of Lorn and his son John Baccach remained opposed to the English interest until 1301, when they were faced not only by Alexander macDonald of Islay and his younger brother Angus Og, Lord of Kintyre, but by a wider alliance of Highland chiefs, including John macSweyn of Knapdale and Hugh Bisset, who held land in the Glens of

Antrim. The prospect of joint action by all these ardent supporters of Edward I so alarmed Alexander macDougall of Lorn that he decided to make his peace with the English King and submit to his authority. Thereafter he acted in the English interest, receiving the rents from the Campbell lands of Lochawe and Ardscotnish in 1304 and acting as a member of the King's council for the administration of Scotland in 1305, along with Robert the Bruce, Earl of Carrick.

Why Angus Og MacDonald, Lord of Kintyre, abandoned his erstwhile allegiance to Edward I in favour of Robert the Bruce in 1306 remains a mystery. The newly crowned King of Scotland was a desperate fugitive, hunted by vastly superior forces loyal to the English Crown and very unlikely to achieve success, or even to evade capture. Up to then Angus Og had followed the dictates of his own self-interest in allying himself with Edward I, along with many other magnates in Argyll and the Western Isles. The sudden shift in his allegiance perhaps marked a sudden resurgence of the support once given by Angus Mor, his father, to the earlier claims of Robert Bruce the 'Competitor' after the death of Alexander III in 1286. Links could even have been forged between the two families, given that the Bruce lands of Carrick were still very much a Gaelic-speaking district at the end of the thirteenth century, and indeed for long afterwards. Kintyre was then only separated from Carrick by the waters of the Firth of Clyde and easily reached by galley. It is even known from Barbour's epic poem *The Bruce* that Robert the Bruce had a foster-brother whose death he mourned. Even if his identity is quite unknown, fostering was a peculiarly Gaelic practice, so that Angus Og macDonald might have been related in some way to Robert the Bruce. His family was also linked by marriage to the Campbells of Lochawe at this time, after Angus Mor mac Donald had married a daughter of Sir Colin Campbell. Angus Og macDonald was thus a nephew of Sir Neil Campbell, who had already joined Robert the Bruce in his perilous attempt upon the Scottish throne. Even apart from any patriotic impulse to support the newly-crowned king of Scotland, which was clearly fraught with great uncertainty, Angus Og macDonald may simply have surrendered himself to the dictates of Celtic hospitality when Robert the Bruce sought refuge with him in the autumn of 1306.

Robert the Bruce in the Western Isles

Tradition asserts that Robert the Bruce was first welcomed by Angus Og macDonald to his castle at Saddell before he was taken for greater security to the castle of Dunaverty at the southern tip of Kintyre, overlooking the coast of Antrim across the narrow waters of the North Channel. Still threatened by the pro-English forces, who were intent on using miners to dig a tunnel to breach its defences, Robert the Bruce apparently escaped to the island of Rathlin, lying just three miles off the coast of Antrim. Forced into hiding, he may have stayed on Rathlin until the spring of 1307. But it could hardly have afforded him much security, since it was held by Hugh Bisset of the Glens, who was still loyal to Edward I. More likely he travelled north through the islands of the Inner Hebrides to seek refuge with Christina MacRuari, daughter of Alan mac Ruari and heiress to the vast territories of Garmoran. She was distantly related to Robert the Bruce by virtue of his first marriage with Isabella, daughter of the Earl of Mar, since she had married Duncan, the Earl's second son. Perhaps he even visited the Norse islands of Orkney during the winter, finding sanctuary under the protection of his sister Isabella Bruce, who had married the King of Norway. His brothers Thomas and Alexander most likely visited Ulster at the same time to muster support and Robert the Bruce may even have accompanied them.

Early in 1307 Robert the Bruce evidently felt strong enough to emerge from hiding, encouraged it is said by the repeated attempts of a spider trying to spin its web. Although Edward I had already learnt of his whereabouts in the Southern Hebrides, giving orders for the dispatch of a large fleet of well-manned ships under Hugh Bisset and Sir John Stewart of Menteith to intercept him, the news came too late. Slipping through their net Robert the Bruce reached Kintyre, from where he set sail to Arran with his own small force of thirty-three galleys. After a signal from the coast of Ayrshire, he managed to return unseen to his lands of Carrick. By then he must have learnt of the dreadful fate meted out to his family and his other adherents, who had been captured in 1306, only to suffer from the implacable hatred of Edward I, who treated them without any mercy as traitors. Yet another disaster followed soon after his return to Carrick when his brothers Thomas and Alexander landed at Loch Ryan, only to be attacked and captured by Dungal MacDowell, who was an ally of the Comyns. Brought into the presence of Edward I at Carlisle, they were summarily executed. If his foolhardy and impetuous action at Dumfries in February 1306 had forced Robert the Bruce to embark on a romantic and chivalrous adventure, perhaps only driven by his own self-seeking ambitions to gain the throne of Scotland, he was now faced by its tragic consequences. Thereafter he took on the mantle of a national hero, redeeming his past behaviour by resolutely pursuing the cause of Scottish independence to a successful conclusion and eventually winning for himself the Scottish throne by strength of arms.

Chapter Seven

ROBERT THE BRUCE AND
SCOTTISH INDEPENDENCE

The very start of Robert the Bruce's campaign to seize Scotland as its self-crowned King came close to disaster in the early months of 1307. Ever likely to be overwhelmed by superior forces of heavy cavalry, Bruce first resorted to guerilla tactics, fighting what was then described as a 'secret war'. The vulnerability of the Scottish forces could be much reduced by choosing carefully where to fight, using the natural features of the terrain to prevent the full deployment of the English cavalry on a wide front and to stop its charge from building up any momentum. It was a tactic later to be adopted in 1314 with overwhelming success at the battle of Bannockburn. Meanwhile guerilla warfare allowed Robert the Bruce to pursue a piecemeal strategy of laying siege to each and every castle occupied by the English forces and their Scottish allies over the years after 1307. Once captured these castles were razed to the ground so that they could not be occupied again by his enemies.

Following an early skirmish in Glen Trool, when he ambushed a small detachment of English cavalry, Robert the Bruce first won a resounding victory over the English forces at the battle of Loudon Hill in May 1307, taking advantage of the terrain to hamper the free movement of the English cavalry. Throughout the previous winter Edward I of England had lain sick at Lanercost Priory. Now he roused himself for one last expedition to crush the Scots. Summoning the English host to rally at Carlisle for a summer campaign, he had only reached Burgh-on-Sands on the southern shores of the Solway Firth when he died on 7 July 1307. Known to history as the 'Hammer of the Scots', his death removed a formidable opponent of Scottish independence. He was succeeded by his son Edward II, who lacked his father's indomitable will to subjugate Scotland. Even if he did not want personal courage, he proved incompetent in the field as a commander, little appreciating military tactics and often irresolute and vacillating in their application.

After his father's death Edward II continued north to Nithsdale, but his campaign was ineffective and he soon afterwards withdrew to England. Meanwhile after raiding the Balliol lands in Galloway to such effect that his enemies were forced into a truce, Robert the Bruce moved into the Scottish Highlands with an army of three thousand men, determined to destroy for ever the northern power-base of the Comyn family and their MacDougall allies. His forces were supported by a fleet of galleys, perhaps under the command of Angus Og macDonald, which sailed up Loch Linnhe.

Robert the Bruce and his Highland Campaign

Among the most powerful magnates in the north was William, Earl of Ross. After taking part in the abortive raid against Carlisle in 1296, he was soon afterwards captured at the battle of Dunbar. Only released from English custody in 1303, two years later Edward I had made him Warden of the country north of the Spey. Even if we only know the Christian name of his wife, his mother was Jean, daughter of William Comyn, Earl of Buchan, while his son Sir John Ross was later to marry Margaret Comyn, younger daughter of Sir Alexander Comyn and a niece of the Earl of Buchan. William, Earl of Ross, had therefore every reason to pursue the English interest in 1306, which he did by seizing Bruce's Queen, his daughter Marjory and his two sisters Mary and Christina, as well as the Earl of Atholl, from within the sanctuary of St Duthac's Chapel at Tain. Now he was threatened by Robert the Bruce, who had already forced the surrender of the Comyn castle of Inverlochy at the head of Loch Linnhe by November 1307. Robert the Bruce then advanced rapidly north-east along the Great Glen. He first captured the castle of Urquhart on the shores of Loch Ness, mostly likely from Sir Alexander Comyn, who was certainly its keeper a few years earlier, and then destroyed the royal castles of Inverness and Nairn. These successes brought William, Earl of Ross, to a temporary truce, which lasted until 2 June 1308, even if he reported in a letter to Edward II of England that he had three thousand men under arms. Sutherland was most likely included in this truce, since the earldom was then held in trust by Sir John Ross, younger son of the Earl of Ross, as William, third Earl of Sutherland, was a minor at the time of his father's death in 1306 or 1307. Farther north, even if the Earl of Caithness had sworn allegiance to Edward I in 1297, he took little part in the turbulent events after 1306.

After bringing the northern earldoms of Ross and Sutherland to a truce, Robert the Bruce was free to move east against the Comyn territories of Buchan and Mar. First he laid siege to the royal castle of Elgin, but without any success. He then marched east along the coast towards the royal castle at Banff, but fell seriously ill on the way, suffering it was said from distemper.

However his illness may well have marked the early onset of leprosy, then common in Scotland, since he suffered from this disease towards the end of his life. Borne on a litter, he turned inland with his army, which perhaps now numbered only seven hundred men. Then on Christmas Day 1307, near Slioch just outside Huntly, he encountered the troops of Sir John Mowbray and John Comyn, Earl of Buchan. The engagement was merely a skirmish and Robert the Bruce perhaps made a tactical retreat when reinforcements arrived on the scene a week later. Nevertheless he crossed the mountains towards his lands in Mar, so alarming the Comyn forces there that they strengthened the castle of Coull, before a truce was arranged between the two sides in February 1308. This break in hostilities allowed Bruce or his followers to attack the widely scattered castles of Mortlach, Duffus, Tarradale and Skelbo, which all fell in the spring of 1308. The siege of Elgin Castle was renewed in April 1308 and it too was captured within a few weeks. Only the castle at Banff held out for another two years, supplied by sea.

Defeat of the Comyns

It was not until 23 May 1308 that a decisive engagement was fought between Robert the Bruce and John Comyn, Earl of Buchan. It occurred at the Hill of Barra, which lies midway between Old Meldrum and Inverurie. After an initial skirmish, when some of his soldiers were put to flight, Robert the Bruce rose from his sickbed and mounted his charger in full armour to lead the attack, supported on each side by two men. Although the Earl of Buchan had a thousand men in the field his army was completely routed by the fury of Bruce's attack. His victory left the way open into Buchan as the heartland of Comyn power. The whole earldom was laid waste with such devastation, and its people slaughtered in such numbers, that the 'herschip' or ravaging of Buchan was vividly recalled with terror by its people more than fifty years later. Finally his campaign in the north-east ended in the summer of 1308 when he captured the burgh and supply-port of Aberdeen, even if he was unable to force the English garrison to surrender its castle.

Bruce's campaign in Buchan had broken the power of the Comyn family for ever in the north-east of Scotland. Even so John Comyn, Earl of Buchan, managed to escape south after the battle at the Hill of Barra. Within a month of this defeat, he was appointed by Edward II of England as Warden of the Western Marches, consisting of Annandale, Galloway and Carrick. When he died later in the same year, he left as his sole heirs only his two nieces by the marriage of his younger brother Alexander Comyn with Joanna de Latimer, who came from England. The younger of his nieces was Margaret Comyn, who not long afterwards married Sir John Ross, younger son of William,

Earl of Ross. She brought him her half-share of her uncle's lands in Buchan, which were erected into the barony of Kingedward, lying to the north of the watershed between the Don and the Ythan in Aberdeenshire. Soon after her marriage, Margaret Comyn was widowed, and perhaps after her own death the barony of Kingedward passed into the hands of William, Earl of Ross after 1333. The elder niece was Alicia Comyn, Countess of Buchan in her own right. She had married Henry de Beaumont by 1310, who was recognised by Edward II as the Earl of Buchan by right of his wife. After the Scottish victory at the battle of Bannockburn in 1314, where he fought for Edward II, they were both disinherited of all the lands they held in Buchan, which were later shared out amongst the loyal supporters of Robert the Bruce. Since he would not abandon his allegiance to Edward II for the lands he held in England, he was judged by the Scots to be 'irretrievably English'.

New Families in the North-east

Sir Robert Keith the Marischal afterwards won the largest share of the Comyn lands in Buchan. The **Keiths** as a family take their name from the lands of Keith in East Lothian, while the family itself was founded by a Norman adventurer called Hervey who received a grant of these lands from David I in 1150, after he had married into a native family. His son became Marischal to Malcolm IV and William the Lion, charged with looking after the stable of royal mares. Indeed the office of Marischal got its name from the French word *marechal*, literally a 'horse-servant', still used in France for a 'farrier'. This office became hereditary to the Keiths, requiring them to act as custodians of the crown jewels and charging them with responsibility for the king's safety in parliament. It was Sir Robert Keith who commanded the Scots cavalry at the battle of Bannockburn, when his forces were able to scatter the Welsh archers before they could mount an effective attack against the Scots. He was afterwards granted the royal forest of Halforest in Aberdeenshire, where he built a castle just outside Kintore, while his brother Edward, who succeeded him as his heir, received lands in what are now the parishes of Methlick, Monquhitter, New Deer, Ellon, Longside and Foveran.

Sir William Keith added to their territories later in the fourteenth century when he married the heiress of Sir Alexander Fraser, who brought to the Keiths great estates in Buchan and Kincardine as well as Lothian. Their eldest son married a daughter of Robert II, while a younger daughter married Sir Adam Gordon around 1380, taking with her substantial estates that later formed the foundations of Gordon power in the Highlands. His brother John Keith likewise married the heiress of Reginald Cheyne, bringing to the family her vast estates of Inverugie in Buchan. It was through this marriage that the Keiths of Inverugie gained the Cheyne estates in Caithness, settling there as the Keiths of Akergill. Meanwhile the descendants of Sir William Keith were eventually elevated to the peerage as Earls Marischal in 1458, even if it had been an office hereditary to their family ever since 1176.

After the downfall of the Comyn family, Sir Gilbert Hay of Errol was made hereditary High Constable of Scotland by Robert the Bruce, an office previously held by John Comyn, Earl of Buchan. The name of Constable originated in Roman times with the office of the *Comes stabuli*, or 'count of the stable', and only later was it given to the royal officer in charge of the king's cavalry. The **Hays** were themselves a powerful Norman family from the district of La Haye in Normandy, who had crossed the English Channel with William the Conqueror in 1066, bringing their name with them. The first on record in Scotland was William de Haya, who was granted the lands of Errol in the Carse of Gowrie by William the Lion around 1172. After marrying into the Celtic aristocracy of the district, the power and influence of the family was recognised when Gilbert de la Haye, third Baron of Errol, became Sheriff of Perth and then co-Regent of Scotland during the minority of Alexander III in the middle of the thirteenth century. He married Idonea, daughter of William Comyn, Earl of Buchan, receiving the lands of Auchtercoul in Mar. The fortunes of the Hays received a further boost during the Wars of Scottish Independence, when Sir Gilbert Haye, fifth Baron of Errol, distinguished himself as a loyal comrade-in-arms of Robert the Bruce. Now holding the hereditary office of High Constable of Scotland, he was later rewarded with the lands of Slains on the coast north of Collieston, where his descendants occupied the Old Castle of Slains until it was demolished by James VI in 1595.

Earls of Mar and Ross

Elsewhere in the north-east there was less change. Robert the Bruce had himself inherited lands in the Garioch from his father, and they were later granted to Andrew Moray of Bothwell, the future guardian of Scotland during the minority of David II. He was not only the son of Wallace's compatriot and ally Andrew de Moray, who had died after the battle of Stirling Bridge in 1297, but he later married Christina, sister of Robert the Bruce, long after she had been released from English custody in 1314. Already twice widowed, she had first been married to Gartnait, Earl of Mar, and then after his death to Sir Christopher Seton. Captured at the battle of Methven, her second husband was executed in 1306 by Edward I for supporting Robert the Bruce, suffering the fate of a traitor to England by being hung, drawn and quartered. Christina Bruce had already borne the Earl of Mar a son Donald who inherited his father's title while still a child. Perhaps captured along with his mother at Tain, he was detained in England by Edward I.

Brought up at the English court, he became so strongly attached to Edward, Prince of Wales, that he refused to return to Scotland when his mother was released from English custody in 1314. Indeed he did not return to Scotland until Edward II was deposed in 1327, when Robert the Bruce with great generosity restored his nephew to the earldom of Mar. He was among the commanders of the Scottish army which invaded England in that year, intent on assisting Edward II to regain his throne.

William, Earl of Ross, faced with the destruction of Comyn power in Buchan, paid homage to Robert the Bruce as the King of Scotland at the castle of Auldearn on 31 October 1308. Almost the first Scots magnate to join Robert the Bruce, apart from the earls of Menteith, Lennox and Atholl, he thereafter remained steadfast in his new loyalties. He prospered greatly, receiving a charter to lands of Dingwall and Ferncrosky as a reward from Robert the Bruce for his staunch support. However it was his son and heir Hugh, who succeeded his father as the Earl of Ross in 1323, who benefited to an even greater degree, since he was held in high regard by Robert the Bruce. Indeed he had married the King's daughter Matilda in 1308, or soon afterwards. He eventually became one of the richest magnates in the kingdom before he died fighting against Edward III at the battle of Halidon Hill in 1333. He held the sheriffdoms and burghs of Cromarty and Dingwall, together with the burgh of Nairn, while he was granted vast estates in the Black Isle and elsewhere in Easter Ross, including Strathglass and Strath-conon, together with baronies and thanages in Buchan, and the Isle of Skye.

Randolph Earls of Moray

Another great magnate who gained much power and influence in the north was Sir Thomas Randolph, described in charters as the King's nephew, but seemingly related rather more distantly to Robert the Bruce by an earlier marriage of his father, Earl of Carrick. He was present at the enthronement of Robert the Bruce in 1306, only to be captured by the English after the battle of Methven. Faced with losing his lands, he submitted to Edward I and entered his service. However he was taken prisoner by Sir James Douglas in 1308, most likely in Selkirk Forest, and brought in front of Robert the Bruce, whom he berated for a lack of chivalry in fighting a guerilla war. Imprisoned for a time by the Scottish King, he was soon released to become one of his most trusted lieutenants. By 1312 he had been made Earl of Moray, gaining jurisdiction over vast territories which encompassed the ancient Pictish province of Moray. They stretched inland from the mouth of the River Spey to Badenoch and Lochaber, and then north through the districts of Locharkaig, Glengarry and Glenelg, from where they shared a march with the earldom of Ross to the north, eventually reaching the east coast at the head of Beauly Firth. Holding this vast domain for the service of ten knights, the Earl of Moray came to exercise all the powers of the Crown in a true 'regality', answerable only to the King himself and not to his royal officials. Later events in the Highlands were to prove it a system of government that only worked well if the king was himself held in high authority, since otherwise it tended to result in the break-up of royal power.

Defeat of the MacDougalls

After returning south from Aberdeen in the summer of 1308, Robert the Bruce determined to confront Alexander macDougall of Lorn, who still remained loyal to Edward II. It now seems likely that Robert the Bruce waged two campaigns in Argyll. The first took place in August 1308 when Alexander macDougall apparently submitted to Robert the Bruce in the face of overwhelming forces, although his son John Baccach in writing to Edward II early in 1309 portrayed this submission as merely an honourable truce between the two sides. Alexander macDougall certainly attended the first parliament that Robert the Bruce was confident enough to call in March 1309 at St Andrews, even if it was mostly attended by his own partisans. This proclaimed him King of Scotland, judging that he had inherited the rightful claim of his grandfather Robert the Bruce the 'Competitor' to rule over Scotland, which in 1292 had been usurped by John Balliol with the force of English arms, thus rewriting history. It justified his accession on the grounds that his cardinal virtues fitted him to rule over Scotland, since 'he has by the sword restored the realm'. Finally it asserted that he had the consent of the faithful people of Scotland to rule as their chosen king, for whom they were prepared to live or to die.

Unlike the other magnates at this parliament, who remained loyal to King Robert the Bruce, Alexander macDougall of Lorn and his son John Baccach proved much less trustworthy. They were both present at the Council of Edward II, held at Westminister on 16 June 1309, along with many other 'loyal' Scots. Faced with the defection of the MacDougalls, Robert the Bruce apparently mounted a second invasion of Argyll in the late summer of 1309, if indeed these events had not already taken place in 1308. Its climax was the battle fought at the Pass of Brander between John Baccach of Lorn, supported by perhaps eight hundred men if not the army of two thousand reported by Barbour, and what was probably a much larger force under King Robert the Bruce.

This narrow defile, through which the waters of Loch Awe escape towards the sea at Loch Etive, lent itself by its very nature to an ambush of any forces marching by way of Dalmally towards the MacDougall stronghold at the castle of Dunstaffnage. Before the battle was even engaged, John

Baccach had stationed his forces to the north on the lower slopes of Ben Cruachan overlooking the narrow pass. King Robert the Bruce countered this move by sending a detachment of archers under Sir James Douglas to gain the heights above them, so that they could attack the MacDougall forces in their rear. His main force then pressed on through the pass, where they came under attack from the MacDougall forces who rolled great and heavy boulders down upon Bruce's men. This onslaught was met by King Robert the Bruce who sent lightly armed men to clamber up the slopes to attack the MacDougalls from below, while the archers lying above the MacDougall forces launched their own attack from the heights. Outflanked, the men of Lorn were put to flight and the great power of the MacDougalls broken for ever in Argyll.

After his victory at the Pass of Brander, the forces commanded by King Robert the Bruce captured the MacDougall castle of Dunstaffnage, where it guarded the entrance to Loch Etive. Rather than razing the castle to the ground Dunstaffnage was left standing, occupied by a loyal garrison under Arthur Campbell. John Baccach and his now-aged father Alexander macDougall of Lorn escaped along with Bishop Andrew of Argyll to exile in England. Alexander macDougall died within a year, but his son John Baccach maintained his steadfast loyalty to Edward II until he too died a pensioner of the English King in 1317. During these years he was made Admiral of the Western Isles, but he was only able to recover the Isle of Man for the English after it had been captured by King Robert the Bruce in 1313. Even though Edward II gave him authority to recover his ancestral lands of the MacDougalls, they had been seized by King Robert the Bruce. He later distributed them amongst his Campbell allies as a reward for their own loyalty after the Scottish victory at Bannockburn.

Rewarding the Campbells

Indeed the younger brothers of Sir Neil Campbell were all given lands in Argyll after they were forfeited by the MacDougalls. Duncan Campbell gained the lands of Duntrune with its castle, while Donald Campbell got the district of Benderloch in return for the service of a ship of twenty-six oars. Dugald Campbell obtained in 1312 the lands of Achnaclioch, Degnish, Kilninver, Clachanseil and the Isle of Torsa. Later he became the sheriff of Argyll. Colin Campbell, as the eldest son and heir of Sir Neil Campbell by his first marriage, received as a free barony the ancestral Campbell lands of Loch Awe and Ardscotnish in 1315, which had been held for the Scottish Crown by his father and grandfather. It was a feudal grant for the service of a birlinn of forty oars and Sir Colin Campbell and his heirs were thereafter known as the Lords of Lochow.

Other kinsmen of Sir Neil Campbell also obtained feudal grants of land in Argyll, including Sir Arthur Campbell, who as the keeper of Dunstaffnage Castle was granted lands in Benderloch, along with the MacDougall stronghold of Dunollie Castle, all for a quarter of a knight's service. It was only around 1338 that John MacDougall, grandson of John Baccach, regained some of the territories forfeited by his family, but he never recovered any of the MacDougall lands held by the Campbells in Argyll. Meanwhile many MacDougalls had settled in Ireland, acting as the commanders of mercenary galloglasses, especially to the O'Neills of Tyrone, and taking the names of MacDowell, Doyle or Coyle.

Sir Neil Campbell, already married to Bruce's sister Mary, and their son John were granted estates in Perthshire, forfeited in 1314 by David of Strathbogie, Earl of Atholl. He had succeeded to the earldom of Atholl in 1306 after his father had been executed as a traitor by Edward I for supporting Robert the Bruce. However the son was equally steadfast in his support for the English cause, married as he was to Joan, eldest daughter of John Comyn the younger of Badenoch, who was murdered by Robert the Bruce in 1306. Only during the course of 1312–14 did the Earl of Atholl appear in the Scottish camp, submitting to King Robert the Bruce, who appointed him Constable of Scotland. But he then quarrelled with Edward Bruce, who had seduced his sister Isobel, making her pregnant, only to abandon her for a daughter of the Earl of Ross. Their quarrel culminated in the treacherous attack made by the Earl of Atholl upon the Scottish supply-camp at Cambuskenneth on the very eve of the battle of Bannockburn. Banished to England, where he received lands in compensation, his title was forfeited in 1314, thus ending the line of the Strathbogie earls of Atholl, themselves a cadet branch of the Earls of Fife. The earldom itself was afterwards bestowed upon John Campbell, son of Sir Neil Campbell, when he came of age. He was killed at the battle of Halidon Hill in 1333 and the title passed first to the Douglases and then to the Stewarts, before it eventually came to the Murrays, afterwards Dukes of Atholl.

Local families in Atholl also benefited from the patronage of King Robert the Bruce. Chief among them were the **Menzies**. They originally came from Mesnieres in Normandy, bringing their territorial name with them. After first settling in England, where they took the name of Manners, now the surname of the Dukes of Rutland, their descendants came north in the early thirteenth century. Robert de Meyners is the first on record in Scotland, witnessing charters at the court of Alexander II in 1224 and 1246, while he was made Chamberlain by 1249. He apparently received a grant of lands in Glen Lyon and Rannoch, perhaps benefiting from an advantageous marriage, while his son Sir Alexander de Meigners received the lands of Aberfeldy and Weem, which remain the stronghold of Clan Menzies to this day. Further honours came to the family after the Wars of Scottish Independence through their support for King Robert the Bruce, when Sir Robert Menzies was rewarded with the ancient lordship of the MacNabs, hereditary lay-abbots of Glen Dochart. They had forfeited their lands of Finlarig, Glendochart and Glenorchy after supporting the Comyns in alliance with the MacDougalls of Lorne. When King Robert the Bruce died in 1329, the Menzies family held lands that stretched from Aberfeldy through Breadalbane and Glen Dochart to Glen Falloch, close to the head of Loch Lomond.

Rise of the Gordons

Apart from his lands in Atholl, David of Strathbogie also held Stratha'an in Banffshire from the Earl of Fife and these lands were granted to Malcolm, Earl of Lennox, who had early rallied to the support of Robert the Bruce in 1306. The lordship of Strathbogie was itself granted to Sir Adam Gordon, perhaps as an inducement for him to support Robert the Bruce, since he had been justicar of Lothian under Edward II. He founded the powerful family of the **Gordons**, afterwards Earls of Huntly. A Lowland family, their origins are a mystery. They perhaps came from Gourdon in the district of Quercy in France, bringing their name with them, unless they simply took it from the district of Gordon in the Merse, where they first settled in Scotland in the mid-twelfth century. Equally they may be the descendants of Waltheof, Earl of Northumberland, since they share the heraldic device of three boars' heads in common with their appositely named neighbours the Swintons, who claim just such a descent.

After Sir Adam Gordon was granted the lands of Strathbogie, they continued to be held by his descendants for several generations. In 1408 they passed by marriage into the possession of Sir Alexander Seton, who belonged to a lowland family that originally came from the village of Sai near Exmes in Normandy. His descendants prospered greatly, especially after his eldest son Sir Alexander Seton was created Earl of Huntly in 1445, later taking the name of Gordon for himself and his family. Thereafter the Gordon earls of Huntly acted as the king's lieutenants in the north, exercising their authority with such vice-regal powers that they eventually earned themselves the illustrious title of 'Cocks o' the North' as the rivals of the Campbells, Earls of Argyll.

Rise of the MacDonalds

The aftermath of the Wars of Scottish Independence saw the MacDonalds faring far better than the Macdougalls, apart from Alexander macDonald of Islay, who remained an ardent supporter of Edward II, along with the

MacSweens of Knapdale. Closely allied by marriage to the MacDougalls of
Lorne, and thus inclined to support the Comyn cause, Alexander macDonald
had fought in Galloway against Edward Bruce in 1308, when he had been
captured after the battle fought on the banks of the River Dee. But he managed to escape from Edward Bruce's custody, fleeing to Argyll where he took
refuge in Castle Sween. There he was besieged in 1309 by King Robert the
Bruce after he had captured Dunstaffnage Castle and forced to surrender.
Imprisoned in the Stewart castle of Dundonald in Ayrshire, he probably
died soon afterwards. All his estates were forfeited, while his sons were all
forced into exile, mostly taking refuge in Ireland as the well-regarded captains of mercenary galloglasses, scattered throughout the country in Ulster,
Connaught and Leinster. The MacSweens of Knapdale suffered much the
same fate, never recovering the lands that they had lost in 1262 and later
settling in Ireland as the MacSweeneys or Sweeneys. They were said to
hold a quarter of all the lands of Tirconnel, now Donegal, as well as lands
elsewhere in Ulster, Munster and Connaught.

Angus Og macDonald profited greatly from the misfortunes of his elder
brother, since he never faltered in his support of Robert the Bruce. However
while Angus Og had previously held much of Kintyre as its lord, his lands
there were afterwards shared out by King Robert the Bruce to several others,
including his own grandson Robert the High Steward and Sir John Stewart
of Menteith. He also departed from his policy of destroying any castle which
could be used by his enemies when he rebuilt the castle at Tarbert on Loch
Fyne and garrisoned it with his own forces, guarding the western approaches
to the Firth of Clyde. Tarbert itself was made a royal burgh but it is not clear
that it ever flourished. Evidently he was not prepared to trust Angus Og mac
Donald with such strategic territories, preferring to keep them in the hands of
the Stewarts as his closest allies. In recompense for his loss of Kintyre, Angus
Og mac Donald was granted the islands of Islay, Jura, Gigha and Colonsay,
along with the mainland territories of Duror, Glencoe, Lochaber, Ardnamurchan and Morvern, which had mostly been forfeited by the MacDougalls or
the Comyns. These lands later formed the foundation on which the
MacDonalds, Lords of the Isles, rose to great power in the Western Isles.

Fortunes of the MacRuaris

There was little change in the territories held by the MacRuaris, who had
always supported Robert the Bruce, even if Lachlan MacRuari now pursued
a distinctly lawless course in the Hebrides, worthy of his Viking ancestors.
His half-sister Christina MacRuari, who gave sanctuary to the newly crowned
King of Scotland, still held Garmoran and the Uists as the only legitimate
heiress of her father Alan mac Ruari. She apparently surrendered all her

territories to King Robert the Bruce, who then bestowed them on her other half-brother Ruari macRuari. He held the lands of Garmoran and the Uists in feudal dependency upon the Scottish Crown in return for the service of a single birlinn of twenty-six oars. It is usually thought that all his lands were forfeited for some unknown reason in 1325, even if his son Ranald later received them back by royal charter from David II in 1334. However the Irish Annals imply that Ruari macRuari had already died at the battle of Dundalk in 1318, while it was Ruari of Islay who lost his lands in 1325. His identity remains a mystery, even if he was most likely a kinsmen of Clan Donald. These lands then passed after Ranald's death in 1346 to his half-sister Amie macRuari. Already in 1337 she had married John MacDonald of Islay, younger son of Angus Og macDonald. Even before he received a papal dispensation for his marriage he was proudly calling himself 'Lord of the Isles' in the manner of his ancestors. All these grants to the Campbells, MacDonalds and MacRuaris, among many others, show that the feudal practices long pursued elsewhere in the Highlands were now applied to Argyll and the Hebrides.

The Years before Bannockburn

The years after 1309 were spent in a long and confused struggle against England. King Robert the Bruce now had control over the countryside but many castles and other fortifications were still held by the English forces and their Comyn allies, especially in Lothian and the Borders. After a year of vacillation and indecision, Edward II of England mounted an abortive invasion of Scotland in September 1310, reaching only as far north as Lithlingow. King Robert the Bruce deliberately avoided being drawn into a pitched battle, drawing back as the English forces advanced and harrying their rear, while denying them supplies in a year of famine by burning the countryside. Discouraged, Edward II retreated to Berwick where he spent the winter, only to make another half-hearted attempt at invasion in 1311, before retiring south to London. King Robert the Bruce took full advance of the English weakness, launching such savage raids for money, cattle and corn into the north of England that the inhabitants paid £2,000 for a truce until February 1312. When it ended the raids were renewed by Edward Bruce and Sir James Douglas, penetrating as far south as Durham and Hartlepool, before another truce was arranged for a large ransom.

North of the Forth, the Scots captured the castle of Dundee in the spring of 1312, but Perth held out until January 1313, when its garrison was surprised by a night attack, led by King Robert the Bruce. By then the castles of Loch Doon, Lochmaben, Caerlaverock, Dalswinton, Tibbers and Buittle in the south-west had all fallen to the Scots and soon afterwards the castle of

Dumfries was surrendered to them as well. The Scots then mounted a campaign to capture the castles in the Lothians that were still held for Edward II, when the castles at Linlithgow, Roxburgh and Edinburgh all fell into their hands. Only an attempt on the castle at Berwick failed when its garrison was alerted by the barking of a dog and it remained in English hands until 1318.

By the spring of 1314 only the castle at Stirling was still held for the English. Marching south to Dumfries in May 1313, where he embarked on his conquest of the Isle of Man, King Robert the Bruce had apparently left his brother Edward in charge of the siege of Stirling Castle. But he was far too impetuous a person to suffer the tedium of a long siege. Renewing a tactic used successfully at Dundee, he entered into a truce with the Scottish knight Sir Philip Mowbray, who held the castle for Edward II of England. The castle would be surrendered to the Scots if it had not been relieved by the English by Midsummer's Day 1314. It was a challenge that Edward II of England could not ignore.

Even as the castles of Linlithgow, Roxburgh and Edinburgh fell in the early months of 1314, Edward II was engaged in planning a large-scale invasion of Scotland. Even so it was not until the middle of June that an English army, consisting of 15,000 foot-soldiers at the very least and perhaps 2,000 or 3,000 heavy cavalry, mustered at Berwick and Wark. The English forces then marched rapidly north by way of Lauderdale and Soutra to Edinburgh, where they turned west towards Falkirk and Stirling Castle. They only had a day to spare when Edward II came within three miles of Stirling Castle, as stipulated for its relief under the terms of the truce made a year earlier with Edward Bruce. Any further advance along the high road towards Stirling was blocked by the Scottish army, which lay behind prepared defences within the woods of New Park, just north-west of Bannock Burn.

The Scots had no more than 10,000 foot-soldiers, mostly spearmen with only a small contingent of archers, augmented by perhaps 500 light cavalry. After mustering his army farther south-east in the Tor Wood near Falkirk, King Robert the Bruce had fallen back as the English army approached on 23 June 1314, uncertain as yet whether to fight a pitched battle. Indeed upon reaching New Park, he had laid out his forces as if hinting at retreat, since the vanguard under Thomas Randolph, Earl of Moray, lay closest to Stirling Castle, while the rearguard under his own command was placed farther to the south-east, guarding the approach to Stirling Castle from Falkirk across the Bannock Burn.

First Skirmishes at Bannockburn

It was there that the first skirmish took place, when the English cavalry first encountered the Scots lying behind their defensive positions. It led to the famous encounter between King Robert the Bruce, mounted upon a sturdy palfrey as he inspected his forward defences, and only armed with a battle-axe, and Sir Henry de Bohun. Facing his opponent in single combat, the Scottish King managed to sidestep Sir Henry's lance, only to raise himself up in his stirrups to deal a fatal blow to the English knight as he passed, cleaving his skull apart with his battle-axe. No doubt this feat of arms did wonders for Scots morale, even if it greatly alarmed the Scots commanders. Indeed all might have been lost had King Robert the Bruce been killed. Nonetheless the English vanguard pressed forward their attack, only to be driven back by the Scots across the Bannock Burn, while another detachment of English cavalry threatened to outflank the Scots army on their left by riding along the low-lying Carse of Stirling.

It drew an urgent if tardy response from Thomas Randolph, Earl of Moray, who moved downhill with his spearmen, packed into a tight 'schiltron', to challenge the English cavalry. Although they repeatedly charged the Scots foot-soldiers, who advanced against them with their spears to the fore, the mounted knights of the English cavalry were quite unable to penetrate this bristling line of defence. Indeed the long spears of the Scots foot-soldiers wreaked such havoc that the English were forced to fall back in disarray. The engagement demonstrated that spearmen could attack and rout cavalry, virtually without any casualties, especially if they themselves were not under attack by archers.

As the day was now late Edward II then led his cavalry down from the higher ground towards the Carse of Stirling. It was a dangerous and indeed fatal move, perhaps dictated by a pressing need to water the English horses, since the weather was hot and sultry, and his army had only just arrived in time to relieve Stirling Castle after several days of forced marches. The English cavalry and perhaps some foot-soldiers forded the lower reaches of the Bannock Burn where it flowed across the flat-lying and marshy ground of the Carse of Stirling. Once across this obstacle he decided to bivouac for the night, even if his army now lay just below the Scots.

Presumably Edward II hoped the next day to continue his march towards Stirling Castle, bypassing the Scots army on its left flank without even giving battle. But he was no general, since he had inadvertently placed his own army in almost an ideal position for an attack by the Scots. Even so King Robert the Bruce was still inclined to withdraw without engaging the English when Sir Alexander Seton defected to the Scots during the night, bringing him the welcome news that morale was very low among the English forces in their exposed position. He urged the Scots to attack at first light, when they had every chance of victory. With the enthusiastic agreement of his commanders, King Robert the Bruce gave the orders to engage in a battle that came to mark the very climax of the struggle for Scottish independence.

Defeat of the English

The battle started at daybreak on 24 June 1314 when three battalions of Scots foot-soldiers commanded by Edward Bruce, Sir James Douglas and Sir Thomas Randolph advanced downhill from their encampment in New Park. It was Barbour who later wrote that the Scots appeared suddenly 'in good array and apertly (or boldly)', suggesting that their attack surprised the English army. Indeed Edward II evidently never thought that the Scots would be rash enough to attack his own much more powerful army. The Scottish advance was countered by the English cavalry under the Earl of Gloucester. As they charged the massed ranks of the Scots spearmen, packed into their tight 'schiltrons', they came up against an inpenetrable forest of spears, which wreaked a terrible toll upon their horses, which were not then protected by mail armour. Among the many casualties were the Earl of Gloucester and John Comyn, son of the murdered John Comyn the younger of Badenoch. Faced by the relentless advance of the Scots foot-soldiers behind their bristling spears, the English cavalry were forced to retreat in disorder, since they lacked any space to manoeuvre. The rest of the English army had little chance to deploy before they too were overwhelmed by the advancing 'schiltrons' of Scots foot-soldiers, bristling like huge hedgehogs behind their spears. Only a small detachment of English archers managed to engage effectively in the battle but they were soon routed by a body of light cavalry under Sir Robert Keith. Seeing that the battle had now reached a critical point, Robert the Bruce threw in his own battalion of foot-soldiers, numbering among its ranks many men from the Highlands and the Western Isles under the command of Angus Og macDonald. There were now four 'schiltrons' of Scots foot-soldiers bearing down upon the English army in a slow but dogged advance over a wide front.

Exactly how the English army broke is uncertain. Even if the chronicles of the Scots record a famous victory by heroic feats of arms, the English accounts of the battle reveal a more prosaic story. The Chronicle of Lanercost describes how the van of the English cavalry was forced back upon the bulk of the English army in its rear, causing such disorder that the whole army panicked in utter confusion and thought of nothing but flight. By now, and perhaps much earlier, the Scots had most likely crossed the bench of flat ground below New Park, spilling down the steep slope at its far edge to gain the flat-lying carseland, where the English army had bivouacked the previous night. There the remnants of the English forces were trapped between the Bannock Burn on their left flank and the meandering course of the River Forth to their rear, while yet another stream obstructed their right flank, even if it was less of an obstacle than the Bannock Burn.

As defeat turned into disaster for Edward II, the English army attempted to flee. No doubt some fugitives managed to escape back across the Bannock Burn where it flowed over the flat-lying carseland, just below its gorge from which it emerged farther upstream. But this stream came to flow in yet another gorge farther downstream, just before its waters became tidal near its confluence with the River Forth, where the English probably suffered the most terrible losses as they attempted to flee from the scene of the battle. Trying to cross the Bannock Burn at this point, they were engulfed by the mud in such numbers that Barbour wrote that men might pass dry over the drowned bodies of men and horses. Yet other fugitives lost their lives as they tried to escape across the waters of the Forth, dragged down by the weight of their armour.

As soon as they realised that the battle was lost, the English commanders hurried Edward II from the field against his protestations, fearful that he would be captured by the Scots and held to ransom. Five hundred knights accompanied the English King as he rode towards Stirling Castle across the Carse of Stirling. Once there Sir Philip Mowbray told him that he could enter, but warned him that he would be surrendered to the Scots on the very next day when the castle itself capitulated. The royal party turned around and crossed behind the Scottish lines to reach the high road near Falkirk. Hotly pursued by a small party of Scots cavalry under Sir James Douglas, Edward II eventually reached the safety of Dunbar Castle, where he took ship to Berwick and the south of England. Another large body of English cavalry managed to reach Bothwell Castle, then held for the English by Walter, Gilbert's son, ancestor of the Hamiltons. They were admitted, only to be imprisoned when he changed sides on hearing of the Scottish victory. Among their number was the Earl of Hereford, who was exchanged for the release of Bruce's Queen, his daughter Marjorie, his sisters Mary and Christina and Robert Wishart, Bishop of Glasgow, now very old and blind. Others in the party were ransomed for large sums of money, including Robert d'Umfraville, Earl of Angus. His lands in Scotland were shared out among Bruce's followers and the title itself became extinct for a time, until it was bestowed in 1329 on Sir John Stewart of Bonkyll.

The Scottish victory at Bannockburn has a resonance which echoes down the centuries, but it did not end the conflict with England, which continued with minor breaks until a thirteen-year truce was agreed in 1323. These years were spent by the Scots in harrying the north of England, even penetrating as far south as Holderness, just north of the Humber estuary, seizing goods and cattle and raising large sums of money as blackmail. Even if the well-defended castles of Carlisle, Norham, Newcastle and Richmond were held at first by the English, all except Richmond eventually fell to the Scots. Berwick was captured in 1318, and the castle heavily fortified. Its loss prompted Edward II to come north in 1319 with an army of perhaps 10,000 men, but he was forced to retreat south to the Trent when the Scots raided as far south as the Vale of York. He mounted yet another abortive invasion of Scotland in 1322, which reached Edinburgh, but hunger and starvation forced his army to retreat and he never again set foot in Scotland.

Edward Bruce in Ireland

Meanwhile Edward Bruce had embarked on a more dangerous adventure by invading Ireland in 1315, after he had been invited by the native Irish to become the High King of Ireland. Indeed after his initial victories against the English and their Irish allies, he was installed to this office at the Hill of Maeldon near Dundalk on 2 May 1316. As the heir-presumptive to the Scottish throne, it opened up the prospect of a dynastic union between the two countries, should the English be driven out of Ireland as well. Doubtless the Scots entertained grandiose plans for a pan-Celtic alliance against England. Letters written by King Robert the Bruce to the leaders of the native Irish stressed the common Gaelic heritage of their two peoples, asserting that both countries shared the same origins, the same language and the same customs and arguing that they should together regain the former freedom of their peoples. Yet Edward Bruce perhaps had more personal ambitions, since he evidently hoped to become the overlord of Wales as well as Ireland. But whatever his motives, the Scottish campaigns in Ireland came to a disastrous end in 1318 when Edward Bruce was himself killed in a battle near Dundalk.

Declaration of Arbroath

Even if Edward II still resolutely refused to recognise Robert the Bruce as the King of Scotland, Pope John decided in 1324 to address him by his royal title. This followed the Declaration of Arbroath of 1320, which took the form of a letter addressed to the Pope in Rome. Signed by eight earls and thirty-one barons, and perhaps written by Bernard, Abbot of Arbroath and Chancellor of Scotland on behalf of the Community of the Realm, it was an eloquent and inspiring document. It argued brilliantly that Scotland was an independent kingdom under the sovereignty of King Robert the Bruce, who was supported by all the people but only if he upheld the cause of Scottish independence. It ended with the stirring words: 'it is not for glory, riches, or honours that we fight, but for freedom alone ... which no man yields up, save with his life.'

Despite this, King Robert the Bruce was not fully absolved of his crimes against the Church until 1328. By then Edward II had been deposed by his Queen Isabella and her paramour Roger Mortimer, who probably arranged for his murder in a peculiarly barbaric manner. They then ruled over England in the name of her son, the youthful Edward III. By ending the truce between the two countries, if only on a legal technicality, his overthrow threatened the English with yet more raids by the Scots upon Northumberland, which looked ever more vulnerable to annexation by the Scottish Crown. After the Scots defeated the English forces in a short-lived campaign in 1327, Queen Isabella was forced to sue for peace on behalf of Edward III.

The Treaty of Edinburgh

The negotiations culminated in the Treaty of Edinburgh, by which the England at last recognised the absolute right of Scotland to exist as an independent kingdom. It further arranged for a marriage to be contracted between David, born in 1324 as the son and heir of King Robert the Bruce and soon to reign over Scotland as David II, and Joanna, daughter of Edward II, even if they were both still children, only a few years old. King Robert the Bruce bound himself to pay Edward III the sum of £20,000 'for the sake of the peace'. Often seen as compensation for the blackmail extracted by the Scots, it was then common enough practice for one party to make such a payment for its lawful rights to be recognised. The treaty also provided for a military alliance between the two countries, whereby the Scots agreed not to help the Irish if they attacked the king of England, and the English agreed not to help anyone in the Isle of Man or the Hebrides who attacked the king of Scotland. The agreement did not affect the Treaty of Corbeil, signed in 1326 as the 'Auld Alliance' between Scotland and France, which bound each country to come to the other's defence if it were attacked by England.

No part of the Treaty of Edinburgh tackled the 'Disinherited'. Already in 1314, soon after his victory at Bannockburn, Robert the Bruce had decreed that all those who would not accept his peace or whose fathers had died in battle against him were to forfeit their lands and titles. Even so, he was magnanimous in victory, willing to be reconciled with any of his opponents who were prepared to serve him alone as King of Scotland. But equally he required absolute and undivided loyalty from his subjects, even the greatest in the land, so that for the first time since the eleventh century, Scottish magnates could no longer be landholders in England, subject to the English king, or vice versa. Any English magnate who held lands in Scotland had these lands forfeited, thus joining the ranks of the 'Disinherited', if they still held lands in England. Backed by the ambitions of Edward III of England to conquer Scotland, they threatened the fragile peace that existed between the two kingdoms after King Robert the Bruce had died in 1329, lamented throughout his whole kingdom.

Chapter Eight

DAVID II AND THE EARLY STEWARTS

Robert the Bruce was succeeded as the King of Scotland after his death in 1329 by his young son David II, then only five years of age, while Thomas Randolph, Earl of Moray, acted as Guardian until his own death in 1332. By then Edward III had seized power in England from his mother Queen Isabella. He never accepted the Treaty of Edinburgh, and once the final instalment of the £20,000 had been paid he encouraged the 'Disinherited' to invade Scotland so that they might recover their lands. Their leader was Henry de Beaumont, who had married Alicia, elder niece of John Comyn, Earl of Buchan. After her uncle had died in 1308 without any issue, she became Countess of Buchan in her own right and her marriage with Henry de Beaumont gave him a claim to the earldom of Buchan. He was joined among many others by his son-in-law, David of Strathbogie, who hoped to recover the earldom of Atholl after its lands had been granted to Sir Neil Campbell in 1314, and Gilbert d'Umfraville, hoping to regain the earldom of Angus which had been granted to Sir John Stewart of Bonkyll in 1329. They planned to invade Scotland by sea, since an expedition north across the border was judged by Edward III as too blatant a breach of the Treaty of Edinburgh between the two countries. Lending some authority to their venture was Edward Balliol, son and heir of John Balliol, who had died in 1313. Even before the expedition set sail in 1332 with eighty-eight ships, he had returned from his family estates in Picardy to England, where he secretly paid homage to Edward III for the kingdom of Scotland that he hoped to win.

Dupplin Moor and Halidon Hill

Although the 'Disinherited' could only muster 500 knights and men-at-arms and perhaps 1,000 foot-soldiers and archers, they landed at Kinghorn in Fife at an opportune moment, since nearly all the chief lieutenants of King Robert the Bruce were now dead. The invading forces marched from Kinghorn by way of Dunfermline towards Perth. They had reached the low banks of the River Earn, a few miles west of the city, when they encountered the hastily raised but much larger forces of the Scottish Crown, ranged against them on the higher ground of Dupplin Moor, north of the river. They were commanded by Donald, Earl of Mar, who had just been made Guardian of the realm in place of Sir Thomas Randolph, Earl of Moray, who had died only a month earlier. The Scottish forces looked forward to an easy victory but allowed themselves to be outwitted, when the 'Disinherited' crossed the river under cover of darkness and took up a stong defensive position to the north. Attacked by the Scots in a confused and disorderly manner, the battle turned into a disaster for the Scots as the English archers took their toll. Donald, Earl of Mar, was killed along with several other earls and high officers of state. Duncan, Earl of Fife, was taken prisoner, and not long afterwards on 24 September 1332, he crowned Edward Balliol as the King of Scotland at Scone.

Edward Balliol only reigned over Scotland for eleven weeks before he was forced to flee the country, after he had nearly been captured at Annan. Nonetheless he now gained the open support of Edward III in pursuing his claim to the Scottish throne. Together they first laid siege to Berwick in early 1333. When the Scots attempted to raise the siege in July 1333, they suffered a crushing defeat at Halidon Hill just outside the town, when five more earls were slain. While Edward III returned south after his victory at Halidon Hill, Edward Balliol was once again established as King of Scotland, and the 'Disinherited' regained their lands. However Henry de Beaumont was disappointed in his claim to the earldom of Buchan, which Edward Balliol granted instead to the Mowbray family, who were like himself allied by marriage to the Comyns. The erstwhile Earl of Buchan retired to Dundarg Castle on the coast of the Moray Firth near Aberdour, which he heavily fortified. Within a few months he was besieged in this stronghold by Sir Andrew Moray, whose father had been Wallace's companion at the battle of Stirling Bridge in 1297.

Renewed Wars of Scottish Independence

Meanwhile Sir Colin Campbell had captured Dunoon Castle with a force of 400 men. This Stewart stronghold had been held for Edward Balliol by David of Strathbogie, after he had regained his earldom of Atholl as one of the 'Disinherited' from John Campbell, who was killed at the battle of Halidon Hill in 1333. Sir Colin Campbell was later rewarded by David II when he was appointed its hereditary keeper, which is an office still held by the Dukes of Argyll. His success prompted the men of Bute to seize Rothesay Castle, which they restored to Robert the High Steward, thus providing him with a base to regain Renfrew and his other possessions in the west of Scotland. Otherwise only the scattered strongholds of Kildrummy, Urquhart, Loch Leven and Loch Doon were held by the Scots, apart from Dumbarton Castle, which sheltered David II and his young queen. They were sent to France for their own safety in 1334.

But Edward Balliol soon found it difficult to rule effectively over the country. He faced an offensive launched by John Randolph, now Earl of Moray after the death of his father and elder brother, and Robert the High Steward, acting together jointly as the Guardians of Scotland. Edward III once again came to the rescue of his protégé. After campaigning in the Borders during the winter of 1334 the English King invaded Scotland from Carlisle with a powerful army of more than 13,000 men in the summer of 1335, while Edward Balliol led a smaller force north from Berwick. After making their headquarters at Perth Edward III offered peace to any Scot who would accept his terms. David of Strathbogie, Earl of Atholl, who had briefly abandoned Balliol's cause, changed sides once again, when he was appointed by Edward III as his Lieutenant in the North. There he besieged Kildrummy Castle, which was held by Christina Bruce, Robert the Bruce's sister, and now the wife of Sir Andrew Moray. This action brought her husband north with 800 men. The two sides encountered one another in the Forest of Culblean near Ballater on St Andrew's Day 1335, when Sir Andrew Moray defeated David of Strathbogie, the erstwhile Earl of Atholl, who it is said was killed defending himself with his back to an oak tree. His death marked the turning point in yet another War of Scottish Independence.

The Scottish Recovery

Thereafter Sir Andrew Moray played a leading role in the struggle against Edward III and Edward Balliol, reverting to the guerilla tactics once employed so successfully against the English by William Wallace and King Robert the Bruce. The tide now turned against the English, even if Edward III came north once again in the summer of 1336. This campaign was marked by his romantic expedition north from Perth with a force of 800 cavalry through Drumochter Pass in four days of forced marches to rescue Katherine de Beaumont, Countess of Atholl, and the daughter of Henry de Beaumont, erstwhile Earl of Buchan. She had sought refuge in Lochindorb Castle after the death of her husband David of Strathbogie at the battle of Culblean, only to be besieged there for the next seven months by Sir Andrew Moray.

After burning Forres and Kinloss and laying waste to the surrounding countryside Edward III returned south by way of Aberdeen, razing its buildings to the ground. Even so the English King was unable to prevent the slow expansion of Scottish power, as each of his strongholds was captured in its turn by forces loyal to Sir Andrew Moray and then destroyed. After returning to Scotland for yet another campaign in 1337, Edward III now embarked on a far greater enterprise than the conquest of Scotland, invading Flanders in 1338 to press his claim to the French throne. It marked the start of the Hundred Years War, which greatly weakened the power of England to attack Scotland, while drawing Scotland into the conflict in support of France by virtue of the Treaty of Corbeil between the two countries. It was perhaps fortunate that Edward III had turned his back on Scotland, since Sir Andrew Moray died in the spring of 1338 thus depriving the country of his leadership. He was succeeded as Guardian of Scotland by Robert the High Steward, who ruled over the country until David II returned from exile in 1341, when Edward Balliol fled across the Border to the safety of England.

David II and his Broken Reign

David II returned in 1341 as a dashing young prince to an impoverished country, racked and weakened by half a century of bitter warfare and civil conflict. Doubtless he hoped to emulate his illustrious father by his own feats of military prowess but he proved himself inadequate to the task. His personal reign began well, when the young King raided Northumberland early in 1342, while the castles at Stirling and Roxburgh were regained by the Scots during the same year. But the troubled state of the country so concerned William, Earl of Sutherland, that he wrote to the Pope in 1342 that 'murders, burnings, depredations, forays and other evils . . . cease not to happen continually, and many churches of these parts have suffered no small damages'. He requested a papal dispensation to marry Margaret, daughter of King Robert the Bruce, and thus the sister of David II. The marriage took place and the Earl of Sutherland received several grants of land in the north to strengthen his position.

Utter disaster struck the country only a few years later when the Treaty of Corbeil drew the Scots into the Anglo-French conflict after the English victory over the French at the battle of Crecy on 26 August 1346. Only a month earlier the Scots had raided Cumberland and Westmoreland and the French defeat at Crecy virtually demanded that they launch another attack upon England. After marching through Cumberland and Westmorland, the Scottish army of only a few thousand men eventually reached the outskirts of Durham, where at Neville's Cross the Scots were heavily defeated by a much larger English army. John Randolph, Earl of Moray, and Sir Maurice Moray, Earl of Strathearn, were slain, along with several of the royal officers of state. The earls of Fife, Menteith and Sutherland were all taken prisoner and the Earl of Menteith was later executed. Even worse David II was himself captured by the English, gravely wounded in the head. Among the Scottish magnates present at the battle, only Robert the High Steward and the Earl of Dunbar escaped from the battlefield, some said with indecent haste.

David II spent the next eleven years in England, while Robert the High Steward ruled as Guardian of Scotland in his absence. Then the Black Death devastated Scotland in 1349, while feuds and dissensions racked the country and its financial administration fell apart. But after protracted negotiations the Scots eventually agreed in 1357 to pay the huge ransom of 100,000 merks for the release of David II, to be paid over ten years, after Edward III had once again invaded Scotland in a devastating campaign known to the Scots as the 'Burnt Candlemass' early in 1356. It followed the dramatic gesture made by Edward Balliol to the English King at Roxburgh, when he removed the crown of Scotland from his head and taking a handful of earth and stones from Scottish soil presented it to Edward III, so resigning his claim to rule over Scotland. It marked the very end of the civil conflict in Scotland between the Bruce and Balliol factions, which had so plagued the country since the death of Alexander III in 1286.

David II was released in 1357, determined to bring law and order to his troubled kingdom. He proved a tough and energetic ruler, but he offended the great magnates by favouring men of lesser status as his councillors, while he summoned burgesses to parliament for the first time. Resenting their loss of influence with the King, dissension came to a head in 1363 when the nobility under the leadership of Robert the High Steward demanded the King's counsellors be dismissed in favour of themselves. However their open resistance to the new order collapsed when David II called their bluff by a show of arms, bolstered by mercenary forces. Yet it did not prevent the northern earls and barons from allying themselves against the interests of the Crown in what became known as the 'Highland Party', refusing for several years to make any payments to the King's ransom.

Accession of Robert II

David II died suddenly in 1371 at the early age of forty-seven, after a broken reign that has often been judged too harshly. As he left no children, despite his two marriages, he was succeeded by his nephew Robert the High Steward, who came to rule over Scotland as the first King of the Stewart dynasty. Even when acting as Guardian of Scotland before David II returned to Scotland in 1341, and later as the King's lieutenant after David II had been captured at the battle of Neville's Cross in 1346, Robert the High Steward had proved himself weak and ineffectual in governing the country.

Matters did not improve greatly after he had gained the throne as Robert II in 1371 at the age of fifty-five. Eventually he became so incapable, perhaps owing to senility, that he was persuaded in 1384 to allow his eldest son John Stewart, Earl of Carrick, to govern the country on his behalf. He later ruled over the country as Robert III of Scotland, after he had abandoned his Christian name, regarded by the Scots as a name of ill-omen. John Stewart, Earl of Carrick, was charged in particular with suppressing the Highland 'caterans', or brigands, whose lawless activities in the north were symptomatic of even more widespread disorder throughout the whole kingdom. It was perhaps a hopeless task since his younger brother Alexander Stewart, Earl of Buchan, and the favourite son of Robert II, was foremost among their leaders as the 'Wolf of Badenoch', despite his official position as Justiciar of the North.

Alexander Stewart, Lord of Badenoch

The turbulent and lawless nature of the Highlands first made itself felt in Moray and its hinterland early in the reign of Robert II. Many years before gaining the throne, Robert the High Steward had married Euphemia Ross as his second wife. She was the daughter of Hugh, Earl of Ross, and the widow of Sir John Randolph, Earl of Moray, who had died at the battle of Neville's Cross in 1346. It seems she brought the Lordship of Badenoch to her second husband as her widow's portion. Even before 1371 Robert the High Steward allowed his fourth son Alexander Stewart to exercise his own powers of lordship over Badenoch, since Alexander entered into an agreement in 1370 with the Bishop of Moray, drawn up at the lordship's *caput* of Ruthven, undertaking to protect the Bishop's lands and men. Then after his accession in 1371 Robert II granted his son the Lordship of Badenoch, with full powers of regality, as well as the lands, forest and castle of Lochindorb, previously held as the *caput* of the Randolphs, Earls of Moray.

Alexander Stewart perhaps hoped to gain the earldom of Moray as well, since three of his brothers were already earls, but it went instead to John Dunbar as the younger grandson of Sir Thomas Randolph, first Earl of Moray. But he did receive the barony of Stratha'an, early in the reign of Robert II, while around the same time he leased the barony of Urquhart from his younger half-brother David Stewart, Earl of Strathearn. He gained even more power and influence in 1372 when he was made King's Lieutenant and Justiciar north of the Moray Firth, and afterwards Justiciar of Scotland north of the Forth, while he was appointed Sheriff of Inverness with its wide powers of jurisdiction throughout the north of Scotland by 1380. In 1382 he married Euphemia Leslie, Countess of Ross in her own right, soon after the death of Sir Walter Leslie, her first husband. Even if the marriage did not last, it brought him ownership of her lands in the earldom of Ross, including the lordship of Skye, the thanage and castle of Dingwall, the barony and sheriffdom of Nairn, and the barony of Kingedward in Aberdeenshire. It gave him supreme power throughout the north of Scotland, exercising vice-regal authority from his castles of Ruthven, Lochindorb, Loch an Eilean, Urquhart, Inverness and Dingwall. Since the barony of Kingedward comprised much of the ancient earldom of Buchan, he styled himself Earl of Buchan and Lord of the earldom of Ross.

Alexander Stewart, Lord of Badenoch, was not much opposed in his rise to supreme power by any other magnates in the north. The earldom of Ross had passed from its ancient line in 1372, so that Sir Walter Leslie as the first husband of Euphemia Ross, Countess of Ross in her own right, lacked any territorial basis of power within the earldom of Ross. He was simply a much-favoured courtier of David II, who it seems spent much of the 1370s abroad on military service, fighting for the French. Equally John Dunbar, now Earl of Moray after the death of John Randolph at the battle of Neville's Cross in 1346, was yet another outsider, more concerned with his southern interests and otherwise engaged in fighting the English along the Borders in the late 1380s. Indeed the earldom of Moray now consisted of little more than the coastal lowlands along the southern shores of the Moray Firth, rendering it especially vulnerable to attack from the Highlands.

Quarrels with the Bishop of Moray

Rather than facing the opposition of other local magnates, the sweeping powers of regality claimed by Alexander Stewart as Lord of Badenoch were challenged by Alexander Bur, Bishop of Moray. The quarrel itself arose from the conflicting claims between the two men for jurisdiction over the Bishop's territories, previously exercised by Sir Thomas Randolph under the powers of regality granted to him in 1312 as the first Earl of Moray. This grant of Moray was however limited to the heirs-male of Randolph's body, so legally such powers of jurisdiction over the bishopric of Moray had lapsed when his younger son John Randolph, third Earl of Moray, was killed at the battle of Neville's Cross in 1346, leaving no male descendants. Evidently the Bishop of Moray, appointed in 1362, was eager to win back the former independence of his bishopric as it had existed before even the earldom of Moray was created. The Bishop was able to resist the legal arguments of Alexander Stewart, who threatened him with forfeiture of all his episcopal lands in Badenoch, but he was forced to surrender his territories of Rothiemurchus in Strathspey, and Abriachan to the west of Loch Ness, into the hands of 'the magnificent, noble and powerful lord Alexander Stewart, earl of Buchan'.

Alexander Stewart gained other lands in these years before his downfall, since he was granted the barony of Abernethy with rights of regality which removed it from the earldom of Moray in 1384, along with the barony of Dochfour at the head of Loch Ness in 1386. By then however the council-general of the kingdom had begun to criticise him for his lack of concern with the due processes of law, after various disputes had broken out over the tenure of his lands. Given the lawless state of the Highlands, which Alexander Stewart seemed unable to contain, despite his position as Justiciar of Scotland north of the Forth, as well as Sheriff of Inverness, the council-general ordered John Stewart, Earl of Carrick, and now the King's lieutenant, to go north with sufficient men to see that justice was done.

There matters rested until late in 1388, when Robert II's second son Robert Stewart, Earl of Fife and Menteith, and afterwards Duke of Albany, was made the King's lieutenant in place of John Stewart, Earl of Carrick, now crippled by the kick of a horse. The same meeting of the council-general dismissed his younger brother Alexander Stewart, Lord of Badenoch, from his post as Justiciar north of the Forth and perhaps appointed Thomas Dunbar, eldest son of John Dunbar, Earl of Moray, as Sheriff of Inverness in his place. Justifying their actions the council-general accused Alexander Stewart of 'being negligent in the execution of his office', judging him with such scathing words as 'useless to the community'. Six months later Robert Stewart, Earl of Fife and Menteith, appointed his eldest son Murdach Stewart as Justicar north of the Forth.

Meanwhile Alexander Stewart had abandoned his wife Euphemia Leslie, Countess of Ross, in favour of a lady called Mairead, daughter of Eachann, often said to be the daughter of Iye Mackay of Strathnaver, despite the lack of any evidence. Alexander Bur, Bishop of Moray, now exercised his spiritual powers over Alexander Stewart, Lord of Badenoch, by persuading him to return to his lawful wife, who was perhaps more interested in regaining the revenues from her estates than her conjugal rights. No doubt Alexander Stewart felt humiliated by this marital settlement, coming as it did just a year after he had lost all his royal offices of state. But then yet another blow to his pride occurred early in 1390, when the Bishop of Moray entered into an indenture with Thomas Dunbar, now Sheriff of Inverness, who agreed to defend the Bishop's possessions and men in return for an annual payment.

Their agreement could have even been directed against Alexander Stewart himself, who had perhaps threatened the Bishop of Moray with revenge for all the humiliations he had received at the Bishop's hands. After all, twenty years earlier, he had entered into just such an agreement with the very same Bishop of Moray, ordering all his own friends and men to protect the Bishop's men and lands, especially in Badenoch and Strathspey, as if they were his own. It was evidently this final insult to his obvious pride and fiery temper that prompted him to launch a series of furious and devastating attacks upon the lowlands of Moray, accompanied by his 'wyld, wykkyd Heland-men', shortly after his father Robert II had died in 1390. They earned him lasting notoriety as the 'Wolf of Badenoch'.

Raids on Forres and Elgin

He first attacked Forres in late May, destroying the town, the choir of St Lawrence's church and the archdeacon's house. Then, emboldened by the success of this raid, he put Elgin to the torch on 17 June 1390. It was perhaps even a grotesque joke on his part, since his teinds as lord of Rothiemurchus had gone for the last 150 years to provide the candles for lighting Elgin cathedral. Maybe he saw himself as fulfilling his responsibility once and for ever.

> [He] burned the whole town of Elgin and the Church of St Giles in it, the hospice beside Elgin, eighteen noble and beautiful mansions of canons and chaplains and, what gives most bitter pain, the noble and beautiful church of Moray, the beacon of the countryside and ornament of the kingdom, with all the books, charters and other goods of the countryside preserved there.

It was a horrendous act of utter sacrilege for which he was sentenced to immediate excommunication by the Church.

The Bishop of Moray was determined to receive full reparation for the great damage done to the cathedral church of Elgin. Soon afterwards Alexander Stewart was brought before his brothers Robert III and Robert Stewart, Earl of Fife and Menteith, along with the other members of the royal council, and forced into submission. He agreed to give full satisfaction to the Church to compensate it for his behaviour, whereupon he was absolved of all his crimes, while the penalty of excommunication against him was lifted. Two years later Euphemia Leslie, Countess of Ross, petitioned for divorce, arguing that her marriage with the 'Wolf of Badenoch' had been 'the cause of wars, plunderings, arson, murders and many other damages and scandals, and it is likely that more will happen if they remain united'. Her petition was granted so that Alexander Stewart lost the earldom of Ross with all its territories. He was deprived of the barony of Urquhart around the same time, while he later lost the barony of Dochfour in 1394 when it was granted by Thomas Dunbar, now Earl of Moray after his father's death in 1392, to Alexander MacDonald, Lord of Keppoch.

Thereafter Alexander Stewart, Lord of Badenoch and still Earl of Buchan, held the lowly office of baillie to the earldom of Atholl before his death in 1405, after which the earldom of Buchan passed to his nephew

John Stewart, as the younger son of Robert Stewart, Duke of Albany. He was laid to rest behind the high altar of Dunkeld Cathedral where his effigy can still be seen. His tumultuous career, culminating in the sacking of the cathedral of Elgin, suggests that he was powerful enough to place himself above the forces of law and order in the Highlands. Yet arguably he acted out of weakness, fearful of losing the powerful position he had perhaps only established for himself as the favourite son of Robert II, or so Alexander Grant has suggested in his account of the 'Wolf of Badenoch'. Certainly he never seems to have exercised his powers effectively as Justiciar north of the Forth and Sheriff of Inverness, since this was the charge repeatedly made against him. Even as a feudal overlord he perhaps lacked the firm basis of kinship which made the ancient earldoms of Scotland so strong, and which was later to prove equally strong a basis for the clan system in the Highlands.

Raid on Angus and its Aftermath

Indeed to judge by the further disorders that broke out in the Highlands after 1390, it seems that Alexander Stewart could not even resolve the feuds that broke out under his own jurisdiction as Lord of Badenoch. Duncan and Robert Stewart as two of his natural sons by Mairead, daughter of Eachann, were almost certainly among the leaders of the Highland 'caterans' who raided Angus in 1392. This armed incursion ended in what was virtually a full-scale battle at Glasclune near Blairgowrie, or perhaps farther north in Glen Brerachan. Sir Walter Ogilvie, Sheriff of Angus, and several other knights-at-arms, together with sixty of their followers, were slain fighting a force of 300 or more Highlandmen. Badly wounded in the battle, Sir Patrick Grey and Sir David Lindsay of Glenesk managed to escape with their lives.

According to the chronicle of Wyntoun, written before 1425, the raid on Angus arose from a 'great discord' between Sir David Lindsay of Glenesk and the chief of the 'Duncansons', as Clan Donnachie or the Robertsons of Struan were then known. Their dispute was apparently over lands that Sir David Lindsay had inherited in Strathnairn from his mother, which were also claimed by Robert de Atholia, who had married another daughter and co-heiress of Sir James Stirling of Glenesk. Indeed he was among the raiders, along with Patrick and Stewart Duncanson. The government reacted by outlawing twenty-two people, putting them to the horn, who were each named in the first recorded instance of what later became known as a Letter of Horning. This was simply a royal decree read out after three blasts had been sounded on a horn.

Four years later an even more notorious event was staged in 1396 as the battle of the Clans upon the North Inch at Perth, when a judicial trial by combat was fought between two clans. Robert III was present, along with many other noblemen and knights, not just from Scotland but from England and France as well. The combatants were variously known to the medieval chroniclers as Clan Qwhewyl or Clan Quhele, later identified as Clan Chattan by Hector Boece, but perhaps then only by the mistaken reading of an earlier Gaelic manuscript, and Claninchya, Clan Ha or Clan Kay, often identified on very little evidence as a sept of Clan Cameron.

Early Feuds in Lochaber

Certainly there was a bitter feud then raging between the MacIntoshes, chiefs of Clan Chattan, and the Camerons, which had arisen much earlier over the lands of Glenloy and Locharkaig. Traditionally they had belonged to the ancestors of the Camerons, who indeed occupied them, but they were granted in 1336 to the MacIntoshes by John MacDonald, first Lord of the Isles. He was then acting under the authority of Edward Balliol, who had made him Lord of Lochaber as the ward of the young son and heir of David of Strathbogie, the erstwhile Earl of Atholl. However Clan Chattan as the ancestors of the MacIntoshes maintained an even earlier claim to these lands, which they had perhaps once inhabited, long before they settled in Badenoch. But they were unable to dislodge the Camerons, who held on to their territories by force of arms, even though David II had confirmed their legal right to these lands in 1359. This feud between the Camerons and the MacIntoshes lasted for more than three centuries and what were virtually full-scale battles were occasionally fought between them.

One such conflict occurred in 1370 at Invernahavon near Newtonmore, where the Spey is joined by the River Truim, flowing north from its head-waters below Drumochter Pass. A raiding party of Camerons, 400 strong, was surprised by Clan Chattan as they returned with their booty from an attack on Badenoch. It is said that Lachlan MacIntosh as the captain of Clan Chattan was accompanied by the chieftains of MacPherson and Davidson, who both claimed the right to command the right wing. The MacPhersons took offence when MacIntosh decided in favour of the Davidsons and with-drew from the battle, which was then joined. Deprived of their support Clan Chattan was close to defeat after nearly all the Davidson clansmen had been killed. But then, taunted for cowardice, the MacPhersons attacked the Camerons, turning defeat into victory. According to some historians such animosity erupted again in 1396 when the judicial combat was fought on the North Inch of Perth between the MacPhersons and the Davidsons, rather than the Camerons and Clan Chattan. But other historians follow Wyntown and the other chroniclers, who later identified Clan Chattan and the Camerons as the combatants in the battle of the Clans, perhaps influenced by the protracted feud still raging between them.

Battle of the Clans

However the chronicles give conflicting and mutually contradictory accounts of the two clans, so their identity is best judged from the historical circumstances. *The Book of Pluscarden*, dating from the fifteenth century, implies the battle of the Clans was connected with the earlier raid upon Angus, when the chieftains of Clan Qwhewyl were among those put to the horn as a result. The trial by combat itself was arranged by Thomas Dunbar, Earl of Moray, and Sir David Lindsay of Glenesk, perhaps acting as the feudal superiors of the two clans in question. It was further said that the clans could not resolve a serious feud between them, which disturbed the whole country north of the Mounth.

Thirty men were chosen from each clan, armed with swords, battle-axes, cross-bows with three arrows and dirks, but without any armour. Their leaders were said to be Christy Johnesone and Scha Ferqwhareisone, or Shaw, Farquhar's son. One combatant apparently escaped by swimming across the River Tay, when his place was taken by a volunteer from the same clan, at least according to the later accounts. Nearly all of Clan Ha were slain, apart from for one or two survivors, while only ten or eleven survived at the very most from the ranks of Clan Qwhewyl, even if the volunteer escaped with his life. Whether this trial by combat settled the dispute is not recorded, but it was said that the Highlands remained at peace for many years afterwards.

Sir Iain Moncrieffe of that Ilk (1967) has argued that Clan Qwhewyl were most likely to be the Cummings of Altyre, rather than a sept of Clan Chattan such as the Shaws or the MacIntoshes, as usually thought. Indeed Clanchewill is even named in 1594 along with Clan Chattane and Clan Chamron as a quite separate clan but there is no mention of the Cummings. They claim descent from Sir Robert Comyn, uncle of John Comyn the younger of Badenoch, who died defending his nephew when he was attacked and killed by Robert the Bruce in February 1306. Equally the identity of Clan Ha, otherwise known as Clan Kay, remains a mystery. The Cummings of Altyre were the traditional enemies of the MacIntoshes of Rothiemurchus, who rallied to the support of King Robert the Bruce after 1306, even though they had earlier served as stewards to the Comyns, Lords of Badenoch. Many years later the Cummings of Altyre had seized Rait Castle, after it had been granted to the MacIntoshes by Sir David Lindsay of Glenesk as the overlord of Strathnairn. It was perhaps this dispute which the battle of the Clans was intended to settle in 1396, or so Sir Iain Moncrieffe of that Ilk (1967) has argued. If so, it apparently continued until 1442, when the MacIntoshes slaughtered nearly all the Cummings of Altyre at what was intended to be a feast of reconciliation and finally gained possession of Rait Castle.

Alexander Stewart, Earl of Mar

Meanwhile Sir Alexander Stewart as the eldest son of the 'Wolf of Badenoch' had gained the earldom of Mar, even before his father's death in 1405. The ancient earls of Mar had died out in 1374, when the title passed first to the last earl's sister Margaret and her husband Sir Willliam Douglas, created Earl of Douglas in 1357. The title then passed after her death to her daughter Isabella, who thus became the Countess of Mar in her own right. Her first husband died in suspicious circumstances and afterwards she attracted the attentions of Sir Alexander Stewart, described as a 'young man of wild tendencies'. He seized her person in 1404, along with Kildrummy Castle, which he besieged with a force of Highland 'caterans', intending to force her into marriage. Indeed she agreed a contract of marriage, designed to bring him and his heirs the rich prize of the earldom of Mar and her other lands in the Lordship of Garioch. But his plans received a setback when Robert III refused to confirm the marriage between them, so rendering it invalid.

The erstwhile Earl of Mar was thus forced a few weeks later to enter into a quite spurious ceremony of marriage, watched by a distinguished company of invited guests. He first surrendered the keys to Kildrummy Castle to the Countess of Mar, who then chose him of her own free will as her husband, making over to him the earldom of Mar and all her other lands. He then embarked on a distinguished career as a professional soldier, especially in Flanders, returning to Scotland in 1409 after his wife had died. Two years later, at the battle of Harlaw, he commanded the forces that repulsed Donald, second Lord of the Isles, in his advance against the city of Aberdeen. After James I had returned to Scotland in 1424, he became the King's confidant and soon afterwards received a charter to the earldom of Mar and Lordship of Garioch in 1426. Another charter granted him the Lordship of Badenoch in the following year, but it seems quite likely that he had acted as its Lord ever since his father's death in 1405. It was during these years that he became the chief agent of the government in the Highlands, who 'ruled with acceptance nearly all the north of the country beyond the Mounth', according to Bower. Indeed along with David Stewart, Earl of Caithness, he was the commander of the royalist forces defeated by Donald Balloch at the battle of Inverlochy in 1431. He died four years later in 1435, leaving no descendants, when James I ignored the claims of Sir Robert Erskine to the earldom of Mar, which remained vested in the Crown until 1458.

Alexander MacDonald, Earl of Ross

Two years after the death of Alexander Stewart, Earl of Mar, his powerful position in the Highlands was taken by Alexander MacDonald, third Lord of the Isles. He succeeded in his claim to the earldom of Ross, which he was granted in 1437 soon after the assassination of James I. Not long afterwards he was made Justiciar of Scotland north of the Forth, and his name appears frequently in the official records during these years while James II was still a minor. As the earldoms of Moray and Buchan remained vacant he was now among the most powerful magnates in the kingdom. Indeed he had apparently entered into a treasonable 'band' with William, eighth Earl of Douglas, and David Lindsay, Earl of Crawford, or his son Alexander, binding them to act together in a defensive and offensive pact against all other men, not even excluding the King. Alexander MacDonald died in 1449, when his son and heir John MacDonald was only fifteen years of age. As we shall see, only two years later he rebelled against James II, even if he escaped the destruction that the King later wreaked on the earls of Douglas and their allies.

Rise of the Gordons, Earls of Huntly

It was the Gordons who ultimately profited from these events. Their original lands of Strathbogie had already been greatly augmented in 1380 when the great-grandson of the first Gordon to settle in the north married Elizabeth Keith, fourth daughter of Sir William Keith, Marischal of Scotland. She brought her husband the valuable lands of Aboyne, Glen Tanar and Glen Muick in Aberdeenshire. Even though Sir Adam Gordon had a son John by his wife Elizabeth, he had died without any issue by 1408, when he was succeeded by his sister Elizabeth Gordon. She became the ward of Sir William Seton of that Ilk, who married her to his second son Alexander Seton. Having fought alongside Alexander Stewart, Earl of Mar, at the battle of Harlaw in 1411, and knighted soon afterwards, Sir Alexander Seton then visited James I in France where the Scots King was held captive by the English. He later negotiated the King's release in 1424, surrendering himself briefly as a hostage for the payment of the King's ransom. After his own death he was succeeded by his eldest son and namesake Sir Alexander Seton, who was created first Earl of Huntly in 1445 during the turbulent regency of William, eighth Earl of Douglas, and his allies, the Livingstons. The newly created Earl of Huntly took his title from his lands of Huntly in Berwickshire and it was only later that the town of Huntly came to be so named. He later adopted the family name of Gordon by which his descendants became known. Even before his elevation to the peerage, he had received the barony of Kingedward in life-rent from Alexander MacDonald, third Lord of the Isles, and Earl of Ross, so adding further to his territories.

Not long after he had been raised to the peerage Sir Alexander Seton, first Earl of Huntly, was staying as a guest of the Ogilvies, from whom he held lands, when he became involved in a quarrel with the Lindsays and their Douglas allies. It concerned the appointment of Sir Alexander Lindsay, Master of Crawford, and known later as the 'Tiger Earl', as justiciar to the Abbey of Arbroath, only to be ousted from his office by Sir Alexander Ogilvie of Inverquharity. As he was still digesting his meal, the newly created Earl of Huntly felt obliged by the customs of the time to accompany his hosts when the two factions marched early in 1446 to an armed confrontation outside the gates of Arbroath. There, David Lindsay, third Earl of Crawford and married to an Ogilvie, was inadvertently killed, attempting to avert hostilities between the two sides. The Earl of Huntly was forced to flee with his Ogilvie hosts after 500 of their number died in the fighting that then erupted.

Earls of Huntly, 'Cocks o' the North'

Since David Lindsay, third Earl of Crawford, was an ally of the Earls of Douglas, the affray at Arbroath virtually forced the newly created Earl of Huntly into the opposite camp, where he found himself among the most loyal supporters of the young King. He greatly benefited from such loyalty when James II granted him the Lordship of Badenoch with its castle at Ruthven in April 1451. It now seems likely that this grant was made only a month after John MacDonald, fourth Lord of the Isles, and the Earl of Ross, had rebelled, or so Alexander Grant (1993) has argued. He was most likely charged as the new Lord of Badenoch with preventing the rebellion from spreading any farther, and perhaps he was made Lieutenant-General of the North in the same year. He was certainly acting in this capacity when he defeated Alexander Lindsay, fourth Earl of Crawford, at the battle of Brechin in 1452, after he had revolted against the Crown in support of the Douglases. Sir Alexander Seton, first Earl of Huntly, then received the lands of Enzie in Banffshire, lying on the eastern bank of the River Spey near its mouth, which he certainly held by 1458, perhaps as a reward for this victory. By then, after taking the family name of Gordon, held afterwards by his descendants, he was among the greatest magnates in the north-east of Scotland. Soon afterwards his eldest son married Annabella, youngest of James I's many daughters. He succeeded to the earldom in 1470 and afterwards acted as Justiciar of Scotland north of the Forth and then as High Chancellor of Scotland. His successors wielded so much power as the king's Lieutenants in the North among their many other offices that the Gordons became known as the 'Cocks o' the North'. They came to rival the Campbell earls of Argyll in their vice-regal powers, at least in the years before the Scottish Reformation of 1560, even if they afterwards suffered from their attachment to the Catholic religion.

The Northern Earldoms

Beyond the earldom of Ross, north of the Dornoch Firth and the valley of the River Okyell, the lands of Caithness and Sutherland existed as a quite separate province of Scotland for much of the Middle Ages, hardly affected by events farther south. Its history was dominated by the earls of Sutherland, descendants of Freskyn of Duffus in the senior line, since the ancient earldom of Caithness was broken apart by dynastic misfortune during the fourteenth century. Indeed the lands of Caithness passed by marriage into the hands of such families as the Keiths of Inverugie and the Sutherlands of Duffus, descended from a junior line of the Earls of Sutherland, as well as the Sinclairs of Roslin, who became the earls of Orkney under the Norwegian Crown after 1379 and eventually the earls of Caithness in 1455.

Much of the history of Caithness and Sutherland during these years is dominated by the almost constant feuds that these various families waged against one another. The **MacKays** of Strathnaver were often at the centre of these conflicts. Although their origins are clouded in obscurity, they claim descent from Iye, whose name is a corrupt form of *Aodh* or *Aedh*. It is said he was the son or nephew of Kenneth macHeth, who lost his life in the MacWilliam rebellion of 1215. The name of MacKay is an anglicised version of MacAoidh in modern Gaelic, meaning 'the son of Aodh', while Aodh comes from the earlier name Aed or Aedh, which was later spelt as Heth. Why MacAoidh became MacKay is simply a quirk of pronunciation, since Aedh came to be spoken as a mere grunt. All this perhaps lends credence to the traditional claim by the MacKays that they were descended from the MacHeths of Moray with their hereditary claims to the Scottish throne.

Indeed the forbears of Clan MacKay could well be the original inhabitants of Moray who it is said were expelled by Malcolm IV in 1160, if they had found refuge in what eventually become their ancestral lands of Strathnaver. Fordun later described them as 'removed from the lands of their birth, just as Nebuchadnezzar, king of Babylon, had dealt with the Jews . . . , so that not even one native of Moray still lived there'. Even so the near contemporary Chronicle of Holyrood records what happened in only four cryptic words, simply stating in Latin 'king Malcolm moved Moray-men'. It was perhaps only later that the story became embellished by such chroniclers as Fordun.

It is perhaps just as likely that the followers of Malcolm macHeth and his descendants sought refuge in Strathnaver and elsewhere, after the failure of their various revolts against the Scottish Crown. Indeed local traditions suggest that Harald Maddadson retreated north by way of Strathnaver after his revolt of 1196 in support of the MacHeth claim and it was there that he was defeated by William the Lion and his army. Another revolt is recorded in 1223, when royal troops pursued the insurgents into Strathnaver and hanged several of their ringleaders. But the inhabitants of Moray could equally well have settled in Ross when Malcolm IV released Malcolm macHeth from captivity in 1157, before they later retreated northwards into Strathnaver in face of the feudalising pressures exerted by William the Lion and his immediate successors, where they established themselves as the MacKays.

Early History of the MacKays

Little is known of the early history of the MacKays, but by 1428 it was reported to James I that they were able to raise 4,000 men from their territories. Indeed when William, fifth Earl of Sutherland, obtained a papal dispensation in 1343 to marry Mary Bruce, sister of David II of Scotland, and youngest daughter of King Robert the Bruce, it described the disturbed state of the country, racked by 'wars, disputes, and many offences, on which account, murders, burnings, depredations, forays, and other evils have frequently happened . . . by the wicked procurings of an ancient enemy'. It is most likely that this ancient enemy of the Sutherland family were none other than the MacKays, who even then disturbed the peace in the far north.

Nearly thirty years later in 1370 an attempt was made to end their protracted feud when Iye MacKay, Chief of MacKay, and his son Donald were given safe-conducts allowing them to come to a meeting at Dingwall with William, fifth Earl of Sutherland, and his brother Nicholas, ancestor of the Sutherlands of Duffus. Despite their safety being guaranteed, both the MacKays, father and son, were murdered in cold blood by Nicholas Sutherland of Duffus, perhaps when it seemed likely that they might succeed in whatever territorial claim they had put forward. Soon afterwards the Earl of Sutherland died as well, perhaps murdered in revenge.

The fifth Earl of Sutherland had been greatly favoured by David II, who indeed hoped that his nephew John Sutherland, born of the Earl's marriage with his sister Mary, would succeed him upon the throne of Scotland. However he died of the plague in 1361 and David II was succeeded instead by his nephew, who then ruled over Scotland as Robert II after 1371. He evidently favoured the MacKay family, rather than the Sutherlands, since his favorite physician was Farquhar the Leech, younger son of Iye MacKay of Strathnaver. He was granted a royal charter to the lands of Melness and Hope in 1379, while he afterwards received another charter in 1386 to the little islands of Strathnaver.

Iye MacKay was succeeded in 1370 as chief of MacKay by his grandson Angus. He married a daughter of Torquil MacLeod of Lewis, who had been granted the lands of Assynt by David II in 1343. Angus MacKay died in

1403, when a violent conflict erupted between his own family and their MacLeod in-laws. His widow was apparently offended by his younger brother Huistean Dubh MacKay, acting as tutor to her young son Angus *Dubh* MacKay. Her brother Malcolm MacLeod invaded the MacKay lands of Braechat, laying waste the country and seizing much plunder. Returning to Assynt with their spoils, the raiding party was surprised by the MacKay forces at Tuiteam Tarvach in Strathoykell and nearly all the MacLeods were slaughtered, including Malcolm MacLeod himself.

Feuds with the Sutherlands of Duffus

Not long after Angus *Dubh* MacKay came of age he was defeated near Dingwall in 1411 by the forces of Donald MacDonald of Harlaw, second Lord of the Isles, who had invaded Ross in pursuit of his claim to the earldom. Taken prisoner during the battle he evidently came to terms with Donald MacDonald, whose sister Elizabeth he is said to have married. Angus *Dubh* MacKay later received a charter from his brother-in-law to the lands of Strath Halladale and Creich. Angus *Dubh* MacKay was now strong enough to pursue his family's ancient quarrel with the earls of Sutherland, and especially its feud with the Sutherlands of Duffus, seeking revenge for his grandfather's murder. After first raiding the Sutherland lands of Duffus in Moray, he then invaded their territories in Caithness, gained by marriage with an heiress of the Cheynes. His campaign ended at the pitched battle of Harpsdale, fought in 1426 just two miles south of Halkirk, even if it is not certain who gained the victory. Two years later James I held a parliament at Inverness where he detained many of the Highland chiefs, including Angus *Dubh* MacKay. Even if he was later released, his eldest son Neil MacKay was held hostage on the Bass Rock for his father's obedience to the Crown, after which he became known as Neil *Vass* MacKay.

Nevertheless it was not long before the MacKays resumed their lawless ways, when Thomas MacKay of Creich, first cousin of Angus *Dubh* MacKay of Strathnaver, and a powerful man in his own right, attacked Mowat of Freswick near Tain. Forcing him to seek sanctuary in the church of St Duthus, Thomas MacKay set it alight, burning Mowat and his party to death. Holding lands in Caithness and Moray, it is quite likely that the Mowats were the allies of the Sutherlands of Duffus as their close neighbours in both these districts. Thomas MacKay of Creich was promptly outlawed for this act of sacrilege, which greatly angered James I. As fate would have it both his brothers were married to daughters of Angus Moray of Culbin, himself closely related to the Sutherlands of Duffus. Divided from their clan they were persuaded to betray their own brother. Thomas MacKay of Creich was captured by Angus Moray of Culbin and taken to Inverness, where he was beheaded. His lands were divided in 1430 between the two brothers and their father-in-law, Angus Moray of Culbin. He was now determined to attack the MacKays in their heartland of Strathnaver in revenge for their earlier raid against Moray.

Battle of Drum nan Coup

Raising a force of 1,500 men in 1433, Angus Moray of Culbin and his two MacKay sons-in-law crossed the Crask and sweeping north around Ben Loyal reached within two miles of the MacKay stronghold at Castle Varrich, overlooking the Kyle of Tongue. They were only stopped by the MacKay forces at Drum nan Coup, just south of Loch Hakel. The two armies were evenly matched but the MacKays were still fresh. Attacking from a defensive position they first discharged volleys of arrows and then drove the enemy downhill. Angus Moray of Culbin and his two MacKay sons-in-law were killed, along with nearly all their men, as they attempted to escape over the slopes of Ben Loyal. It is said that only nine Morays escaped south with their lives. Owing to age and infirmity Angus *Dubh* MacKay of Strathnaver did not take part in the battle, which he watched from a litter, but he was killed by an arrow as he was carried away from the field.

The death of Angus *Dubh* MacKay in 1433 left his son Neil *Vass* MacKay to succeed him as the chief of the MacKays. Still held prisoner on the Bass Rock, the young chief managed to escape soon after the murder of James I in 1437. Returning north to Strathnaver he found that the men of Caithness had launched an attack against Strathnaver after the battle of Drum nan Coup in 1433, which however was repulsed at Tom nan Dris in Strath Halladale. Neil *Vass* MacKay then joined with his younger brother Ian Aberach in yet another expedition against Caithness in 1437. Penetrating as far east as Thurso they fell back to Sandside, just west of Dounreay, where they turned and defeated once again the men of Caithness in what was probably another blow in their bitter feud with the Sutherlands of Duffus.

Gunns and the Keiths

It was around this time that the MacKays allied themselves with the Keiths of Ackergill, as the Keiths of Inverugie were known in Caithness, when they came into conflict with the **Gunns**. They take their Norse name from Gunni, son of Olav, or so it is said. The family traditions once identified him with a younger son of Olav the Black, Norse King of Man, who died in 1237, but the Orkneyinga Saga makes him a grandson of Swein Asleifsson, last of the Vikings, who was killed in 1171 whilst on a raid against Dublin. Gunni's wife Ragnhild inherited great estates in Caithness and Sutherland after her brother, Earl Harald the Younger, was killed fighting Harald Maddadson in 1198. Little is known of the early history of Gunni's descendants, except that his son Snaekoll Gunnison was among the murderers of Earl John Haraldson in 1231. Even so the family still retained their vast estates in the north of Scotland during the time of the Angus earls of Caithness, stretching from their stronghold at Halberry Head, north of Lybster, to Dirliot Castle around the headwaters of the River Thurso. Afterwards they lost much of their territories to their more powerful neighbours, until they only held the hinterland of Braemore along the borders between Caithness and Sutherland, and the Strath of Kildonan.

Tradition has it that the feud between the Gunns and the Keiths first erupted when Duncan Keith of Ackergill abducted Helen, daughter of Lachlan Gunn. She killed herself by throwing herself from the battlements of Ackergill Tower after she had been ravished by the 'brutal and licentious Keith'. The first skirmish recorded in this feud supposedly occurred in 1438 when the MacKays marched across country to attack the Gunns at Tannach Moor, just south of Wick, and defeated them with heavy losses. It is said that another battle was fought later at the Hill O'Many Stanes near Clyth, when the Gunns avenged this defeat by the Keiths and their allies, the MacKays. Afterwards the feud between the Gunns and the Keiths reached a bloody climax at the Chapel of St Tear near Ackergill, most likely in 1464.

There are conflicting accounts of what exactly happened, but all agree that the Gunns were tricked by the Keiths. Tradition has it that the heads of the two families agreed to meet peacefully to settle their differences, attended by only twelve horsemen on each side. George Gunn the Crowner duly kept the appointment as arranged, but when the Keiths reached the rendezvous, two men were seen mounted on each horse, so that the Gunns were out-numbered. Seeking sanctuary in the chapel itself, George Gunn the Crowner was killed along with several of his sons. It is said that the surviving Gunns took their revenge the very same night at Dirlot Castle, when they killed the Keith chieftain by shooting him with an arrow through an open window, piercing his heart. It is perhaps more likely that fifty years passed before the Gunns waylaid the Keiths of Ackergill in an ambush and slaughtered them all, so bringing their ancient line to an end. After the death of George Gunn the Crowner, his descendants lost their independence, forced to become the vassals of their more powerful neighbours, who held their lands by feudal charter.

The lawless state of the country during these years perhaps arose from the absence in England of John, seventh Earl of Sutherland. Held hostage at Pontefract Castle for many years after 1427 to guarantee the payment of James I's ransom, he was only released after 1445, when he returned north with an English bride. Equally the earldom of Caithness had been granted out twice since it was forfeited in 1344 by Malise, Earl of Strathearn, firstly in 1375 to David Stewart, Earl of Strathearn, who was succeeded by his daughter Euphemia after his death in 1389, and then in 1401 to his brother Walter Stewart, Earl of Atholl. Both men were presumably more concerned with their southern territories, closer to the centres of power, and indeed the earldom of Caithness was almost an honorific title by this time, lacking much territory. Then after passing briefly in 1428 to Walter Stewart's youngest son Alan Stewart, who was killed at the battle of Inverlochy in 1431, the earldom itself was forfeited in 1437 after the downfall of Walter Stewart, Earl of Atholl, implicated in the murder of James I. It was only in 1455, after it had been held very briefly by George Crichton, that the earldom of Caithness was granted to William Sinclair, Earl of Orkney and Lord Chancellor of Scotland.

Sinclairs, Earls of Caithness

According to their traditions the **Sinclairs** first brought their name to England from Saint-Clair-sur-Elle in Normandy during the Norman Conquest of 1066. They first appear in Scotland during the reign of David I, while they were granted the barony of Roslin just south of Edinburgh in 1163. A century later Sir William Sinclair came to exercise great power during the reign of Alexander III, when he was made sheriff of Edinburgh, Linlithgow, Haddington and Dumfries, and Justiciar of Galloway. After the Wars of Scottish Independence, the Sinclairs rose to great prominence in the far north of Scotland after his grandson Sir William Sinclair married Isabel, daughter and co-heiress of Earl Malise of Strathearn, Caithness and Orkney, who was forfeited in 1344. Their son Henry Sinclair was recognised in 1379 as the first of the Sinclair earls of Orkney under the Norwegian Crown.

The Sinclair family held the Norse earldom of Orkney for three generations until 1470, when William Sinclair, third Earl of Orkney of his line, and already Earl of Caithness under the Scottish Crown, resigned his title into the hands of James III, soon after Scotland had gained sovereignty over Orkney and Shetland in 1468. The Sinclair earls of Caithness afterwards rose to very great power in the far north during the sixteenth century by virtue of their lands, as well as holding the offices of justicar, chamberlain and sheriff for all the bishopric of Caithness north of the Dornoch Firth. Even if they afterwards fought a losing battle against the Gordon earls of Sutherland in the early seventeenth century, they continued to hold the earldom until 1765, despite a brief interlude in the years after 1677 when the title was claimed by John Campbell of Glenorchy, afterwards Earl of Breadalbane.

Feud with the Rosses

Meanwhile Neil *Vass* MacKay died around 1460, when he was succeeded by his eldest son Angus Roy. It seems likely that Angus Roy MacKay came to terms with the Sutherlands of Duffus, since he allowed his daughter to marry Sutherland of Dirlot, who was a scion of that family. He may well have realised that the creation of William Sinclair as Earl of Caithness in 1455 had changed the balance of power in the far north. Whatever the reason Angus Roy MacKay now embarked on a feud with the Rosses of Balnagown, most likely over their claim to the lands of Creich. Attempting to reclaim these lands, he eventually penetrated deep into Ross in 1486 after much mutual raiding had taken place. His foray south ended in disaster when he was overwhelmed at Tarbet and burnt to death in the church where he had taken sanctuary.

The next year the MacKays avenged the death of their chief at the battle of Alt'a Charrais, north of Strath Oykell, where the Rosses of Balnagown were put to flight, and Alexander Ross, laird of Balnagown, was slain along with seventeen other landed gentlemen and a great number of common soldiers. After James IV had ascended the throne in 1488 their dispute came to the attention to the King, acting through his brother James, now Duke of Ross. The lands of Strathoykell and Strathcarron, which had once belonged to Thomas MacKay of Creich, were granted in 1490 to David Ross, heir of the Rosses of Balnagown. Iye Roy MacKay was now chief of the MacKays following the murder of his father at Tarbet in 1486. He probably led yet another raid against the Rosses of Balnagown, which took place in 1493. Even so it was only a year later that he received a pardon for all his crimes from James IV. He in turn bound himself to the King's service for maintaining law and order in the far north, for which he was paid the yearly sum of £20. Despite this the Rosses of Balnagown afterwards pursued a claim against him for the loss of 1,200 cattle, 100 horses and mares and 1,000 sheep and goats, taken in the 1493 raid, amounting in value to 6,000 merks. Not long afterwards Iye Roy MacKay was rewarded with royal charters to his lands of Strathnaver and elsewhere, after he had assisted the Crown in putting down the rebellion of Donald Dubh, grandson of John MacDonald, one-time Earl of Ross, who had himself forfeited the Lordship of the Isles in 1493.

Rise of the Gordons, Earls of Sutherland

Soon afterwards the ancient line of the earls of Sutherland, descended from Freskyn of Duffus, came to an end, brought down by the machinations of the Gordon earls of Huntly. The eighth Earl of Sutherland was John, who succeeded to the title in 1460. Even if his tenure of the earldom had been uneventful, despite the many feuds then raging in the far north, he was suddenly declared unable to conduct his own affairs in 1494, owing to mental infirmity. Quite likely his downfall was engineered by George Gordon, second Earl of Huntly, acting in his capacity of Justiciar of Scotland north of the Forth. Shortly before his own death in 1501, George Gordon arranged for the marriage of his younger son Adam Gordon to Elizabeth Sutherland, only daughter of the eighth Earl of Sutherland, whose affairs was now handled by a curator. After the Earl of Sutherland had died in 1508, he was succeeded by his eldest son and namesake John as the ninth Earl of Sutherland, but he too was judged incapable of managing his own affairs. Even so he was sufficiently *compos mentis* to assert that his sister Elizabeth and her husband Adam Gordon were his closest heirs, thus effectively disinheriting his half-brother Alexander, who was afterwards killed. When John, ninth Earl of Sutherland, died in 1514, just a month after these proceedings, he was succeeded by his sister Elizabeth as the Countess of Sutherland, who thus carried the earldom to her Gordon husband and his descendants. The Gordon earls of Sutherland afterwards came to wield great power in the far north, often acting in unison with the Gordon earls of Huntly and eventually overcoming the Sinclair earls of Caithness in the early decades of the seventeenth century.

Chapter Nine

LORDSHIP OF THE ISLES

The turbulent years after the death of King Robert the Bruce in 1329 saw the rise of Clan Donald under four successive chieftains, who proudly styled themselves Lords of the Isles, ruling over their vast territories in quasi-regal fashion. Indeed before James III first established the nucleus for a Scottish navy under Andrew Wood, the Lords of the Isles could afford to ignore the authority of the Scottish Crown whenever it suited them, since they were effectively beyond its reach. Commanding as they did the sea-lanes of the Western Isles with their powerful fleets of galleys, it was only when they gained the earldom of Ross in 1437 that they came within its sphere of influence. Until then they doubtless recognised the allegiance that they owed to the Scottish Crown, even if they were able to ignore its authority over them. Indeed, were they not the descendants of Somerled, who himself claimed descent from the kings of Dalriada according to the ancient traditions of Clan Donald? Not even the Stewart kings of Scotland could claim such an illustrious pedigree, except distantly through the female line.

The Lords of the Isles evidently regarded themselves as sufficiently independent of the Scottish Crown to pursue what was in effect a foreign policy, which often challenged the national interests of the Scottish monarchy. Since England was then the only real enemy facing Scotland in its alliance with France, it was perhaps inevitable that the MacDonalds reacted by allying themselves with the kings of England. Indeed it was obviously in the English interest to detach the MacDonald Lords of the Isles from their allegiance to the kings of Scotland, since England would inevitably benefit. Equally the actions of Clan Donald were often driven by only what they perceived to be the dictates of their own self-interest, not tempered in any way by any sense of allegiance to the Scottish Crown. Even when they acknowledged its sovereignty, the Lords of the Isles often only submitted to its authority if circumstances forced them to do so. Otherwise they took full advantage of its every weakness and profited from the long minorities and regencies which afflicted Scotland during the fourteenth and fifteenth centuries. It was only when the Lords of the Isles gained the earldom of

175

Ross, thus overstretching their resources, while exposing themselves to the more effective exercise of royal authority, and later entered into an audacious but ill-advised treaty with England, that their downfall perhaps become inevitable.

Nature of the Lordship Charters

Even if many of their Latin charters were couched in conventional terms, pledging allegiance to the Crown against whom service was specifically excluded, others omitted such an important qualification, perhaps quite deliberately. As Alexander Grant (1988) writes:

> Four [such grants] are particularly significant: Donald [second Lord of the Isles] in 1415 to Angus MacKay, 'for homage and service ... against all mortals of this life', Alexander [third Lord of the Isles] in 1427 to Gilleownan MacNeill, 'for homage and service ... against all men and women of whatever status ... in peace and war on land and sea', John [fourth Lord of the Isles] in 1456 to Somerled son of John, 'for homage and service ... against any mortal whatsoever' and John [fourth Lord of the Isles] in 1469 to Hugh his son, 'for homage and service ... in war and peace on sea and land as is required ... against any mortal male or female whatsoever'.

Such phraseology, specifying service to the lord against everyone else, not even excepting the king, is unique among late medieval Scottish charters. By omitting such an exemption, unlike all other fifteenth-century charters and bonds of man-rent, the Lords of the Isles seemingly did not recognise even their conventional obligations towards the Crown. In fact they often ignored these conventions, just as the last Lord of the Isles, and his father before him, administered inheritances on their own, as if the Lordship was a regality independent of the royal officers of state. Yet they were content to receive numerous charters to their lands from the Crown, doubtless thinking that such grants would bolster their own power and influence, while they were not averse to pursuing their own claims under feudal law to such territorial honours as the earldom of Ross.

Feudal Practices in a Kin-based Society

Much of the strength of Clan Donald under the Lordship of the Isles arose from their adoption of feudal practices, such as the principle of primogeniture, so that eldest sons came to succeed their fathers. Their territories were therefore not partitioned as they had been earlier, certainly at the time of Somerled's death in 1164, and perhaps even later during the thirteenth and

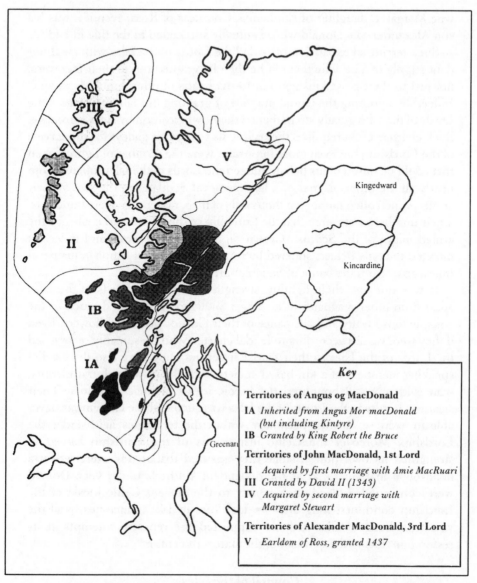

FIGURE 9.1   *Territorial expansion of Clan Donald under the Lordship of the Isles*
(after Kermack)

early fourteenth centuries. Equally accepting the feudal principle that
heiresses could transmit land and titles to their husbands allowed territorial
aggrandisement on a grand scale. Indeed, John MacDonald of Islay as the
first MacDonald Lord of the Isles gained the territories of Garmoran and the
Outer Isles through his first wife, while his son Donald MacDonald of
Harlaw, second Lord of the Isles, claimed the earldom of Ross by right of his

wife Margaret, daughter of Euphemia, Countess of Ross, even if it was his son Alexander MacDonald who eventually succeeded to the title in 1437.

Such territorial expansion provided the Lords of the Isles with an abundant supply of land which could be then be granted out to their followers, not just to their close kinsmen but to the heads of other kindreds as well. Indeed by adopting the feudal practice of granting out land by charter the Lords of the Isles greatly strengthened their own position by such patronage. Such charters often required the recipients to provide galleys for the service of the Lordship, but even more important were the number of fighting men that could be raised on its behalf. Indeed the Lords of the Isles differed from nearly all the other magnates in late medieval Scotland in the size of their armies, which often numbered thousands of men, rather than mere hundreds. Their numbers were such that the Lordship of the Isles could challenge the armed might of the Scottish Crown on almost equal terms and indeed it inflicted the only defeats suffered by royal forces at rebel hands in medieval times, apart from the battle of Sauchieburn in 1488.

It was not just their fighting strength that set the Lords of the Isles apart from other magnates in medieval Scotland. They owed much to the conspicuous loyalty and allegiance of their Gaelic-speaking followers. Even if they were vassals according to feudal charter, who presumably recognised the Lords of the Isles as their feudal superiors, they were also the Gaelic-speaking members of a kin-based society with their own cultural identity, who evidently still honoured the heroic ideals of their ancestors. Their steadfast loyalty to the Lords of the Isles was such that the Crown was never able to exercise its own patronage within the territories held under the Lordship. Moreover the Celtic institutions of the Lordship served to strengthen its own power, since they ensured that it was exercised in a benevolent manner as far as the dependent kindreds under Clan Donald were concerned. Indeed such loyalty to the ancient Celtic ideals of the Lordship continued long after its forfeiture in 1493, since nearly all the vassal kindreds of Clan Donald supported the repeated attempts at its restoration during the first half of the sixteenth century.

Council of the Isles

Foremost among these institutions was the so-called Council of the Isles. Such an institution was not unique to the Lordship. Other great magnates drew on such councils for advice in administering their territories in late medieval times. However the Council of the Isles may well have evolved from the body known as *Principes Insularum*, or Chiefs or Princes of the Isles, which is recorded on many occasions from the Norse kingdom of Man and the Isles before 1266. Its members did not all have the same standing for they were divided into an distinct hierarchy of three or four different grades, reminiscent of the hierarchal status accorded to the different classes in the uppermost levels of ancient Irish society, as described in the law-tracts of the seventh and eighth centuries and mirrored in the Scots society of Dalriada around the same time.

The uppermost rank in the Council of the Isles consisted of four kinsmen of Clan Donald: 'four great men of living of thair royal blude of Clan Donald lineally descendit', who were represented in the fifteenth century by MacDonald of Dunnyvaig and the Glens, MacDonald of ClanRanald, MacDonald of Keppoch and MacIain of Ardnamurchan. Below them were: 'four greatest of the Nobles callit Lords', namely, MacLean of Duart, MacLaine of Lochbuie, MacLeod of Dunvegan and Harris, and MacLeod of Lewis, who had all gained great power and influence as the chieftains of vassal kindreds under the Lordship of the Isles by the second half of the fifteenth century. Below them came: 'four thanes of less living and estate', namely, MacKinnon of Mull, MacQuarrie of Ulva, MacNeill of Gigha and MacNeill of Barra. Finally there were according to one account: 'freeholders or men who had their lands in factory', prominent among whom were MacFie of Colonsay, MacKay of the Rhinns, MacNicol of Portree, MacEarchern of Killelan, MacKay of Ugadale, MacGillevray in Mull and MacMillan in Knapdale. The Bishop of the Isles and the Abbot of Iona were also councillors, at least according to Dean Munro, writing in 1549. The presence of four representatives in each rank of membership, apart from the lowermost level, may well be a survival from earlier times, when the Norse kingdom of the Isles was divided by Alexander III after 1266 into four great baronies, centered on Lewis, Uist, Mull and Islay, which may even reflect its earlier partition dating from the time of Somerled.

The Council of the Isles is only occasionally mentioned in the surviving charters and other documents of the Lordship. They mostly date from the time of John MacDonald, fourth and last Lord of the Isles, and then more often than not they deal with the affairs of the earldom of Ross, which he held until 1476. Even so nearly all the island chieftains already named as high-ranking members of the Council were witness to the Lordship charters, some only once but others much more frequently. They were evidently members of the Lordship's entourage, not just in the Isles but also in the earldom of Ross. Indeed we find many men from the distant Hebrides witnessing charters in Inverness and Dingwall, almost to the total exclusion of such local magnates as Munro of Fowlis and the members of the Chisholm and Fraser families.

What role the Council played in the Lordship of the Isles is now difficult to determine from the scanty records of the time. It seemed more concerned with domestic matters than public affairs. There is no evidence that negotiation of treaties or alliances ever fell within its province, except that the Council might be called upon to decide the delicate matter of marriage, even within the ruling family of Clan Donald, by which different families with their competing ambitions allied themselves with one another. Rather clearer is its concern with justice since it was said later: 'There is a judge in every island for the discussion of all controversies, who had lands from MacDonald for their trouble, and likewise the eleventh part of every action decided. But there might be still an appeal to the Council of the Isles.' Dean Munro described its deliberations when he wrote in 1549 that its members

Discerned [judged], decreed, and gave forth suits upon all debateable matters according to the Laws made by Reginald mac Somhairle [son of Somerled] called in his time King of the Occident [Western] Isles, and albeit their Lord was at his hunting or at any other games, yet they sat every one at their Council ministering justice. In their time there was great peace and wealth in the Isles through the ministration of justice.

Ceremony of Inauguration

It is almost certain that the Council of the Isles played a prominent role in the ceremonials at which the Lords of the Isles were inaugurated. As Hugh MacDonald of Sleat wrote in the seventeenth century:

At this [ceremony] the Bishop of Argyll, the Bishop of the Isles, and seven priests were sometimes present; but a bishop was always present, with the chieftains of all the principal families, and a *Ruler of the Isles*. There was a square stone, seven or eight feet long and the tract of a man's foot cut thereon, upon which he stood, denoting that he should walk in the footsteps and uprightness of his predecessors, and that he was installed by right in his possessions. He was clothed in a white habit to show his innocence and integrity of heart, that he would be a light to his people and maintain the true religion ... Then he was to receive a white rod in his hand, intimating that he had the power to rule, not with tyranny and partiality, but with discretion and sincerity. Then he received his forefather's sword, or some other sword, signifying that his duty was to protect and defend them from the incursions of their enemies in peace as in war, as were the obligations and customs of his predecessors. The ceremony being over, Mass was said after the blessings of the bishop and the seven priests, the people pouring out their prayer for the success and prosperity of their new created Lord. When they were dismissed, the Lord of the Isles feasted them for a week thereafter; [and] gave liberally to the monks, poets, bards and musicians. You may judge that they spent liberally without any exception of persons.

Early History of the Lordship

Tradition has it that Angus Og macDonald, faithful ally of Robert the Bruce after 1306, died around 1330 at his residence of Finlaggan on Islay and it is said that he was buried on Iona among the graves of the former kings of the Isles. Even so, it now seems more likely that he was dead by 1318 at the very latest, when he was succeeded by the shadowy figure of his eldest son Alexander, who according to the Annals of Ulster died with Edward Bruce at the battle of Dundalk in 1318, if not earlier. Even before then the leadership of Gaelic society of the Western Isles may well have passed to Ruari macRuari, who was himself the great-grandson of Somerled's son Reginald by his son Ruari, but he almost certainly died as well at the battle of Dundalk in 1318. The history of the next few years is obscure but the leadership of Clan Donald most likely passed by 1325 to John MacDonald of Islay as the eldest-surviving son of Angus Og macDonald, after the mysterious figure of another kinsman known to us only as Ruari of Islay had forfeited his lands in the same year. John MacDonald of Islay came to rule over what was still in effect a petty kingdom, founded by Somerled in the twelfth century, but which perhaps had its roots much earlier in the ancient Celtic kingdom of Dalriada itself.

John MacDonald of Islay

Known to Clan Donald as 'Good John of Islay' for his many benefactions to the Church, John MacDonald first pursued a tortuous course during the renewed wars with England during the 1330s. It was possibly triggered by the refusal of Thomas Randolph, first Earl of Moray, and Guardian of Scotland after the death of King Robert the Bruce in 1329, to confirm his possession of the widespread territories that he had inherited from his father. Indeed he may well have felt that his father had not been rewarded sufficiently by King Robert the Bruce, who had granted the MacDonald lands of Kintyre and Knapdale to his grandson Robert the High Steward, among several others. Much of the MacDougall lands in Argyll were given to the Campbells of Lochawe, while the islands of Skye and probably Lewis as well went to Hugh, Earl of Ross. Even his father's lordship of Lochaber

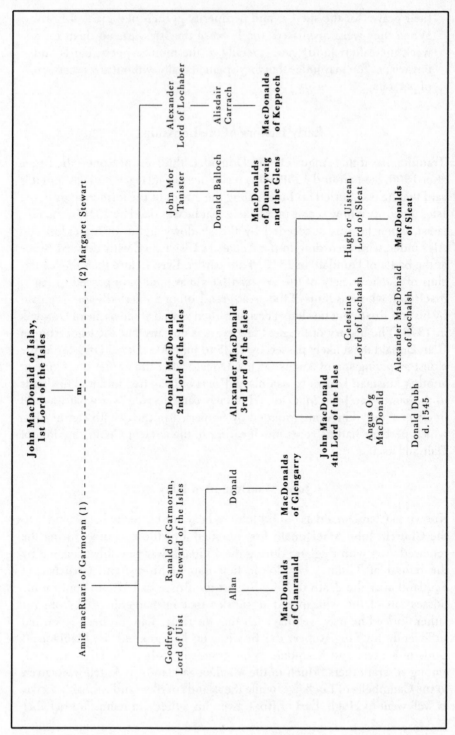

FIGURE 9.2 *MacDonald lords of the Isles and their descendants (after Munro and Munro)*

came to be held under the superiority of Thomas Randolph, first Earl of Moray, as did his own territories of Morvern and Ardnamurchan, which had been forfeited from the MacDougalls.

All these rival magnates were related by marriage to King Robert the Bruce and his family, since the King's sister Mary was married to Sir Neil Campbell of Lochawe, another sister Matilda was married to Hugh, Earl of Ross, his daughter Marjorie was married to Walter the High Steward and Thomas Randolph was the King's nephew by marriage. John MacDonald of Islay must have felt excluded from the territorial hegemony so created by King Robert the Bruce in the western Highlands. Doubtless it encouraged him to support Edward Balliol and the English cause, hoping to profit from the weakness of the Scots after they had been defeated at the battles of Dupplin Moor and Halidon Hill. Indeed after he had rejected the overtures made to him in 1335 by John Randolph, second Earl of Moray, acting on behalf of David II, Edward Balliol rewarded him in 1336 with a grant not only of the islands that he already held, consisting of Islay, Gigha, half of Jura, Colonsay and Mull, but also of Skye and Lewis, which were to be forfeited by the Earl of Ross. He was further confirmed in possession of his mainland territories of Ardnamurchan and Morvern, and granted Kintyre and Knapdale, which were to be forfeited by Robert the High Steward. Moreover he was to hold the wardship of Lochaber until the son and heir of David of Strathbogie, last Earl of Atholl, should come of age. Edward Balliol likewise confirmed Ranald macRuari in his possession of Garmoran, north of Ardnamurchan, while he attempted to restore the MacDougalls to their lands in Argyll, if not Lorn itself, only to be foiled by the opposition of John MacDonald of Islay. All these agreements were ratified by Edward III as Lord Superior of Scotland, who wrote to John MacDonald of Islay as his 'dearest friend' with honeyed protestations of his good faith, and granted him a safe-conduct to come to England with a retinue of 100 men. Indeed it was at the urging of John MacDonald of Islay that Edward III in 1338 granted lands in Antrim to Hugh Bisset, his kinsman, which eventually came by marriage into the hands of his own son John Mor Tanister, ancestor of the MacDonalds of Dunyvaig and the Glens, as well as the Earls of Antrim.

Despite the subsequent downfall of Edward Balliol, and the triumphant return to Scotland of David II in 1341, John MacDonald of Islay managed to retain possession of all the territories held in his own right before 1336 and indeed he made further gains. Admittedly he apparently lost Kintyre and Knapdale to Robert the High Steward, even if these lands were later restored to him after his second marriage with Margaret, the Steward's daughter, while the lordship of Skye was regained by the Earl of Ross, but he simply ignored the attempt of David II to deprive him of Islay, Gigha and Colonsay in favour of his kinsman Angus MacIain of Ardnamurchan. Thus even before launching his ill-fated invasion of England in 1346, David II was forced to come to terms with John MacDonald of Islay whom he confirmed in all his previous possessions, including the islands of Islay, Gigha, Mull and Colonsay, along with the lands of Morvern, Lochaber, Duror, Glencoe, and the custody of what were now called the royal castles of Cairnaburgh and Dunchonnel. He was also granted the rest of Jura as well as the islands of Coll, Tiree and Lewis. Such a generous settlement was only made 'after diligent discussion and bearing the common utility and peace of our realm in mind', so it seems that David II was less than enthusiastic in rewarding John MacDonald of Islay with such vast territories. Nonetheless the recipient of these territories seemingly did not support David II in his campaign of 1346, since there is no evidence that he was present at the battle of Neville's Cross, evidently preferring to remain aloof from both sides in the conflict.

John MacDonald as Lord of the Isles

Even before the Scottish defeat at Neville's Cross, the territories already gained by John MacDonald of Islay were greatly augmented by the violent outcome of the quarrel between Ranald macRuari and William, Earl of Ross. It probably arose over the grant of lands in Kintail to Ranald macRuari by David II, which he had previously held from William, Earl of Ross. The climax to their feud occurred in 1346 when the Scottish army was mustering at Perth prior to its invasion of England. William, Earl of Ross, murdered Ranald macRuari and seven of his followers after breaking into their quarters at the nunnery of Elcho during the dead of night. Ranald macRuari died without any issue, so that his territories passed to John MacDonald of Islay, who had married his half-sister and sole heiress Amie macRuari by papal dispensation in 1337. Even if he did not receive a feudal grant to these lands until much later, he occupied all the MacRuari territories that David II had already granted to Ranald macRuari. They consisted of the Uists, Barra, Rhum, Moidart, Arisaig and Knoydart, together with the island of Eigg and part of Lochaber, so that he now held even more territory than his illustrious ancestor Somerled.

Indeed ten years earlier John MacDonald of Islay had already proudly styled himself 'Lord of the Isles' in the manner of his ancestors, when he gave himself this title in writing to Edward III of England in September 1336, before adopting it in later charters. The letter itself suggests that he regarded himself as the equal of Edward Balliol, then puppet King of the Scots, with whom he was willing to ally himself. Indeed he may well have adopted such a title to demonstrate his independence, just as Edward III of England called himself *Dominus Hibernie*, or 'Lord of Ireland'. Even so it was an ancient Celtic title borne by many of his ancestors. Translated into

Latin as *Dominus Insularum*, the wording almost certainly has the meaning of the Gaelic *Ri Innse Gall*, or 'King of the Western Isles', or perhaps more accurately 'Ruler of the Isles', since the Gaelic word *Ri* lacks the connotations of sovereignty usually implied by the English title of 'King'. As emphasised by Professor Barrow, it seems very likely that he adopted the title by virtue of his marriage with Amie macRuari of the Isles, even if he used it before receiving a papal dispensation for this marriage in 1337, or even the lands themselves, which were still held by Ranald macRuari until his death in 1346. Strictly speaking, he was not the first Lord of the Isles, since the title had already been used by his ancestors, but we shall adopt the convention that gives him such a title as the first in line of the MacDonald lords of the Isles.

Alliance with the Stewarts

The captivity of David II in English hands after 1346 meant that Robert the High Steward, afterwards Robert II of Scotland, was now acting as Guardian of the country. Soon afterwards John MacDonald of Islay, first Lord of the Isles, evidently decided to ally himself with the growing power and influence of the Stewart family. Tradition has it that he repudiated Amie macRuari as his first wife, even if he kept her lands of Garmoran and the Uists. But there is no evidence she was not dead by 1350, when he received a papal dispensation to marry Margaret Stewart, daughter of Robert the High Steward of Scotland. He thus became the son-in-law to the future King of Scotland and incidentally gained possession of Knapdale and Kintyre, now or later. It is said that he sailed up the Clyde to claim his bride, accompanied by sixty galleys. The younger sons born of this marriage included John Mor Tanister, ancestor of the MacDonalds of Dunnyvaig and the Glens, as well as Alexander, Lord of Lochaber, from whose son, Alastair Carrach, the MacDonalds of Keppoch are descended. Meanwhile his sister Mary had married William, fifth Earl of Ross, while his eldest son John married Ellen, daughter of Archibald Campbell, so allying the first Lord of the Isles with two families who had previously been his rivals. Afterwards John MacDonald of Islay, first Lord of the Isles, entered into an agreement in 1354 with John Mac-Dougall, great-grandson of Alexander MacDougall of Lorn, who renounced his family's claim to the islands of Mull, north Jura and Tiree, together with the castles of Cairnaburgh in the Treshnish Islands and Dunchonnel in the Garvellachs, provided they were not occupied by the MacKinnons. In return John MacDougall of Lorn was granted the island of Coll and certain lands in Tiree and Duror to be held as the vassal of John MacDonald of Islay, first Lord of the Isles.

It is said by the seannachies of Clan Donald and other historians that

John MacDonald of Islay, first Lord of the Isles, now pursued an anti-English policy in close alliance with Robert the High Steward of Scotland as his father-in-law. But he has perhaps been confused with another person, who appears in the records as John de Lisle, rather than John *de Yle*, as John MacDonald of Islay was known in the records of the time. Supposedly he was among a party of Scottish knights who went to the aid of the French king in 1356 and were captured by the English forces after their victory at the battle of Poitiers. Released more than a year later, he is then thought to have returned to Scotland under a safe-conduct, afterwards playing a prominent role in the negotiations which eventually gained the release of David II in 1357. Indeed he was named in the Treaty of Berwick. However it seems much more likely that he was then being cajoled by the English King into entering his service, and indeed trading privileges were granted by England to six merchants from the Isles at John's request around this time.

Emergence of the 'Highland Party'

Finding himself in royal favour, it is then said that he was made Constable of Edinburgh Castle in 1360, while he supposedly served as High Steward of the Royal Household in 1364, after Robert the High Steward as the hereditary holder of this office was involved in an abortive rebellion against the Crown in 1363. Three years later, he was apparently even sent by David II to Flanders to act as his envoy, where he negotiated with the Flemish merchants for the sale of fleeces and wool, which proceeds were intended to pay for the King's ransom to Edward III of England. Whatever the truth of the matter, and much of the record is hearsay, it was certainly not long afterwards that he fell from royal favour, when he joined the other members of what later became known as the 'Highland Party' in refusing to collect the rents and other taxes needed to pay for the King's ransom, and then absenting himself from the parliaments called by David II to discuss the matter.

The northern earls and barons who made up the 'Highland Party' were all related to one another by a complex web of marriage alliances. John MacDonald of Islay, first Lord of the Isles, had perhaps placed himself at its centre in 1350 when he married Margaret, daughter of Robert the High Steward, as his second wife. A few years later in 1355 Robert the High Steward had married Euphemia Ross, sister of William, Earl of Ross, after Elizabeth Mure of Rowallane, his first wife, had died, while William, Earl of Ross, was already married to Mary, sister of John MacDonald of Islay, first Lord of the Isles. Other diplomatic marriages and political alliances bound together John MacDougall of Lorn and Archibald Campbell of Lochawe as two more members of the 'Highland Party'.

In 1366, apart from Robert the High Steward, they all reneged on their allegiance to the Scottish Crown by refusing to contribute any further revenues for the payment of David II's ransom. Faced with this challenge to his own authority David II ordered their arrest, after they had wilfully failed to attend his parliaments, and then passed an act in 1367 revoking all the grants of land made on behalf of the Crown since the death of King Robert the Bruce in 1329. Even if this act of revocation was only used with discretion by David II, it placed him in a powerful position to bargain with his more recalcitrant subjects. Indeed John MacDougall of Lorn and Archibald Campbell of Lochawe both submitted to royal authority soon afterwards and Archibald Campbell received a grant to all his lands that he had resigned in favour of the King. Even if John MacDonald, first Lord of the Isles, still persisted in his opposition to David II, his position *vis-à-vis* royal authority was greatly weakened in 1369 by a truce between Scotland and England, since he was no longer able to rely on the tacit support of Edward III in his dealings with the Scottish Crown. Faced with this difficulty John MacDonald of Islay, first Lord of the Isles, was persuaded by Robert the High Stewart to submit to David II, which he did in 1369, when the King himself came in force to Inverness to take his 'most complete and unqualified submission'. He surrendered his son Donald and his grandson Angus as hostages for his own good behaviour in the future and agreed that he would no longer obstruct the royal officials in their duties. Then in 1370 William, Earl of Ross, was forced to recognise his son-in-law Sir Walter Leslie, who had married his elder daughter and heiress Euphemia Ross at the King's insistence, as the rightful heir to his earldom of Ross, thus disinheriting his younger brother Hugh, ancestor of the Rosses of Balnagowan.

John MacDonald and Robert II

A year later in 1371 David II died suddenly at the early age of forty-seven, and Robert the High Steward of Scotland came to the throne as Robert II, aged around fifty-five years. The very next year John MacDonald of Islay, first Lord of the Isles, received a charter from his royal father-in-law confirming all his MacRuari possessions, which included Moidart, Arisaig, Morar and Knoydart on the mainland, as well as the islands of Rhum, Eigg, Barra and the Uists. Three more charters were granted to him in 1376 which confirmed his possession of all his remaining territories, while he also received Knapdale and Kintyre from the Stewart family in the same year, if he had not gained these territories much earlier at the time of his marriage with Margaret Stewart. Even so the seeds of future trouble were sown when John MacDonald of Islay, first Lord of the Isles, was required to resign his lands into the hands of the Crown, only to receive them back jointly with his wife. Equally he received no grants of public office from Robert II, who

appointed his own son Alexander Stewart as the King's lieutenant and justiciar north of the Forth, admittedly with disastrous results as he was none
other than the 'Wolf of Badenoch', while he assigned Archibald Campbell of
Lochawe to much the same position in Argyll. John MacDonald of Islay may
well have expected such a prestigious office as the King's lieutenant in the
Western Isles. Nevertheless he had now regained nearly all of Somerled's
territories in the Western Isles apart from Skye, which was still held under
the earldom of Ross.

Donald MacDonald, Second Lord of the Isles

The final years before the death of John MacDonald of Islay in 1387 were
evidently a time of peace and prosperity for the Lordship of the Isles.
Indeed Gaeldom would later look back with romantic nostalgia to a heroic
age established by John MacDonald of Islay as the first Lord of the Isles and
his three successors at the Headship of the Gael, before the Lordship itself
was finally forfeited by the Scottish Crown in 1493. After his death at
Ardtornish Castle his body was taken to Iona and laid to rest with great
pomp and ceremony among the graves of his ancestors in the Reilig Oran.
His successor as Lord of the Isles was his eldest son Donald by his second
marriage with Margaret Stewart, daughter of Robert the High Steward, now
ruling as Robert II over Scotland. The matter of the succession had already
been decided during his father's lifetime and, no doubt, it was a politic
decision to pass over Ranald and Godfrey as the two surviving sons of his
first marriage to Amie MacRuari in favour of their half-brother, who was so
closely related by marriage to the Scottish throne. In recompense Ranald
was granted the lands of Garmoran and the Outer Isles in 1373, if not earlier,
together with Sunart, Ardgour and sixty merklands in Lochaber, to be held
as the vassal of John MacDonald, first Lord of the Isles, and his heirs, while
Godfrey apparently received North Uist as his share around the same time.
When the first Lord of the Isles died in 1387, presumably at a great age,
Ranald as his eldest son from his first marriage was acting as 'High Steward'
of the Isles. Calling a Council of the Isles he surrendered all his rights and
privileges in the Lordship of the Isles to his half-brother Donald at a ceremony held at Kildonan on the island of Eigg. Witnessed by all the principal
men of the Isles, and despite their apparent opposition, Donald MacDonald
of Harlaw was nominated to succeed his father as chief of Clan Donald and
second Lord of the Isles.

Donald's accession to the Lordship of the Isles brought conflict in its
train since his younger brother, known as John Mor Tanister, became
dissatisfied with his own inheritance, said to consist of a grant of 120
merklands and the castles of Saddell and Dunnaverty in Kintyre and 60

merklands and the castle of Dunnyvaig in Islay, received from their father during his lifetime. He revolted against his elder brother but he was pursued first to Galloway and then to Ireland, where he was forced to take refuge in great hardship. There he entered the service of Richard II of England in 1395, most likely as the commander of Highland galloglasses. It was while he was living in Ireland that he married Mary Bisset, daughter and heiress of John Bisset, Lord of the Glens of Antrim, whose death is recorded in the annals of 1383. This inheritance gave him vast territories in Ulster which, combined with his lands in Kintyre and Islay, were enough to found the fortunes of his descendants, known as the MacDonalds of Dunnyvaig and the Glens. He had returned to Scotland by 1401 after he was reconciled with his brother. Indeed his title of Tanister suggests that he was recognised as his brother's successor during his lifetime, most likely until Donald's son Alexander came of age.

Donald MacDonald of Harlaw, as the second Lord of the Isles became known to Gaeldom from the victory he later claimed at the battle of Harlaw in 1411, pursued just as independent course as his father. Even if he was the grandson of Robert II, his early life and later circumstances apparently caused him to favour English interests, especially during the long years of intermittent warfare between the two countries during the reigns of Robert II and Robert III. Donald himself is first mentioned in 1369 as a young boy around ten years of age, when he was surrendered as a hostage to David II by his father as a guarantee of his own good conduct. His enforced residence in Dumbarton Castle for the next two years, after which he was released on the death of David II in 1371, evidently did not engender in him any feelings of loyalty to the Scottish Crown. It is said that his pro-English susceptibilities were further encouraged by the education he received at Balliol College in the University of Oxford, after which he returned home in 1378 under a safe-conduct issued by Richard II of England. More likely it was his half-brother, born of an unknown woman, but also called Donald, who received such an education. Thereafter Donald MacDonald of Harlaw, second Lord of the Isles, and his brothers appeared several times at the English court, where they were treated with much pomp and ceremony, despite the repeated outbreak of hostilities between Scotland and England. Indeed soon after he succeeded his father as Lord of the Isles, Donald MacDonald entered into an alliance of friendship, mutual defence and trade with Richard II of England in 1388, along with two of his brothers.

Conflict with the Stewarts

Such a breakdown in the friendly relations between the Lord of the Isles and the Scottish Crown, which had previously existed between John

MacDonald of Islay and his royal father-in-law Robert II, first became evident in 1389. A complaint was made in parliament by John Stewart, Earl of Carrick and then heir-apparent to the throne, insinuating that his sister Margaret Stewart, widow of the first Lord of the Isles, had been ill-treated by her own sons and their adherents, among whom was Donald MacDonald, second Lord of the Isles. Most likely a dispute had arisen over the lands previously held jointly with her husband under the charters issued during the reign of Robert II, namely Colonsay, Lochaber, Kintyre and Knapdale. Holding land in joint tenure was quite alien to the kin-based nature of Gaelic society, so the arrangement was probably imposed upon the first Lord of the Isles against his wishes by Robert II. Her claim to these lands evidently caused such a serious breach between the Lords of the Isles and the Scottish Crown that a state of outright hostility existed between them for nearly forty years, until Alexander MacDonald, third Lord of the Isles, was forced to submit to the authority of James I in 1429. Meanwhile the dispute itself reached a crisis point in 1394 when the Earl of Carrick, now ruling as Robert III after the death of Robert II in 1390, ordered Robert Stewart his brother, Earl of Fife and Menteith, who was still acting as the Guardian of the country, to protect their widowed sister.

By then yet another source of trouble had arisen in the Highlands when Thomas Dunbar, now Earl of Moray, complained to parliament that he was forced to pay protection money to Alexander MacDonald of Keppoch, Lord of Lochaber, and the younger brother of Donald MacDonald, second Lord of the Isles. Indeed he had agreed to pay eighty merks each year to protect his earldom and its church-lands from such attacks. Alexander MacDonald of Lochaber reacted angrily to such a complaint by seizing Urquhart Castle on the shores of Loch Ness. Thereafter matters went from bad to worse, since it was decided in 1398 that David Stewart, now Earl of Carrick as the eldest son of Robert III, or his uncle Robert Stewart, now Duke of Albany, should mount an expedition to the Western Isles. Even if it never took place, parliament agreed that the submission of the rebels could only be accepted if Donald MacDonald, second Lord of the Isles, his brothers John Mor Tanister and Alexander of Lochaber and their chief counsellors and other notables, together with all the robbers and marauders associated with them, surrendered themselves to the justice of the King and his council or gave hostages for their own good behaviour.

Even if Donald MacDonald of Harlaw now agreed to act as a surety for the good conduct of his kinsmen, his younger brother Alexander, Lord of Lochaber, launched a armed raid against Moray in 1402, when he and his followers sacked the canons' houses in the cathedral close of Elgin and set fire to the nearby burgh, just as the 'Wolf of Badenoch' had done in 1390. Only three months later Alexander was forced to return ignominiously to

Elgin with a large following, now seeking absolution for his sins. Meanwhile Donald MacDonald of Harlaw, second Lord of the Isles, still retained his pro-English stance, since after Richard II was deposed by Henry IV in 1399 he entered into further treaties of perpetual peace and friendship with the king of England. Indeed he apparently visited the English court in 1400, accompanied by 100 horsemen, after receiving a safe-conduct from the English King.

Skye and the Earldom of Ross

It was perhaps during these years, not long after Donald MacDonald of Harlaw had succeeded his father as second Lord of the Isles in 1387, that conflict broke out in Skye with the MacLeods of Harris and Dunvegan. Ever since the time of Alexander III the island of Skye had been held as part of the earldom of Ross. The MacLeods of Harris and Dunvegan were therefore the vassals of the earls of Ross for the lands they held around Dunvegan in the north of the island. But the marriage of Donald MacDonald, second Lord of the Isles, to Mary Leslie, granddaughter of William, fifth and last Earl of Ross in the ancient line, meant he had a claim to the earldom of Ross itself, which came to a head at the battle of Harlaw in 1411. But it seems likely that this marriage also encouraged him to lay claim to the island of Skye, even before Alexander Leslie, who was his wife's brother and Earl of Ross in his own right, had died in 1402, leaving only his daughter Euphemia Leslie to succeed him. Indeed the troubles in Skye seemingly occurred around 1395, when Alexander Leslie succeeded to the earldom of Ross after the death of his mother Euphemia, Countess of Ross in her own right. A few years earlier she had been granted a Crown charter to the islands of Skye and Lewis, to be held jointly with her second husband Sir Alexander Stewart, Earl of Buchan, even though Lewis had previously been held by John MacDonald of Islay, first Lord of the Isles.

It may well be that Donald MacDonald of Harlaw felt himself free to enforce his rights over the MacLeods of Harris and Dunvegan as their feudal superior, once his wife's mother had died in 1395. Whatever the reason for their struggle the battle of Sligachan was fought around this time between the MacDonalds, most likely under the leadership of Alexander MacDonald of Keppoch, Lord of Lochaber, rather than his son Alastair Carrach as usually thought, and the MacLeods of Harris and Dunvegan, after the MacDonalds had landed from their galleys at Loch Eynort and laid waste to the surrounding countryside. According to the traditional accounts of this battle, which are all we have, the MacLeods gained a great victory over the MacDonalds with the help of the MacAskills, who seized the MacDonald galleys to prevent their escape.

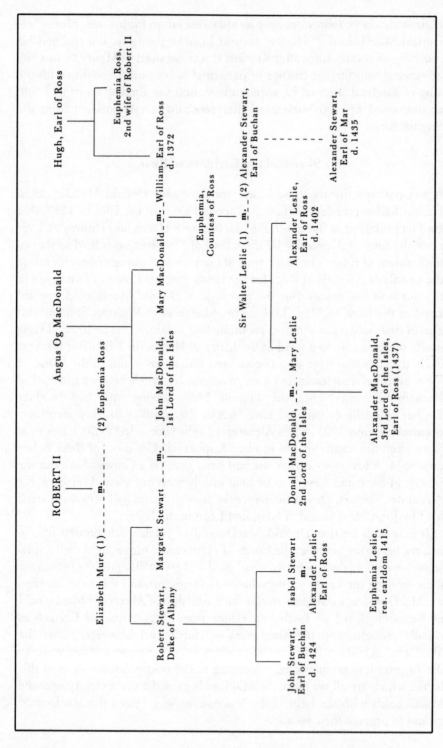

FIGURE 9.3 Family alliances and the succession to the earldom of Ross (after Munro and Munro)

Godfrey the Usurper

Even if they were defeated at the battle of Sligachan in 1395 Clan Donald had already gained a foothold on the island of Skye, since Godfrey, who was the half-brother of Donald MacDonald of Harlaw by their father's first marriage with Amie MacRuari, had earlier seized the MacLeod lands of Sleat in the south of Skye. Indeed he had seized not only Sleat but all the MacRuari lands of Garmoran, which were originally held by his brother Ranald. These events presumably occurred before 1389, when the usurper described himself in a charter as Godfrey of Sleat, which he signed at 'our castle of Tioram' in Moidart, originally held by his brother Ranald as Lord of Garmoran. Godfrey perhaps did not accept the accession of his half-brother Donald to the Lordship of the Isles with the same grace as his elder brother Ranald, who had died only a few years later after acting as 'High Steward of the Isles'. It has even been suggested that Godfrey was older than Ranald, who since he was prepared to accept the feudal superiority of his half-brother Donald as the second Lord of the Isles was rewarded with a grant of Garmoran and the Outer Isles. Godfrey himself only received North Uist, whereas he might have expected to inherit the Lordship itself, if indeed he was the eldest son of John Macdonald of Islay by his first marriage with Amie MacRuari.

According to the MacLeod traditions all this happened in the years after 1392, or perhaps even later, when it is said that the MacDonalds invaded not only Sleat, seizing the MacLeod strongholds of Dunskaith and Castle Camus, but North Uist as well, where they defeated the MacLeods of Harris and Dunvegan at the great battle of Cailus, driving them from their lands on the island. Indeed the MacDonalds were so successful that they forced the MacLeods under their tutor to take refuge on the remote island of Pabbay, while they laid siege to Dunvegan Castle, where the young heir of the MacLeods had sought safety with his mother. It was Torquil MacLeod of Lewis who rescued his kinsmen of Harris and Dunvegan. Landing in Skye with a large force of clansmen he defeated the MacDonalds with heavy losses at the battle of Feorlig. Later known as Iain *Borb* MacLeod, meaning 'Surly' or 'Truculent', the young chief of Harris and Dunvegan was taken by Torquil MacLeod with his mother to Lewis, until he came of age.

Then, after assuming the leadership of the MacLeods of Harris and Dunvegan, Ian *Borb* MacLeod collected a large fleet of galleys and sailed towards Islay, intending to attack Donald, second Lord of the Isles. However he was dissuaded from such an action by his uncle Hector MacLean of Duart and Donald's nephew, such were the marriage alliances between their families. He persuaded him not only to abandon his claim to the disputed lands in North Uist but also to recognise the second Lord of the Isles as his

feudal superior over the MacLeod lands of Skye. In return his possession of
these lands was acknowledged by the Lord of the Isles, even if there is no
record of any charter. Their agreement was probably made much easier by
the death of the renegade Godfrey in 1401, since it seems that afterwards the
MacLeods regained their lands in Sleat. Thereafter for the next fifty years
the MacLeods of Harris and Dunvegan were just as loyal vassals of the
MacDonalds, Lords of the Isles, as the MacLeods of Lewis. Indeed Iain
Borb MacLeod of Harris and Dunvegan and Torquil MacLeod of Lewis
were both present at the battle of Harlaw in 1411, fighting with great valour
on behalf of Donald, second Lord of the Isles.

Prelude to the Battle of Harlaw

The bitter quarrel between Donald, second Lord of the Isles, and Robert
Stewart, Duke of Albany, which reached such a bloody climax at the battle
of Harlaw in 1411 first arose over their conflicting claims to the wardship of
Donald's niece Euphemia Leslie, heiress to the earldom of Ross. Hunch-
backed and sickly, or so it was said, she was the only daughter of Alexander
Leslie, Earl of Ross, who had died in 1402, leaving no other issue. Although
still a minor at her father's death, on coming of age she would become
Countess of Ross in her own right, while her maternal grandfather was none
other than Robert Stewart, now Duke of Albany, since her mother was his
elder daughter Isabel. Even so Donald MacDonald of Harlaw stood to gain
the earldom himself by right of his wife Mary Leslie, brother of Alexander
Leslie, Earl of Ross, should his niece Euphemia renounce the title or die
without any heirs. But despite his opposition it was Robert Stewart, Duke of
Albany, and now acting as Guardian of Scotland for his ailing and inept
brother Robert III, who eventually gained the wardship of his granddaughter.

Invasion of Ross

Donald MacDonald of Harlaw reacted by invading the earldom of Ross in
1411, fearful that the Albany Stewarts were about to claim it for their own.
Quite possibly he had heard of plans by Robert Stewart, Duke of Albany, to
persuade Euphemia, Countess of Ross, to resign her title into his own
hands, thus depriving his wife Mary of her own claim to the earldom. But it
was only later in 1415 that Euphemia actually resigned her title by taking the
veil, so becoming legally dead to the world as a nun, after which the Regent
was able to confer the title in 1417 upon his own son John Stewart, Earl
of Buchan. Whatever his reasons Donald MacDonald of Harlaw mustered
his forces in 1411 at Ardtornish Castle in Morvern. Answering his call to
arms were the MacLeans of Duart and Lochbuie, the MacLeods of Harris

and Dunvegan, the MacLeods of Lewis, the Camerons of Lochaber and the MacIntoshes of Clan Chattan, among a host of lesser clans who owed allegiance to the Lord of the Isles. His forces may well have numbered 10,000 men, even if we dismiss as apocryphal the engaging story that he chose only two out of every three men who rallied to his banner, such was his military strength.

After embarking by galley from Ardtornish, Donald MacDonald of Harlaw sailed north to Strome in Wester Ross and then marched inland through the Glens of Ross towards Dingwall. There he encountered the hastily raised forces of Angus *Dubh* MacKay from Strathnaver, said to number over 2,000 men, who was virtually alone among the Gaelic-speaking community in opposing his claim to the earldom of Ross. After a hard-fought engagement his opponents were routed with many casualties and Donald, second Lord of the Isles, took possession of Dingwall Castle. He was joined there by the Rosses of Balnagown, whose family had lost the earldom of Ross in 1372, and several other clans, who evidently objected to the designs of the Stewart family upon the earldom of Ross. Donald MacDonald of Harlaw then marched towards Beauly, where he turned aside to ravage the lands of the Frasers of Lovat, against whom he probably had a feud concerning the lands of Glenelg. He then proceeded to Inverness, where he seized the castle and raised his standard.

March towards Aberdeen

The second Lord of the Isles now marched eastwards with his forces through the Laigh of Moray towards Aberdeen, which he had threatened to sack. His strategy is difficult to understand unless he had hopes of help from the English, who might have landed at Aberdeen. Indeed he had already signed a treaty of peace and friendship in 1408 between Henry IV of England and his subjects, on the one hand, and himself, together with John Mor Tanister and all their subjects, on the other hand, after his nephew Hector MacLean of Duart was given a safe-conduct in 1407 to visit James I in England, where he was held captive. He may simply have wished to gain a decisive victory over the forces loyal to the Regent, forcing the government to recognise his claim to the earldom of Ross, and hoping to seize its lands in Buchan, such as the barony of Kingedward. His advance through the lowlands of Moray evidently met with little opposition, since the army under the second Lord of the Isles came within twenty miles of Aberdeen. There its further advance was blocked at Harlaw near the village of Inverurie by forces under the command of his own cousin Alexander Stewart, Earl of Mar.

The approach of the second Lord of the Isles through Moray greatly alarmed the burgesses of Aberdeen and the landed gentry of the surround-

ing districts. Apart from his own retinue of armed followers, Alexander
Stewart, Earl of Mar, had the support of the Lords Marischal and Errol, Sir
James Scrymgeour, Constable of Dundee, Sir Alexander Ogilvie, Sheriff of
Angus and their armed retainers, together with such Lowland families as the
Lindsays, the Carnegies, the Leslies, the Lyons, the Irvings, the Gordons,
the Abercrombies, the Arbuthnots, the Bannermans, the Leiths, the
Douglases, the Barclays, the Mowats, the Duguids, the Fotheringhams, the
Frasers and the Burnets. Together with their retinues they may only have
numbered 1,000 or 2,000 men but they made up a cavalry force of mail-clad
knights, heavily armed with lances, maces and battle-axes. The Islemen
were foot-soldiers, more lightly armed with broad-swords, battle-axes and
bows and carrying wooden shields covered in bull-hide for their protection.
Only their leaders wore the high, conical helmets known as bascinets to
protect their heads, along with an apron of chain-mail around their necks
and shoulders, while their bodies and lower arms were most likely protected
by quilted tunics or surcoats made of heavy cloth or leather, stuffed with any
suitable material, which reached down to their knees.

The Battle of Harlaw

There are no trustworthy accounts of the battle of Harlaw and both sides
later claimed a victory. Even before the battle started Lachlan Mor
MacMhuirich, chief bard to the Lord of the Isles, recited the renowned
brosnachadh catha, or 'incitement to battle', accompanied by the playing of
a clarsach, or Highland harp, in front of the Highland army. It was a battle-
song which worked its way in Gaelic through the alphabet in a series of
alliterative couplets, given here in a much abbreviated and freely translated
version, exhorting the clansmen of Clan Donald to emulate the warlike feats
of their distant ancestor, Conn of the Hundred Battles:

> O Children of Conn, remember
> Hardihood in time of battle,
> Be strong, nursing your wrath,
> Be resolute and fierce,
> Be forceful, standing your ground,
> Be nimble and full of valour,
> Be dour, inspiring fear,
> Be exceedingly fierce, recklessly daring,
> Be spirited, inflicting great wounds,
> Be venomous, implacable,
> Be glorious, nobly powerful,
> Be exceedingly fierce, king-like,
> Be vigorous, nimble-footed,

In winning the battle
Against your enemies.
O Children of Conn of the Hundred Battles.
Now is the time for you to win renown,
O raging whelps,
O sturdy bears,
O most sprightly lions,
O battle-loving warriors,
The Children of Conn of the Hundred Battles,
O Children of Conn, remember
Hardihood in time of battle.

Taken up as hypnotic chant by the Highland host, it must have had a powerful and demoralising effect upon the Lowland army under the Earl of Mar.

The battle itself apparently lasted all day, and only ended when darkness fell. By then Donald of Harlaw had lost perhaps 1,000 men at the very most, including Hector MacLean of Duart, his nephew and second-in-command as the Lieutenant-General of his army, and several other chieftains of lesser degree. But relative to their numbers much greater losses were sustained by the forces under the Earl of Mar, who was himself seriously wounded in the battle, while many other men of high rank on his side died in the bloody encounter. Yet both sides held their ground and it was only during the night after the battle that Donald, second Lord of the Isles, withdrew his forces from the battlefield, thus effectively conceding victory to Alexander Stewart, Earl of Mar. Soon after Donald returned to the Isles with his own men, Robert Stewart, Duke of Albany, belatedly came north with a large army which recaptured Dingwall Castle and installed his own garrison there. Next year he raised such a show of force that Donald, second Lord of the Isles, felt obliged to submit to the Regent's authority at Lochgilphead, where he handed over hostages and agreed to keep the peace, or so it was said in a later chronicle. It was only after his death in 1423 that his son Alexander MacDonald, third Lord of the Isles, eventually became Earl of Ross in 1437.

Chapter Ten

DOWNFALL OF CLAN DONALD

Donald MacDonald of Harlaw, second Lord of the Isles, spent the final years of his life in religious seclusion, or so it was said, like so many of his predecessors. He most likely died in 1423, when he was succeeded by his eldest son Alexander MacDonald. Just a year later in 1424 James I returned to Scotland after his long captivity in England, determined to end the chronic disorder that now existed within his kingdom. By then Robert Stewart, Duke of Albany, was dead, but his son Murdach Stewart had succeeded him as the second Duke of Albany and Regent of Scotland. Soon after his return James I acted ruthlessly to destroy for ever the power of the Albany family, when he arrested Murdach Stewart, Duke of Albany, together with Murdach's elder sons, Walter and Alexander, and their aged grandfather Duncan, Earl of Lennox. Arraigned before a jury, among whose members was Alexander MacDonald, third Lord of the Isles, they were all found guilty of treason and executed in 1425. Only Sir James Stewart as the youngest son of the second Duke of Albany escaped capture, but he was forced to take refuge in Ireland after he had attacked the burgh of Dumbarton with a sizeable body of men from the Highlands and killed John Stewart of Dundonald, governor of Dumbarton Castle, who was the illegitimate uncle of James I.

Alexander MacDonald, third Lord of the Isles

After his ruthless destruction of the Albany family James I turned his attention to pacifying the Highlands, hoping especially to curb the power of the Lordship of the Isles under its new chief, Alexander MacDonald, third Lord of the Isles. He first passed an ordinance in 1426 requiring all the lords of parliament with lands beyond the Mounth to repair their castles, fortalices (or strongholds) and manor-houses with the aim of implementing the good and efficient government of the country. The King then became implicated in a plot which ended with the murder of John Mor Tanister by a certain James Campbell. After his reconciliation earlier with Donald MacDonald of Harlaw, second Lord of the Isles, it is said that John Mor Tanister quarrelled again over some lands in Kintyre shortly before his brother's death in 1423. It seems likely that James I was prompted to use James Campbell as his intermediary to approach John Mor Tanister, perhaps suggesting that he should seize for himself the territories of his young nephew Alexander MacDonald, third Lord of the Isles. Alternatively it may be that John Mor Tanister was implicated in the escape of Sir James Stewart to Ireland after his raid on Dumbarton. Whatever the circumstances he was killed in 1427 when he apparently resisted arrest by James Campbell, acting as he said later in the name of the King, after a meeting between the two men on Islay.

Meanwhile Alexander MacDonald, third Lord of the Isles, renewed his family's claim to the earldom of Ross, after John Stewart, Earl of Buchan, who had gained the title in 1417, was killed at the Battle of Verneuil in 1424 fighting for the French. Since his only surviving son did not claim the earldom, perhaps overawed by the King's execution of his own uncle in 1425, the title should have reverted to Mary Leslie, now the widow of Donald MacDonald of Harlaw, second Lord of the Isles, and she indeed styled herself Countess of Ross after this date. The earldom itself remained in Crown hands until 1437. This rebuff may well have prompted Alexander MacDonald, third Lord of the Isles, to enter into negotiations with the King of Norway, hoping to restore Norse sovereignty over the Western Isles, after Scotland itself had failed to keep up its payments of the 'Annual of Norway' for these territories. Faced with such a prospect James I soon afterwards mounted a decisive show of force against his more recalcitrant subjects in the Highlands. Raising a formidable army James I marched north to Inverness in 1428, where he summoned some fifty Highland chieftains to attend his parliament.

Royal Expedition to Inverness

Despite a warning from the Earl of Douglas, Alexander MacDonald, third Lord of the Isles, and his mother Mary, now entitled the Countess of Ross, obeyed the King's summons, along with such other notables as Angus *Dubh* MacKay and his four sons, Kenneth *Mor* MacKenzie of Kintail, John Ross of Balnagowan, William Leslie, Angus Moray of Culbin, Alexander MacRuari, John MacArthur and James Campbell. After lodging for some days in the town they were all summoned separately into the King's presence, whereupon they were promptly arrested and held prisoner in solitary confinement. The King was evidently delighted by the success of his scheme, jubilantly composing a doggerel verse in Latin:

> Let us carry that gang to a fortress strong,
> For Christ's own lot, they did deadly wrong.

Several of the captives were summarily executed without any trial, including James Campbell who was beheaded for the murder of John Mor Tanister, despite the likely involvement of the King himself in plotting the latter's death. Among the other victims of such arbitary justice were Alexander MacRuari and John MacArthur, who had quarrelled with one another over the lands of North Uist. It is only surmise that identifies Alexander macRuari as the son of Godfrey and therefore the grandson of John MacDonald, first Lord of the Isles, by his marriage with Amie macRuari. As already recounted Godfrey was given North Uist after he and his brother Ranald were passed over in favour of their half-brother Donald when he inherited their father's mantle as the second Lord of the Isles. After Ranald's death Godfrey seized his brother's lands of Garmoran from his two nephews, as well as the MacLeod lands of Sleat. The fortunes of his family declined after his death in 1401, since Ranald's heirs had already been confirmed in their possessions by a royal charter of 1394. It seems likely that John macArthur received a charter to Godfrey's lands of North Uist around the same time, reviving his family's claim to lands in Garmoran and the Outer Isles, which had supposedly been granted to his ancestor Sir Arthur Campbell, Constable of Dunstaffnage Castle, by Christina macRuari of the Isles, who had sheltered Robert the Bruce in the winter of 1306–7. Evidently James I thought his interests best served by their mutual destruction, especially as they were both able to bring 1,000 men into the field. It was also to the benefit of the MacDonalds of Clan Ranald, descended from Ranald, eldest son of John MacDonald, of Islay by his first marriage with Amie macRuari, who regained their lands of Garmoran. Alexander MacDonald, third Lord of the Isles, was himself taken in custody to Perth, where he was forced to attend the King's court. He either escaped or gained his release within a couple of months, but his mother was kept in captivity on the island of Inchcolm in the Firth of Forth as a hostage for her son's good behaviour.

Revolt and Submission of Alexander MacDonald

Returning to the Western Isles, and obviously rankling with anger and indignation at his humiliating treatment by James I, Alexander MacDonald rather unwisely raised an army of 10,000 men in 1429 and proceeded to sack Inverness. James I promptly retaliated by leading another army north to suppress the rebellion, invading Lochaber where he put Alexander MacDonald, third Lord of the Isles, to flight after his cause had been deserted by the Camerons of Locheil and the MacIntoshes of Clan Chattan, who defected upon sight of the royal standard. There is no account of the battle and it is not even known where exactly it was fought, if indeed the two sides ever engaged one another, but it evidently brought the fortunes of the Lordship of the Isles to a very low ebb indeed.

It was perhaps as a final and despairing attempt to restore his fortunes that now prompted Alexander MacDonald, third Lord of the Isles, rather than taking refuge in Ireland, to throw himself upon the mercy of James I, who demanded his abject surrender. Not long after his defeat in Lochaber, Alexander came into the presence of James I with his Queen when at prayer in Holyrood Palace on Easter Sunday in 1429, clad only in a shirt and drawers as penitential garb and carrying his sword by its point. Kneeling in front of the King, the once-proud Lord of the Isles offered James I his sword in an humiliating act of utter submission to royal authority. It was most likely just a spectacle, craftily stage-managed by the King, who it is said only spared Alexander's life after the Queen and his nobles had pleaded with him for mercy. He was afterwards held captive in Tantallon Castle near North Berwick under the custody of William Douglas, Earl of Angus, while his territories of Kintyre and Knapdale were given briefly into the custody of two Ayrshire magnates, who acted as the constables of the castles at Sween and Skipness.

Donald Balloch and the Battle of Inverlochy

James I now decided to press home his advantage in the north. Next year in parliament it was decreed that all the magnates who held lands along the seaboard of the western Highlands were to have galleys ready for the King's service by May 1431. Evidently a great expedition was planned against the Western Isles. But beforehand Alexander Stewart, Earl of Mar, who was still acting as the King's chief lieutenant in the north, raised an army of local levies with the intention of seizing Lochaber from Alastair Carrach of Keppoch, son of Alexander MacDonald, Lord of Lochaber, whose troublesome activities we have already mentioned. Yet it was his cousin Donald Balloch, eldest son of the murdered John Mor Tanister, and now Lord of Dunnyvaig and the Glens, who took up arms on behalf of Clan Donald, hoping to avenge his father's death.

Donald Balloch first raised his own standard on the island of Carna at the mouth of Loch Sunart, where he was joined by MacIain of Ardnamurchan, Alan macAlan of Moidart, John MacLean of Coll, MacDuffie of Colonsay, MacQuarrie of Ulva and MacGee of the Rhinns of Islay, together with a force said to number around 6,000 men. They made their way towards Lochaber, perhaps sailing up Loch Sunart, and then using the porterage of the aptly named Glen Tarbert to gain the waters of Loch Linnhe. Sailing up Loch Linnhe, they landed from their galleys just south of Inverlochy, where Alexander Stewart, Earl of Mar, was encamped with his much-superior forces. Even so Donald Balloch apparently managed to surprise the enemy, unless it is true that the Earl of Mar was so confident of victory that he refused to leave a game of cards with MacIntosh, Captain of Clan Chattan, rather in the manner of Sir Francis Drake when faced by the ships of the Spanish Armada. Supported by Alistair Carrach of Keppoch, whom it is said had 220 archers under him, Donald Balloch routed the royalist forces, inflicting many casualties upon the enemy. Alan Stewart, Earl of Caithness, was killed and Alexander Stewart, Earl of Mar, was forced to flee across country from the battlefield, seriously wounded by an arrow.

The victory in 1431 of Donald Balloch at the first battle of Inverlochy (there was another battle there in 1645) did not end the matter, since James I was still determined to bring Clan Donald to heel. He proposed yet another expedition to subdue the Western Isles and it may well have reached Dunstaffnage Castle in Lorn. There he received the submission of many Highland chiefs, who declared that they had been forced to act as the unwilling accomplices of Donald Balloch in his recent rebellion. Legend has it that 300 freebooters were executed after they had been surrendered into the King's hands by the clan chiefs. Donald Balloch retired to the safety of the Glens of Antrim, where James I apparently tried to have him arrested. However the King was appeased when he was presented with the severed head of some unfortunate Gael, said to have graced the shoulders of Donald Balloch, even if he did not die until 1476. According to MacDonald traditions six Campbells were beheaded before the exact colour of Donald Balloch's hair could be matched.

Assassination of James I

Soon afterwards James I evidently realised the futility of trying to subjugate the Western Isles by force, since he released Alexander MacDonald, third Lord of the Isles, from captivity, and allowed him to return to his island territories. In revenge for his desertion by Clan Cameron, Alexander MacDonald granted their lands in Lochaber to the MacLeans of Coll. Even if the third Lord of the Isles thereafter remained a loyal and obedient servant of the King, his treatment was symptomatic of the headstrong and wayward attitude of James I in dealing with his Gaelic-speaking subjects. His government became increasingly autocratic and dictatorial, since he was not averse to flouting his own laws when it suited him. His nemesis came to pass on the night of 21 February 1437, when he was assassinated in his apartment within the Dominican friary of Perth.

The regicide of James I greatly benefited Alexander MacDonald, third Lord of the Isles, even if he was not directly implicated in the plot against the King. James II was himself only six years old in 1437 when his father was murdered by a small clique of disaffected noblemen, led by Sir Robert Stewart, who probably hoped to place his aged grandfather, Walter Stewart, Earl of Atholl, and the last-surviving son of Robert II, if not himself, upon the throne. They evidently hoped for popular acclaim for ridding the country of a 'tyrant'. Instead the perpetrators of the crime were arrested, tried for high treason and savagely put to death. The long regency which followed the death of James I was dominated by the Earls of Douglas, despite their internecine quarrels, until their final downfall at the hands of James II when he eventually came to rule in person after his marriage in 1449.

Alexander MacDonald, Earl of Ross

The government of the country during the minority of James II was first placed in the hands of Archibald, fifth Earl of Douglas, but he died of the plague in 1439. It was most likely under his patronage that Alexander MacDonald, third Lord of the Isles, was finally granted the earldom of Ross, soon after the death in 1436 of his mother Mary Leslie, Countess of Ross in her own right, when it seems that the Lord of the Isles adopted the title of Earl himself. Indeed, Alexander MacDonald joined the ranks of a much reduced aristocracy, since Archibald, Earl of Douglas, and David Lindsay, Earl of Crawford, were otherwise the only earls still living as adults in Scotland in the autumn of 1437. Such a power vacuum allowed the rise of such families as the Erskines, the Crichtons and the Livingstons, while encouraging claims to the various earldoms that were vacant, such as Lennox and Mar. Further favour was shown to Alexander MacDonald when he was made Justiciar of Scotland north of the Forth in 1439, once the death in 1435 of Alexander Stewart, Earl of Mar, had deprived the Crown of its chief agent in the north. Even if it seems he performed his duties in an able and conscientious manner, his tenure of this office evidently did not prevent Alexander's followers from launching several attacks beyond the borders of his own territories. One such raid was made against the earldom of Lennox in 1439, possibly led among others by Lachlan MacLean of Duart, when John Colquhoun of Luss was killed, while another attack against Arran came from Knapdale and Kintyre in the years around 1443.

Nevertheless when he died in 1449 Alexander MacDonald, third Lord of the Isles, exercised almost as much power and influence as any of his ancestors, holding as he did not just all of the Western Isles, including Skye and Lewis, but the vast estates of the earldom of Ross as well. By then he was amongst the greatest of all the landowners in the kingdom and the equal of such magnates as the Earl of Douglas and the Earl of Crawford. Indeed it was recorded much later that the eighth Earl of Douglas entered in 1445 or 1446 into an 'offensive and defensive league and combination against all none excepted, not [even] the king himself, with the Earl of Crawford and [Alexander] Lord of the Isles'. Such a triumvirate exercised great influence over their own territories and Alexander MacDonald was himself the dominant power in the north of Scotland.

Indeed once the Lords of the Isles had gained the earldom of Ross in 1437, it seems that they virtually abandoned their power-base in the west for their eastern territories. Three-quarters of all their charters and other legal documents issued after 1437 deal with land-holdings in the east, and a similar proportion of these documents were witnessed at such places as Inverness, Dingwall and Tain. Even so many of these documents are witnessed by the followers of Clan Donald from the Western Isles, showing that these vassal chieftains accompanied Alexander MacDonald and his son John, fourth and last Lord of the Isles, when they moved east to occupy the earldom of Ross. Indeed when he died at Dingwall in 1449 Alexander MacDonald was buried, not with his ancestors on Iona, but at the Chanonry of Ross on the Black Isle, prompting the apt comment from J. Munro (1986) that 'he seems to have died as he had lived, as Earl of Ross, rather than . . . Lord of the Isles'.

Succession to the Lordship

Alexander MacDonald, third Lord of the Isles and Earl of Ross, was succeeded after his death in 1449 by his eldest son John. Although perhaps only fifteen years of age and still a minor when he gained the Lordship of the Isles, John MacDonald as the fourth Lord of the Isles and Earl of Ross soon became embroiled in the turbulent events that occurred when James II first came to rule in person after the long years of his minority. These years had been dominated by the powerful Douglas family and latterly by William, eighth Earl of Douglas, often acting in alliance with the Livingstons against the Crichtons, and helped by the Lindsays, Earls of Crawford. The Lowlands especially were racked by conflict and lawlessness. Soon after James II had married Mary of Guelders in 1449 he marked the end of his minority by destroying the power of the Livingston family. Charged with treason, two of its leading members were executed in 1450 and several others were imprisoned and forfeited of all their lands and offices. The King then acted with equal vigour against the Black Douglases early in 1451, when the absence abroad on pilgrimage in Rome of William, eighth Earl of Douglas, prompted James II to mount an ill-advised attack upon the Douglas lands in Galloway in an attempt to seize the earldom.

Murder of the Earl of Douglas by James II

Although this foray ended in an uneasy compromise between the young King and his 'over-mighty subject', their quarrel reached a climax early in 1452 when William, eighth Earl of Douglas, was summoned by James II into his presence at Stirling Castle under the security of a safe-conduct. There he was charged by James II to break the band of loyalty that he had apparently signed in 1445 or 1446 with the Earl of Crawford and Alexander MacDonald, third Lord of the Isles and Earl of Ross, before the latter's death in 1449, and which he may have renewed later with their sons and heirs. When the Earl of Douglas contemptously refused to renege on his agreement, he was struck down by James II and murdered in cold blood. The crime was all the more heinous, and judged so at the time, because it was committed under trust in contravention of a solemn undertaking by the King that the Earl of Douglas would not be harmed.

John MacDonald, fourth Lord of the Isles and Earl of Ross, was drawn into these events firstly by his marriage in 1449 with Elizabeth Livingston, eldest daughter of the Chamberlain of Scotland, and then by the 'band' that it seems his father had made earlier with William, eighth Earl of Douglas, and the Earl of Crawford. Within a month of the Earl's murder, the Douglases rose in open rebellion against the Crown under the leadership of James, ninth Earl of Douglas, and the eldest-surviving brother of the murdered Earl, together with his three other brothers. It is often thought that their revolt was joined almost immediately by John MacDonald, fourth Lord of the Isles and Earl of Ross, who certainly mounted a rebellion in the north of Scotland around this time. However, as argued by A. Grant (1981), it may be that he actually rebelled a year earlier in 1451, reacting to the downfall of his father-in-law Sir James Livingston. It seems he was further angered by James II who had broken a promise to give him custody of the strategic castles of Urquhart and Ruthven, which guarded the routes west from Inverness, linking the earldom of Ross with his western territories. If so, it may well explain why James II acted so strongly against William, eighth Earl of Douglas, when he refused to abandon his band of loyalty with the Lord of the Isles in 1452, thus committing what was no doubt an act of treason by continuing to support a rebel, who was himself guilty of treason against the Scottish Crown.

Rebellion of John MacDonald, Earl of Ross

Whenever this rebellion actually took place, John MacDonald, fourth Lord of the Isles and Earl of Ross, first captured the royal castles of Urquhart and Inverness with a large force of his own clansmen and then demolished the castle at Ruthven in Badenoch. After placing a garrison in Inverness Castle, he left Urquhart Castle in the charge of his father-in-law, Sir James Livingston, who had now escaped from royal custody. It was evidently in reaction to these events that James II appointed Sir Alexander Seton of Seton, first Earl of Huntly, as Lord of Badenoch. After the murder of William, eighth Earl of Douglas, probably in the following year, Alexander Lindsay, now the Earl of Crawford, and known as the 'Tiger Earl', was defeated at Brechin by the newly created Lord of Badenoch, who was virtually the only supporter of the King in the north apart from William Sinclair, Earl of Caithness and Orkney, and George Douglas, Earl of Angus. Even if the Earl of Huntly was victorious at Brechin his territories of Strathbogie were attacked by Archibald Douglas, who was another brother of the murdered Earl of Douglas, as well as being Earl of Moray by virtue of his marriage with Elizabeth Dunbar, heiress of the Dunbar earls of Moray,

Meanwhile James, ninth Earl of Douglas, had come to Knapdale to parley with John MacDonald, fourth Lord of the Isles, bringing with him 'right great gifts' of clothes, wine, silk, English cloth and silver. They apparently prevailed upon the veteran Donald Balloch of Dunnyvaig and the Glens to mount a raid on the islands in the Firth of Clyde with a fleet said to number 100 galleys. Sailing from his territories in Antrim, he first landed at Inverkip in Renfrew, where the Bishop of Glasgow had some lands and then he harried the Cumbraes and Arran, burning the castle at Brodick to the ground. Next he attacked Rothesay on the island of Bute and demanded blackmail from its inhabitants. Finally he sailed north to Lismore where he attacked the lands of George Lauder, Bishop of Argyll, who had made himself obnoxious to the men of Argyll with his Lowland ways. The Bishop only escaped with his life by taking sanctuary in his own church, while many of his servants were slain. The plunder from this campaign was reputed to consist of 100 bolls of meal, 100 bolls of malt, 100 merks of silver, 500 horses, 10,000 oxen and cows and more than 1000 sheep and goats. It was perhaps to support Donald Balloch that John MacDonald, fourth Lord of the Isles, now invaded Sutherland with a force of 500 or 600 men. This invasion was renewed after his forces had been repulsed but they were finally defeated with much loss of life at the battle of Strathfleet.

Final Destruction of the Earls of Douglas

James II reacted to these events by launching yet another expedition against the Douglas lands of Galloway in the summer of 1452, which was just as ineffective as his earlier foray into the south-west. An accommodation was then apparently reached with James, ninth Earl of Douglas, which lasted until the final showdown took place in 1455 between James II and the Black

Douglases, when James II launched a third and final attack against his enemies. The Earl of Douglas himself managed to escape to England, where he was soon afterwards joined by one of his brothers, who had escaped after his defeat in a decisive skirmish with royalist forces at Arkinholm on the banks of the River Esk near Langholm. His second brother was killed and his third and last brother was executed after his capture at the same affray. The Earl of Crawford was already dead and his earldom forfeited to the Crown.

By then John MacDonald, fourth Lord of the Isles and Earl of Ross, had evidently had the good sense to seek a reconciliation with James II. Indeed the King had already been forced to reinstate his father-in-law Sir James Livingston to his old office of Chamberlain. Nonetheless the fourth Lord of the Isles remained aloof during what was effectively a civil war waged by the King against the Black Douglases, which ended with the forfeiture of James, ninth Earl of Douglas. He himself was fortunate enough to escape such a fate on this occasion, even if he was deprived of the castles at Urquhart and Inverness. Even so he regained Urquhart Castle next year in return for an annual rent of 100 merks, while he received at the same time the surrounding lands of Urquhart and Glen Moriston, as well as Abertarf and Stratherrick. Further signs of royal favour were shown in 1457, when he was made a Warden of the Marches, even if this appointment was perhaps intended to weaken his power by forcing him to reside outside his territories in the north. The next year he was appointed to the powerful office of Sheriff of Inverness, while he had the sheriffdom of Nairn as well in his gift. Such a conciliatory policy pursued by James II towards the fourth Lord of the Isles had its reward at the siege of Roxburgh Castle in the summer of 1460, when John MacDonald brought a force of 300 men, which he intended should act as an advance guard to 'take the first press and dint of battle' in the proposed invasion of England. But the campaign itself had scarcely got under way when James II was killed by the bursting of a cannon as he was demonstrating its capabilities to his queen.

The Treaty of Ardtornish

The early death of James II in 1460 just a few months before his thirtieth birthday, after an effective reign of only a few years, ushered in yet another long minority. James III was only eight years old when he succeeded to the throne of Scotland and the country was first ruled jointly by the dowager queen Mary of Guelders and Bishop Kennedy of St Andrews. The early years of the regency were overshadowed by the Wars of the Roses in England, after Henry VI of Lancaster had first been captured in 1460 and then deposed in the following year in favour of Edward IV of York. Bishop

Kennedy favoured the defeated Lancastrians, some of whom took refuge with Henry VI as exiles in Scotland, while Mary of Guelders was more far-sighted in her support of the Yorkists. It was perhaps the surrender of Berwick to Scotland by the Lancastrian exiles and their promise to give up Carlisle which prompted Edward IV of England to send the disinherited Earl of Douglas north as his emissary to negotiate on his behalf with John MacDonald, fourth Lord of the Isles, and John Balloch of Dunnyvaig and the Glens. The result of their deliberations was the Treaty of Ardtornish of 1462, later ratified at Westminister, whereby John MacDonald, Earl of Ross, Donald Balloch of Dunyvaig and the Glens, and the latter's son and heir John Mor MacDonald, each agreed to become the vassals of Edward IV of England, along with all their subjects. In return the Earl of Ross was to receive £200 every year in time of war and 100 merks during peacetime, while Donald Balloch and his son John Mor were each to receive annual payments of £40 and £20 in time of war but only half these amounts during peacetime. Such payments were then often made in the Lowlands of Scotland under the system of land-holding known much later as 'bastard feudalism', under which the obligations of service to a lord-superior were replaced by annuities paid to a vassal for his loyalty.

Yet the Treaty of Ardtornish went very much further, since it also envisaged 'if it so be' the conquest of Scotland by Edward IV of England, aided by John MacDonald, fourth Lord of the Isles, and Donald Balloch of Dunnyvaig and the Glens, as well as James, ninth Earl of Douglas. If this ever came to pass it was agreed that Scotland north of the Forth should be divided equally between James Douglas, John MacDonald and Donald Balloch, holding their lands from the English King, while James Douglas would himself be restored to the earldom that he had forfeited to James II.

Role of Donald Balloch

It is difficult to understand why John MacDonald, fourth Lord of the Isles, ever entered into such a treasonable league with James Douglas, since he was later described as 'a meek, modest man, brought up at Court in his younger years . . . and a scholar, more fit to be a churchman than to command so many irregular tribes of people'. Indeed the veteran Donald Balloch of Dunnyvaig and the Glens may well have been the real power at this time behind the Lordship of the Isles, acting as an *eminence gris* in manipulating the policies pursued by the fourth Lord. Already it had been reported that men from the Western Isles were attacking Caithness and Orkney in large numbers around this time, while it was certainly under his leadership that the men of the Isles mounted yet another attack upon Inverness in 1463. Then after capturing Inverness Castle he assumed the powers of regality throughout the northern counties. The spoils of this expedition included nearly £1,500 collected in rents from the Crown lands of Moray, as well as very large quantities of grain and cattle. The young James III came north in 1464 with Bishop Kennedy to Inverness, where he summoned John MacDonald, fourth Lord of the Isles, to account to a royal council for the depredations done in his name. It seems that a reconciliation was reached with the government and he evidently continued in his office of Sheriff of Inverness. Indeed James III or Bishop Kennedy as his Regent confirmed several charters made earlier by John, fourth Lord of the Isles, in favour of his two half-brothers.

John MacDonald and his Grants

John MacDonald, fourth Lord of the Isles, first confirmed his elder half-brother Celestine of Lochalsh in his possession of the lands of Lochbroom, Lochalsh, Torridon, Lochcarron and Kishorn in the earldom of Ross, once part of North Argyll, while a year later in 1464, he granted him the lands of Ferincoskry in Braechat, north of the Kyle of Sutherland. Both grants were evidently intended to strengthen the MacDonald presence on the northern frontiers of the earldom of Ross. Likewise he granted out in 1469 to his other half-brother Hugh MacDonald the MacLeod lands in Sleat, and the lands of North Uist, Benbecula and parts of South Uist, previously held by the descendants of Godfrey of Uist, who had seized these lands before his death in 1401. It was a grant apparently made with the full agreement of William MacLeod of Harris and Dunvegan and Ruaridh MacLeod of Lewis, who both witnessed the charter. Hugh founded the family known as the MacDonalds of Sleat, which later came to hold the chiefship of Clan Donald itself, as indeed it still does. All these lands were resigned by Hugh's son John in 1498, when they came into the possessions of the MacDonalds of Clan Ranald. No doubt it was becoming ever more difficult to find lands on which to settle younger sons, since this could often only be done by seizing land from the more distant branches of the family. Indeed Sleat had already been resigned into the hands of John, fourth Lord of the Isles, by his half-brother Celestine of Lochalsh, before it was granted out to Hugh MacDonald, presumably for this very reason. Thereafter it remained in the hands of the MacDonalds of Sleat despite the repeated attempts of the MacLeods of Harris and Dunvegan to recover what was their ancient patrimony

Another grant said to have been made around this time by John, fourth Lord of the Isles, acting in his capacity as the Earl of Ross, gave Alexander MacKenzie of Kintail lands in the Braes of Ross, including Killin, Garve and Kinlochluichart. Even if it was perhaps intended to reward Alexander

MacKenzie for reconciling the Earl of Ross to James III, as MacKenzie tradition would have it, the grant itself was apparently made six months earlier. It therefore seems more likely that it was an attempt to persuade this powerful family to give their support to John, fourth Lord of the Isles. The same motive may well have been behind the granting of lands in Lochaber and the office of bailie in Lochaber to Duncan MacIntosh, captain of Clan Chattan. But all such attempts by John MacDonald, fourth Lord of the Isles, to strengthen his position came to nought when the Treaty of Ardtornish came to light in 1475, six years after James III started to rule in his own right in 1469.

Loss of the Earldom of Ross

The Treaty of Ardtornish was revealed to James III of Scotland after he had concluded a treaty of friendship with Edward IV of England. When the full extent of his treasonable actions became known, John MacDonald, fourth Lord of the Isles and Earl of Ross, was summoned to appear before parliament to answer a long list of charges, including one of high treason, arising not just from the Treaty of Ardtornish in 1462 but from his previous acts of rebellion against the Crown as well. When he failed to appear he was sentenced to death, while his lands, rents, superiorities and offices were all forfeited to the Crown. He was now faced with the forcible seizure of his lands by Sir Colin Campbell, Earl of Argyll, and threatened by land and sea with the dispatch of an expeditionary force under the command of John Stewart, Earl of Atholl, and David Lindsay, Earl of Crawford. Already his castle at Dingwall had been seized early in 1476 by an expedition led by George Gordon, second Earl of Huntly.

Faced with such threats to his position, John MacDonald was forced to submit to royal authority. Pleading humility and contrition for his earlier actions he appeared in person before parliament in July 1476, when he resigned to the Crown the earldom of Ross, except for the lordship of Skye along with the lands of Knapdale and Kintyre, all of which he held by feudal grant, and the hereditary sheriffdoms of Inverness and Nairn, so that he still possessed Morvern and the lands of Garmoran along with Lochaber, Glencoe and Duror. In return he was granted a feudal title to his ancient territories under the once-proud title of Lord of the Isles, which he now held as a mere Lord of Parliament. James III also agreed that his possessions should pass on his death to his natural son and heir, Angus Og MacDonald of Islay, failing any legitimate issue. The earldom of Ross was annexed to the Crown, while some of its rents were granted during her lifetime to Elizabeth Livingston, estranged wife of the Lord of the Isles, who had earlier taken refuge at the royal court. A few years later it was granted out in 1481 to James Stewart, second son of James III, who held it afterwards as a dukedom until his death in 1504.

Now holding the Lordship of the Isles under royal charter, John MacDonald promised to render due rights and services to the Crown and, together with the tenants and other inhabitants of his lands, to observe the laws and customs of the realm like all other barons and freeholders. But it was easier said than done. When he exchanged his ancient title of *Ri Innse Gall* for what were known contemptuously as sheep-skin charters, he greatly weakened his own prestige and authority among the clansmen of Clan Donald. They still adhered to the ancient traditions of Gaeldom and looked to the Lord of the Isles to protect their Gaelic heritage as *Buchaille nan Eilean*, or Herdsman of the Isles. Resenting deeply his humiliating submission to royal authority, they soon came to regard his natural son and heir Angus Og MacDonald as the true champion of their ancient ways. Matters were made worse by the granting out of MacDonald lands to such vassals of John MacDonald, fourth Lord of the Isles, as the MacLeans, the MacLeods and the MacNeils, in return for their support. Such actions by his father were greatly resented by Angus Og MacDonald, since they threatened to reduce further his patrimony, already severely curtailed by the loss of Kintyre, Knapdale and the earldom of Ross.

Tradition has it that animosity between father and son came to such a pitch that Angus Og MacDonald hounded his father from his residence at Finlaggan on Islay, forcing him to take shelter for the night under an upturned boat, and then to seek refuge with Colin Campbell, Earl of Argyll. But even if he did not rebel openly against his father until 1481 at the very earliest, Angus Og was possibly behind the troubles that broke out immediately after 1476. Arran was laid waste in raids by the Islemen in 1477 and 1478, while Angus Og MacDonald almost certainly seized Castle Sween in Knapdale, which was garrisoned by MacDonald forces around the same time. Summoned before parliament in 1478 John MacDonald, fourth Lord of the Isles, managed to procure a pardon for his rebellious son and later that year he received back some of his own lands in Kintyre, when he was also confirmed in all his other possessions. Perhaps then, if not earlier in 1476, Angus Og MacDonald married Mary, younger daughter of Colin Campbell, first Earl of Argyll. The next three years were peaceful. John MacDonald even received back some more of his old lands in Knapdale and Kintyre in 1481, but they were only to be held for his lifetime under the newly created sheriffdom of Tarbert, itself now a royal burgh. Six months earlier Colin Campbell, Earl of Argyll, was granted other lands in Knapdale, to be held by his heirs after his own death, together with the custody of Castle Sween. However these years were just the lull before the storm which was about to break around the Lordship of the Isles, driven by the ambitions of Angus Og

MacDonald to regain the earldom of Ross, once he had the whole strength of Clan Donald behind him.

Rebellion of Angus Og MacDonald

The expedition mounted in 1481 by Angus Og MacDonald against the earldom of Ross was evidently intended to curb the rising power of the MacKenzies of Kintail, which had greatly increased after the MacDonald forfeiture of 1476. Legend has it that a pretext was found when Kenneth, eldest son of the MacKenzie chief, repudiated his wife Margaret, supposedly the sister of Angus Og MacDonald and perhaps blind in one eye, after a quarrel had broken out between the two brothers-in-law. More likely she was Finvola, sister of Alexander MacDonald of Lochalsh and thus Angus Og's cousin. She was sent packing by her husband, mounted on a one-eyed horse, attended by a one-eyed servant and followed by a one-eyed dog, or so it was said. Angered by such an insult Angus Og MacDonald gathered together a large force from the Isles, which was augmented by MacDonald clansmen from the districts of Knoydart, Moidart, Glengarry and Lochaber, and marched against Inverness where he seized the town and castle. He then advanced upon Dingwall where he installed himself for the next two years. Faced with this insurrection James III despatched an army north under John Stewart, Earl of Atholl. It was heavily defeated by the MacDonalds at the battle of *Lagabraad*, or Logiebride, somewhere near the head of the Cromarty Firth. The King then ordered another army north under the joint command of David Lindsay, Earl of Crawford, and George Gordon, second Earl of Huntly, now Justiciar north of the Forth, which may have succeeded in dislodging Angus Og MacDonald from Easter Ross and forced him to retreat to Lochaber. The details of this campaign are very sketchy and it is even possible that they refused to carry out their orders, given the strength of the MacDonald forces and the unsettled state of the country.

Internecine Battle of Bloody Bay

It was after these events, if not even earlier, that Colin Campbell, first Earl of Argyll, who was the father-in-law of Angus Og MacDonald, who had earlier married his daughter Mary, together with John Stewart, Earl of Atholl, attempted to mediate between the chief of Clan Donald and his only surviving son. Perhaps acting at the behest of John MacDonald, fourth Lord of the Isles, who had earlier sought his sanctuary, Colin Campbell, first Earl of Argyll, arranged a meeting between father and son off the island of Mull, where they gathered with their powerful fleets of galleys. John MacDonald, Lord of the Isles, was supported by his vassal kindreds, among whom were the MacLeans of Duart, Lochbuie and Ardgour, the MacLeods of Harris and Dunvegan and Lewis and the MacNeils of Barra, while his son had the support of Clan Ranald and the MacDonalds of Sleat as well as the men of Clan Donald. But instead of the intended reconciliation between father and son, the two sides resolved to settle their differences by battle, perhaps because the Earls of Argyll and Atholl were unable to meet the demands of Angus Og MacDonald that his father should be restored to the earldom of Ross.

The battle of Bloody Bay, which followed the breakdown in these negotiations, was fought off the coast of Mull just north of Tobermory. Significantly it was almost the first such conflict fought within the confines of the Lordship of the Isles for well over two centuries, such had been the power of Clan Donald to keep the peace. Angus Og MacDonald gained a resounding victory, even if the details of the battle only come from traditional accounts. William MacLeod of Harris and Dunvegan was mortally wounded by the MacDonalds of Clan Ranald, while MacLean of Ardgour would have been hanged after he was captured by Angus Og MacDonald. His life was only saved after Ranald Ban, master of Clan Ranald, objected, saying that 'he would have no-one to bicker with if MacLean were gone'.

After his victory at the battle of Bloody Bay, Angus Og MacDonald was known as Master of the Isles and Captain of Clan Donald. Even if he did not entirely supplant his father he certainly came to play a very significant role in the affairs of the Lordship, which it seems they divided between themselves. Angus Og MacDonald maintained himself mostly in the north, even if he also held Islay at its very heart, while his father occupied the more southerly parts of his territories, especially Kintyre and Knapdale. It was during these years that Angus Og MacDonald apparently invaded the MacLeod lands in the north of Skye, seizing the castle of Duntuilm in Trotternish, which later became a stronghold of the MacDonalds of Sleat. By 1482 he evidently felt secure enough in the possession of these lands to describe himself as the 'Lord of Trotternish' in a charter to the monks of Iona. Even if the MacLeods of Harris and Dunvegan attempted time and again to recover Trotternish in later years their efforts never had any lasting effect.

Abduction of Donald Dubh

It was perhaps immediately after the battle of Bloody Bay that John Stewart, Earl of Atholl, kidnapped the Earl of Argyll's daughter from Finlaggan on Islay, where she had been living as the wife of Angus Og MacDonald, and delivered her up to her father. He seemingly connived in abducting his own daughter, furnishing the Earl of Atholl with boats, so that he could cross secretly over to Islay. Afterwards he kept his daughter and her infant son under strict guard in the Campbell stronghold of Innischonnell on Loch Awe. The child, who was later known as Donald Dubh, may even have been born after his mother was abducted and every attempt was made by the Campbells to deny that Angus Og MacDonald was his father. No doubt Colin Campbell, first Earl of Argyll, had his eye upon the MacDonald estates and indeed he convinced the Government that Donald Dubh was illegitimate. In revenge Angus Og MacDonald now launched a devastating attack upon the Earl of Atholl and his countess, who took refuge within the santuary of the Church of St Bridget. They were abducted and held prisoner on Islay for a year. According to tradition Angus Og MacDonald returned to Atholl where he did penance for violating the sanctity of the Church. He evidently feared divine retribution after several of his plunder-laden galleys had foundered in a storm, sailing back to Islay.

Revolt of Alexander MacDonald of Lochalsh

Given his military prowess Angus Og MacDonald might well have restored the fortunes of Clan Donald had he lived to succeed his father, but he was murdered when staying at Inverness by Diarmid O'Cairbre, who was an Irish harper in his retinue. There is perhaps some truth in the romantic story that the assassin acted at the behest of Kenneth MacKenzie of Kintail, who promised him the hand of his daughter in marriage if he was successful. After the death of Angus Og MacDonald, which occurred in 1490 at the very latest, his mantle fell upon Alexander MacDonald of Lochalsh, nephew of John MacDonald, Lord of the Isles, who had inherited the lands of Lochalsh, Lochcarron and Lochbroom from his father Celestine. Aided by Farquhar MacIntosh, son of the Captain of Clan Chattan, together with Clan Ranald of Garmoran, the MacDonalds of Keppoch and Clan Cameron of Locheil, Alexander MacDonald of Lochalsh raised yet another large army from the Western Highlands and Islands in 1491. Advancing from Lochaber through Glean Spean into Badenoch and Strathspey he attacked Inverness, where the castle was captured and destroyed. His forces then ravaged the Black Isle, where they were joined by the Roses of Kilravock, plundering the lands of Sir Alexander Urquhart, Sheriff of Cromarty. But after turning west into Strathconon the MacDonalds were surprised at night by the MacKenzies, whose lands they had hoped to plunder, and utterly defeated at the battle of *Blair na Pairc*, which was fought near Strathpeffer. Although the MacKenzies of Kintail had already begun their long rise to power and influence, they committed such great excesses in the aftermath of their victory over the MacDonalds that George Gordon, second Earl of Huntly, was compelled to intervene as Lieutenant of the North.

This further outbreak of disorder in the north occurred three years after the troubled reign of James III had come to a violent end at the battle of Sauchieburn in 1488, when he 'happinit to be slane' in the quaint words of the time. The battle itself was fought by the King and his loyal supporters against a confederacy of discontented noblemen, among whom was Colin Campbell, first Earl of Argyll. They probably hoped to force James III to abdicate in favour of his eldest son, whose person they had seized earlier, but events turned out otherwise. The King was killed, most likely during the course of the battle itself, and not by an unknown assailant as he fled wounded from the battlefield as tradition would have it. Although only fifteen years of age at the time of his father's death, and implicated in the rebellion against him, James IV soon began to take over the reins of government. Almost his first act of government after attaining his majority in 1493 was the final forfeiture of John MacDonald, fourth and last Lord of the Isles.

Forfeiture of the Lordship

It is not known if the Lord of the Isles had condoned the actions of Alexander MacDonald of Lochalsh when he mounted his insurrection against the earldom of Ross in 1491, or whether he had acted entirely independently of his uncle. Yet there was every reason for the government to deprive John MacDonald of the Lordship of the Isles. If he had encouraged the insurrection of 1491 he was still an incorrigible rebel, whereas if he had failed to dissuade his nephew from disturbing the peace of the realm he was equally at fault, since he was then quite unable to maintain law and order within his own domains. Parliament in 1493 therefore took the momentous decision so fateful to Clan Donald to forfeit John MacDonald by annexing all his territories to the Crown, which in fact he surrendered voluntarily early in 1494. Afterwards he lived as a humble pensioner at court for the next ten years, only to die in obscure and impoverished circumstances in a Dundee lodging-house in 1503. He was a broken man, dependent on James IV for charity. He lies buried in Paisley Abbey, which had benefited so generously from the gifts of his more illustrious predecessors.

After John MacDonald, fourth Lord of the Isles, had forfeited the earldom of Ross in 1476 and then the Lordship of the Isles in 1493, Clan Donald entered into a rapid decline as a unifying force in Gaelic society. The sense of impending loss was well expressed in the elegiac poem written during these years by Giolla Coluim mac an Ollaimh (cited in MacInnes; 1981):

> Alas for those who have lost that company;
> Alas for those who have parted from their society;
> For no race is as Clan Donald,

A noble race, strong of courage.
There was no counting their bounty;
There was no reckoning of their gifts;
Their nobles knew no bound,
No beginning, no end of generosity.
In the van of Clan Donald learning was commanded,
And in their rear were service of honour and self-respect.
For sorrow and for sadness,
I have forsaken wisdom and learning;
On their account, I have forsaken all things:
It is no joy without Clan Donald.

By then other families were in the ascendant, such as the Campbells, the Gordons and, latterly, the MacKenzies, who all took full advantage of the downfall of Clan Donald to pursue their own interests, often acting for the Crown as the King's lieutenants in the Highlands and Western Isles. As Clan Donald itself broke up into separate clans, these agents of royal authority were able to exploit the divisions between the once-solid ranks of Clan Donald and its vassal kindreds. Feuds broke out that lasted until the early years of the seventeenth century, while the surviving septs and branches of Clan Donald revolted time and again in a vain attempt to regain their former glory as Lords of the Isles.

BIBLIOGRAPHY

All the titles are given in full except for the *Scottish Historical Review*, cited as *SHR*.

Historical Background

The *Edinburgh History of Scotland* gives the most authoritative account of Scottish history now available. A. A. M. Duncan, *Scotland: The Making of a Kingdom* (Edinburgh, 1975) and R. Nicholson, *Scotland: The Later Middle Ages* (Edinburgh, 1974) cover the period to 1513. They give full details of most of the primary sources quoted in the present work. These two works may be augmented by W. Croft Dickinson, *Scotland from the Earliest Times to 1603* (Oxford, 1977, 3rd edn, rev. by A. A. M. Duncan). More popular but just as useful as background reading are the relevant volumes in the *New History of Scotland*: A. F. Smyth, *Warlords and Holymen, Scotland AD 80-1000* (Edinburgh, 1984), G. W. S. Barrow, *Kingship and Unity, Scotland 1000-1306* (Edinburgh, 1981) and A. Grant, *Independence and Nationhood, Scotland 1306-1469* (Edinburgh, 1984). See also G. Donaldson, *Scottish Kings* (London, 1967) and G. Menzies (ed.), *Who are the Scots?* (London, 1971). Apart from clan or family histories, few recent books deal in any detail with the history of the Highlands and Western Isles during the Middle Ages. W. F. Skene's masterly three-volume work *Celtic Scotland* (Edinburgh, 2nd edn, 1886-90) deals with historical matters in *Book One: History and Ethnography*, while the other two volumes are more concerned with the nature and institutions of Celtic society. Other books on Highland history include the all too concise account by W. R. Kermack, *The Scottish Highlands: A Short History, c.300-1746* (Edinburgh, 1957) and several nineteenth-century works, such as D. Mitchell, *History of the Highlands and Gaelic Scotland* (Paisley, 1900), as well as W. C. MacKenzie, *The Highlands and Isles of Scotland: A Historical Survey* (Edinburgh, 1949). They may be augmented by such local histories as C. M. MacDonald, *The History of Argyll* (Glasgow, 1950), which provides a well-documented account of events not just in Argyll but throughout the Western Highlands and Islands, especially useful for Chapters 5, 9 and 10. See also W. C. MacKenzie, *History of the Outer Hebrides* (Paisley, 1903) and A. Nicholson, *History of Skye* (Glasgow, 1930). There is a valuable series of short articles by several different authors in P. G. B. MacNeill and R. G. Nicholson (eds), *An Historical Atlas of Scotland, c.400-c.1600* (St Andrews, 1975, new edn forthcoming). The primary sources for the study of Highland history during the Middle Ages are reviewed by G. W. S. Barrow in L. MacLean (ed.), *The Middle Ages in the Highlands* (1981).

Biography and Family History

An invaluable guide to the bibliography of Scottish family history is provided by M. Stuart, *Scottish Family History* (Edinburgh, 1930), augmented by J. P. S. Ferguson, *Scottish Family Histories* (Edinburgh, 1982, 2nd edn). Biographical details of Scottish kings and their nobility are given by J. Balfour Paul, *The Scottish Peerage* (Edinburgh 1904–14, 9 vols), augmented by the Royal Historical Society's *Handbook of British Chronology* (1986, 3rd edn by E. B. Fryde). See also G. F. Black, *The Surnames of Scotland: Their Origin, Meaning and History* (New York 1946, reprinted 1993). Such works may be supplemented by more popular books such as F. Adams, *The Clans, Septs and Regiments of Scotland* (Edinburgh, 1952), Sir I. Moncrieffe of that Ilk, *The Highland Clans* (London, 1967), I. Grimble, *Scottish Clans and Tartans* (Edinburgh, 1973) and G. Way of Plean and R. Squire, *Scottish Clan and Family Encyclopedia* (Glasgow, 1994), even if they often fail to distinguish historical fact from what must pass as myth and legend.

Ancient Celtic Kingdoms

A. P. Smyth, *Warlords and Holymen: Scotland AD 80–1000* (Edinburgh, 1984) gives a spirited account of the first millennium in Scotland's history, accompanied by a very full bibliography. The nature of Celtic society is the subject of a great many publications, among which may be cited the introduction by N. Chadwick, *The Celts* (Harmondsworth, 1970) and the more recent account by L. Laing and J. Laing, *The Picts and the Scots* (Gloucester, 1993), as well as more detailed treatments, such as M. O. Anderson, *Kings and Kingship in Early Scotland* (Edinburgh, 1973) and B. T. Hudson, *Kings of Celtic Scotland* (Connecticut, 1994). See also F. T. Wainwright, *The Problem of the Picts* (Edinburgh, 1955), J. W. M. Bannerman, *Studies in the History of Dalradia* (Edinburgh, 1974) and B. E. Crawford, *Scandinavian Scotland* (Leicester, 1987). The reign of Macbeth is treated by P. B. Ellis, MacBeth, *High King of Scotland 1040–57AD* (London, 1980), by G. W. S. Barrow, 'Macbeth and other mormaers of Moray', in L. MacLean (ed.), *The Hub of the Highlands* (Edinburgh, 1975) and by E. J. Cowan, 'The historical MacBeth', in W. D. H. Sellar (ed.), *Moray: Province and People* (Edinburgh, 1993). W. J. Watson, *The History of the Celtic Place-Names of Scotland* (Edinburgh, 1926, reprinted) gives a classic account of this important but often neglected topic. It is now covered more analytically by W. F. H. Nicolaisen, *Scottish Place-Names: Their Study and Significance* (London, 1976), citing his many earlier articles.

Malcolm Canmore and the Norman Conquest

R. L. G. Ritchie, *The Normans in Scotland* (Edinburgh, 1954), provided the first modern account of the Norman Conquest of Scotland, now augmented by G. W. S.

Barrow, *The Anglo-Norman Era in Scottish History* (Oxford, 1980), among his many other works. The Celtic ceremonials at the inauguration of Alexander III are analysed by J. W. M. Bannerman, 'The king's poet and the inauguration of Alexander III' in *SHR*, **68** (1989) as part of a wider discussion concerning the survival of Celtic institutions in medieval Scotland. What evidence place-names provide for the decline of Gaelic throughout Lowland Scotland during the Middle Ages is discussed by W. F. H. Nicolaisen, 'Gaelic and Scots 1300–1600: some place-name evidence', in D. S. Thomson (ed.), *Gaelic and Scots in Harmony* (Glasgow, 1990), while the linguistic make-up of medieval Scotland is reviewed by D. Murison, 'Linguistic relations in medieval Scotland', in G. W. S. Barrow (ed.), *The Scottish Tradition* (Edinburgh, 1974).

Passing of the Ancient Earldoms

Biographical details of all the ancient earls of Scotland are given by J. Balfour Paul, *The Scottish Peerage* (Edinburgh, 1904–14, 9 vols), augmented by reference to the Royal Historical Society, *Handbook of British Chronology* (London, 1986, 3rd edn by E. B. Fryde). The title of *mormaer* and its derivation are discussed by K. H. Jackson, *The Gaelic Notes in the Book of Deer* (Cambridge, 1972), while the Celtic origins of the earls of Fife are treated by J. W. M. Bannerman, 'MacDuff of Fife', in A. Grant and K. J. Stringer (eds), *Medieval Scotland: Crown, Lordship and Community* (Edinburgh, 1993). The later history of the Scottish earldoms is discussed by A. Grant, 'Earls and earldoms in late medieval Scotland (c. 1310–1460)', in J. Bossy and P. Jupp (eds), *Essays Presented to Michael Roberts* (Belfast, 1976) and 'The development of the Scottish Peerage', in *SHR*, **57** (1978). See also K. Stringer (ed.), *Essays on the Nobility of Medieval Scotland* (Edinburgh, 1985) and A. Young, 'Noble families and political factions in the reign of Alexander III', in N. Reid (ed.), *Scotland in the Reign of Alexander III* (Edinburgh, 1990).

Conquest and Settlement in the North

The histories already cited, including W. R. Kermack, *The Scottish Highlands: A Short History* (Edinburgh, 1957), only give brief details of the revolts in Moray and Ross against the Canmore kings, but there are few more detailed accounts apart from W. F. Skene, *Celtic Scotland: History and Ethnography* (Edinburgh, 1886). The early history of Caithness during the Middle Ages is discussed by B. E. Crawford, 'The earldom of Caithness and the kingdom of Scotland, 1150–1266', in K. J. Stringer (ed.), *Essays on the Nobility of Medieval Scotland* (Edinburgh, 1985). G. W. S. Barrow, 'Badenoch and Strathspey, 1130–1312' in *Northern Scotland*, **8** (1988) documents the feudal settlement of Badenoch and Strathspey, while A. Young, 'The earls and earldom of Buchan in the thirteenth century', in A. Grant and K. J. Stringer (eds), *Medieval Scotland: Crown, Lordship and Community* (Edinburgh, 1993) gives a detailed account of Comyn power in north-east Scotland. The source quoted by Professor Barrow for the existence of Rainaldus Canis is L. Delisle (ed. M. Berger), *Recueil des Actes de Henri II: Volume II*, p. 179 (Paris, 1920).

Kings of the Western Isles

Among the histories already cited only G. W. S. Barrow, *Kingship and Unity: Scotland 1000–1306* (Edinburgh, 1981) describes in any detail the Scottish acquisition of Argyll and the Western Isles in his Chapter 6, 'The winning of the west'. See also A. MacDonald, 'The Kingdom of the Isles: Scotland's Western Seaboard c. 1000–1336', *SHR* monograph (forthcoming). Somerled's pedigree is discussed by W. D. H. Sellar, 'The origins and ancestry of Somerled', in *SHR*, 45 (1966), but see D. O'Corrain, 'Review of studies in the history of Dalriada by J. W. M. Bannerman', in *Celtica*, 13 (1980), as discussed by B. T. Hudson, *Kings of Celtic Scotland* (Connecticut, 1994), casting doubt on the existence of Godfrey mac Fergus. The ancestry of other early families in Argyll is discussed by W. D. H. Sellar, 'Family origins in Cowal and Knapdale' in *Scottish Studies*, 15 (1971). R. A. McDonald and S. A. MacLean, 'Somerled of Argyll: a new look at old problems', in *SHR*, 71 (1992) discuss Somerled's career more objectively than the fulsome accounts of MacDonald historians, such as D. J. MacDonald of Castleton, *Clan Donald* (Loanhead, 1978), largely based on oral sources first recorded in the seventeenth century. The subsequent history of Argyll and the Western Isles is discussed by A. A. M. Duncan and A. L. Brown, 'Argyll and the Isles in the early Middle Ages', *Proceedings of Society of Antiquaries of Scotland*, 90 (1956–7), which may be augmented by reference to G. Broderick and B. Stowell (eds), *Chronicle of the Kings of Man and the Isles* (Douglas, 1981). See also R. A. MacDonald, 'Images of Hebridean lordship in the late twelfth and early thirteenth centuries: the seal of Ranald MacSorley', in *SHR*, 74 (1995). King Hakon's expedition to the Western Isles and his defeat at Largs (1263) are discussed by E. J. Cowan, 'Norwegian sunset – Scottish dawn: Hakon IV and Alexander III', in N. H. Reid (ed.), *Scotland in the Reign of Alexander III* (Edinburgh, 1990). The thirteenth-century castles of the region are briefly described by J. G. Dunbar, 'The medieval architecture of the Scottish Highlands', in L. MacLean (ed.), *The Middle Ages in the Highlands* (Inverness, 1981). See also J. G. Dunbar and A. A. M. Duncan, 'Tarbert Castle: a contribution to the history of Argyll', in *SHR*, 50 (1971). The recent excavations at Finlaggan are described in a progress report by D. H. Caldwell and G. Ewart, 'Finlaggan and the Lordship of the Isles: an archeological approach', in *SHR*, 72 (1993).

Edward I, Hammer of the Scots/Robert the Bruce and Scottish Independence

Apart from the histories already cited, and especially R. G. Nicholson, *Scotland: The Later Middle Ages* (Edinburgh, 1974), G. W. S. Barrow, *Robert the Bruce and the Community of the Realm* (Edinburgh, 1988, 3rd edn) is essential reading for this period of Scottish history, as reviewed in an earlier edition by A. A. M. Duncan, in *SHR*, 45 (1966). P. M. Barnes and G. W. S. Barrow, 'The movements of Robert Bruce between September 1307 and May 1308, in *SHR*, 49 (1970), reconstruct his Highland campaign in the light of new evidence. Reference may usefully be made to E. M. Barron, *The Scottish War of Independence: A Critical Study* (Inverness, 1934, 2nd edn, 1934) for an earlier account which stresses the role played by Scotland north of the Forth. See also J. Bain, *The Edwards in Scotland: AD 1296–1377* (Edinburgh, 1901) for details of their Highland campaigns.

David II and the Early Stewarts

The career of Alexander Stewart, Earl of Buchan, is the subject of A. Grant, 'The Wolf of Badenoch', in W. D. H. Sellar (ed.), *Moray: Province and People* (Edinburgh, 1993). There is no recent account of the Battle of the Clans, but see W. F. Skene, *Celtic Scotland: Land and People* (Edinburgh, 1890), I. F. Grant, *Social and Economic Development of Scotland before 1603* (Edinburgh, 1930) and Sir I. Moncrieffe of that Ilk, *The Highland Clans* (London, 1967), who all discuss the likely identities of the combatants. The history of Sutherland and Caithness for this period is best documented by A. MacKay, *History of the Province of Cat* (Wick, 1914), as supplemented by his *The Book of MacKay* (Edinburgh, 1906), and by other clan histories. The reigns of Robert II and Robert III have been considered by S. Boardman, *The Early Stewart Kings: Robert II and Robert III, 1371–1406* (East Linton, 1996), which appeared too late to be consulted for the present book.

Lords of the Isles and Downfall of Clan Donald

The essential source for studying the MacDonald lordship of the Isles is J. Munro and R. W. Munro, 'Acts of the Lords of the Isles', *Scottish History Society* (1986), which not only gives full details of all their known charters, but much biographical and other information as well. See also the historical accounts by J. Munro: 'The Lordship of the Isles', in L. MacLean (ed.), *The Middle Ages in the Highlands* (Inverness, 1981); and 'The Earldom of Ross and the Lordship of the Isles', in J. R. Baldwin (ed.), *Firthlands of Ross and Sutherland* (Edinburgh, 1986). Reference should also be made to R. W. Munro (ed.), *Monro's Western Isles of Scotland: 1549* (Edinburgh, 1961) for further details of the Council of the Isles. J. W. M. Bannerman discusses the historical and cultural aspects of the Lordship in two important papers: 'The Lordship of the Isles: historical background', in K. A. Steer and J. W. M. Bannerman (eds), *Late Medieval Sculpture in the Western Highlands* (Edinburgh, 1977); and 'The Lordship of the Isles', in J. M. Brown (ed.), *Scottish Society in the Fifteenth Century* (1977). The separatist pretensions of the Lordship are considered by A. Grant, 'Scotland's Celtic fringe in the late Middle Ages: the MacDonald Lords of the Isles and the kingdom of Scotland', in R. R. Davies (ed.), *The British Isles 1100–1500* (Edinburgh, 1988). See also A. Grant, 'The revolt of the Lord of the Isles and the death of the Earl of Douglas 1451–1452', in *SHR*, **60** (1981) for the likely course of events during the revolt against James II. I. F. Grant, *The MacLeods: The History of a Clan 1200–1956* (London, 1959) gives a plausible account of the conflicts between Clan Donald and the MacLeods, which I have followed. See also her entertaining travelogue, *The Lordship of the Isles* (Edinburgh, 1935, reprinted 1982), laced with history. The quotation at the end of the book comes from J. MacInnes, 'Gaelic poetry and the historical tradition', in L. MacLean (ed.), *The Middle Ages in the Highlands* (Inverness, 1981).

INDEX

Numbers in bold italics refer to figures.